Gift from JAW
June 1945

HARVARD HISTORICAL STUDIES

PUBLISHED UNDER THE DIRECTION OF
THE DEPARTMENT OF HISTORY

FROM THE INCOME OF

THE HENRY WARREN TORREY FUND

VOLUME LII

HARVARD HISTORICAL STUDIES

HARVARD UNIVERSITY PRESS
CAMBRIDGE, MASS., U. S. A.

THE REVOLUTIONARY COMMITTEES

IN THE DEPARTMENTS OF FRANCE
1793–1794

BY

JOHN BLACK SIRICH
INSTRUCTOR IN HISTORY IN THE UNIVERSITY OF ILLINOIS

CAMBRIDGE
HARVARD UNIVERSITY PRESS
LONDON : HUMPHREY MILFORD
OXFORD UNIVERSITY PRESS
1943

PRINTED AT THE HARVARD UNIVERSITY PRINTING OFFICE
CAMBRIDGE, MASSACHUSETTS, U.S.A.

To
MY FATHER

ACKNOWLEDGMENT

It is very pleasant to be able to thank in this way Stringfellow Barr, of St. John's College, and Crane Brinton, of Harvard, because to them I owe my introduction to history and to the Revolution. More than that, I have encountered in their company thinking which was adventurous and ideas which were unhackneyed — a heartening experience in the academic world.

Moreover, along with millions of others, I owe a debt to the French people for having gone to the trouble of having a revolution. They have created a tradition of revolt against selfishness and stupidity which still holds forth, in the midst of oppression and despair, the promise of hope and good fortune.

J. B. S.

University of Illinois
December, 1942

CONTENTS

AUTHOR'S NOTE

Unless otherwise indicated, all dates given according to the Gregorian calendar are for the year 1793, all those in Revolutionary style are for the Year II. Laws, unless indicated otherwise, are quoted from Duvergier's *Collection des lois*. To avoid lengthening the many notes, the following abbreviations for the titles of periodicals have been adopted from Caron and Stein's *Bibliographie des travaux publiés depuis 1867*.

A. Bretagne	*Annales de Bretagne*
A. H. Révol.	*Annales historique de la Révolution française*
Anjou. Hist.	*Anjou historique*
A. Révol.	*Annales révolutionnaires*
A. Soc. St. Malo	*Annales de la société de l'arrondissement de Saint-Malo*
B. Acad. Delphinale	*Bulletin de l'Académie delphinale*
B. Com. Hist.	*Comité des travaux historiques, Bulletin philologique et historique*
B. Comm. Mayenne	*Bulletin de la commission historique et archéologique de la Mayenne (Laval)*
B. Soc. Arch. Nantes	*Bulletin de la société d'archéologie de Nantes*
B. Soc. Bayonne	*Bulletin de la société des sciences, lettres et études régionales de Bayonne*
B. Soc. Draguignan	*Bulletin de la société départementale d'études scientifiques et archéologiques de Draguignan*
B. Soc. Oise	*Bulletin de la société d'études historiques et scientifiques de l'Oise*
B. Soc. Pau	*Bulletin de la société des sciences, lettres et arts de Pau*
M. Acad. Nîmes	*Mémoires de l'académie de Nîmes*
M. Soc. Beaune	*Mémoires de la société d'histoire, d'archéologie, et de littérature de l'arrondissement de Beaune*
M. Soc. Savoisienne	*Mémoires et documents publiés par la Société savoisienne d'histoire et d'archéologie*
R. Anjou	*Revue de l'Anjou*

R. Bas-Poitou	Revue du Bas-Poitou
R. Bretagne, Anjou	Revue de Bretagne, de Vendée et d'Anjou
R. Bretagne, Vendée	Revue de Bretagne et de Vendée
R. Gascogne	Revue de Gascogne
R. H.	Revue historique
R. H. Révol.	Revue historique de la Révolution française
R. H. Ouest	Revue historique de l'Ouest
R. Pyrénées	Revue des Pyrénées
Révol. Fr.	La Révolution française
Révol. Vosges	La Révolution dans les Vosges
Soc. Emul. Vendée	Société d'émulation de la Vendée

THE REVOLUTIONARY COMMITTEES IN THE DEPARTMENTS OF FRANCE
1793–1794

CHAPTER I

INTRODUCTION

THE provinces follow Paris. That observation epitomizes so neatly a phenomenon frequently observed in the French Republic that constant repetition has converted it into something accepted as a historical fact. Its proponents declare that political and intellectual movements originate at Paris, are disseminated from that point, and die when they are ridiculed there, for all judgments are made by the standards of the metropolis. Much of the history written in France rests on this assumption. The events of the court, the acts of ministers and assemblies, the opinions of the capital are bundled together and the result is declared to be a history of France, when in fact it is merely a history of French politics.

The historian of the Revolution does not escape this fallacy. His eyes are focused on Paris; like the Mountain, he forgets that Paris was only one eighty-third of France. He pays slight attention to the provinces save when they have burst into prominence as rebels and have sought to compel Paris and its leaders to go back along the road by which they had come. He writes the story of those tormented years from the *Moniteur*, he accepts at their face value the decrees of the Convention and assumes that throughout France laws operated in every respect as the assembly intended. Consequently, for him the government of France during the Terror was simply the material incarnation of countless debates and decrees. He imagines that the laws passed down the line into the departments in orderly fashion, that bureaucrats in unison leapt this way and that and then — still in an orderly fashion — poured back on Paris reports of their gyrations.

Surely only a very credulous person can have faith in a description of this kind, can believe that the officials of the Republic followed meticulously the orders of the Convention. Even in time of peace bureaucracies have a way of transforming, even nullifying, legislation by the manner in which they put it into execution; "special circumstances," "further study," "local conditions" are familiar phrases too often employed to explain delays and exceptions, and to conceal at the same time the real feelings of officialdom. By such tactics the bureaucracy can sabotage an entire legislative program, or, as happened in France repeatedly in the nineteenth century, annul a revolution.

Such administrative nullification was undoubtedly widespread in France during the Revolution, when old prejudices and old institutions which once had protected large groups of the population were being attacked by the legislation of the assemblies. To what extent these obstructionist tactics were operative throughout France as a whole no one has bothered to inquire. Yet there exists abundant material from which one can discover the effectiveness or ineffectiveness of laws and instructions sent down from the capital. In addition to source materials in archives, there exist countless volumes written by local historians, often the archivist, the professor of the university or *lycée*, men whose scholarship can be trusted. Lefebvre's *Les Paysans du Nord*, the work of Lallié at Nantes, of Gabory and Chassin on the Vendée, of Richard on the Basses-Pyrenées, of Schnerb in the Puy-de-Dôme, may serve as examples. Supplementing these more ambitious studies are the countless periodicals published by the learned societies of the departments.

Nevertheless, since the French have avoided the task of constructing comprehensive works on the institutional history of the First Republic, these unordered monographs, although they still have value as contributions to local history, offer no answer to the recurring problem of just how and how well France was governed during the Terror. For the practice of an isolated organization, its vices and its virtues, are inevitably deceptive when attributed to hundreds of such organizations.

The famous drowning committee of Nantes is a case in point, for in the minds of many it has become, unjustly, the archetype of all committees of surveillance.

This study, therefore, was undertaken as an attempt at establishing a comparative outline of the activities of the committees of surveillance, indicating to what extent they conformed to the instructions of the Convention, and discovering periods or districts characterized by special types of activity. At the same time it has attempted to reveal the nature of their duties, their methods of performing their functions, in short, to depict the actual machinery of the Terror in the departments. It has endeavored to complete, in a sense, Mr. Crane Brinton's study of the Jacobin Societies and Mr. Donald Greer's monograph on the social incidence of the Terror by presenting the third instrument of the Revolution at work in the departments.

In such an ambitious task, there are necessary limitations. First, as regards material. There are twenty or twenty-five articles, of varying detail and value, which present the results of research on certain committees. There are, also, the communal and departmental histories, whose accounts of the committees are based on some knowledge of the remaining documents. There are, last of all, the departmental archives, whose collections vary from that of the Marne with the records of 304 committees to that of the Deux-Sèvres with a single document of one committee.[1] It was impossible to visit even the majority of these archives; consequently, after an examination of their inventories, those were chosen which demanded attention, either because of the richness of their collection or because of their importance in Revolutionary history. Lyon, Bordeaux, Marseille, and La Roche-sur-Yon (Vendée) were, of course, inevitable choices. Nancy, Lille, Grenoble, and Carcassonne were chosen because they were directly involved in the military defense of the Republic. Dijon, Orléans, Châlons-sur-Marne, Rouen, Châteauroux (Indre), and Limoges were

[1] See Appendix I.

chosen as relatively quiet centers. Caen was a federalist center which escaped the repression visited upon the other Girondist cities.

Realizing that the investigation was circumscribed to this extent, one may wonder whether it was worth while, whether any validity can be claimed for the general conclusions reached. The final choice is, of course, between no light and some light, whether to continue to rely upon rhetoric to leap across the gaps in one's knowledge or to construct a bridge which may not last for eternity but which, if conscientiously built, will at least give relative safety. Several years ago Belloni in his long study on the Committee of General Security observed that "the law of suspects, in substituting them [the committees of surveillance] for the municipal administration in the pursuit of suspicious persons, recompensed them for the implacable ardor they had displayed in the fight against foreigners." In the next sentence he cited a file of the Archives of the Côte d'Or in regard to the organization of such a committee at Dijon. If M. Belloni had consulted the register of proceedings of one of those committees, that of the Section du Centre, he would have discovered that all the persons entered as "foreigners" were native Frenchmen. M. Belloni's suspicions might have been aroused, and if he had searched further, he would have found that this anomaly is no anomaly at all, for throughout France the overwhelming majority of those persons who made their declarations were native French.[2]

In 1930 Georges Lefebvre wrote in his section of *La Révolution française* that after 14 Frimaire "the revolutionary committees remain, but they are purely communal and are confined to their police functions. . . ."[3] At least ten departments have been discovered, with no particular effort, in which even after 14 Frimaire there existed no village committees whatsoever, the committee of the canton or district capital exercising its

[2] G. Belloni, *Le Comité de Sûreté Générale de la Convention* (Paris, 1924), p. 303 and note, citing Arch. Côte d'Or L IV a 47 i/1; the register of the committee is Arch. Côte d'Or L IV a 47/a.

[3] Lefebvre, Guyot et Sagnac, *La Révolution française* (Paris, 1930), p. 231.

surveillance over all the communes of its canton or district. Similarly, after 14 Frimaire the powers of the committees were not confined, but extended; and extended to matters which were administrative rather than police.

This much and more we have discovered in our researches, and though arguing from the experience of several hundred committees may seem presumptuous to the "hundred per-center," we modestly present this study as a closer approximation of the ideal he demands, confident that we have avoided all the grosser blunders and most of the lesser.

CHAPTER II

THE LAW OF 21 MARCH 1793

THE REVOLUTION'S ATTITUDE TOWARD FOREIGNERS

IT IS one of the misfortunes of the French Revolution that with a few important exceptions the realities of earthly existence forced the men of 1793 to renounce the high principles so proudly proclaimed during the first years of the reign of liberty. The Constituent Assembly bade farewell to absolutism and its bureaucracy, but by the end of 1793 France had as effective a tyranny, as tightly centralized a government, as had any of the Louis'. In May 1790 wars of ambition were declared foreign to the principles of fraternity; by March 1793 three new departments had been added to the French Republic.

The cosmopolitanism of the early years went the same way. Even before the Revolution, Paris was the intellectual haven of Europe; while after 1789 political refugees and idealists such as Wordsworth and Humboldt, exalted spirits who hoped to share in the regeneration of society, swelled the foreign population of the capital. Signs of the changing attitude toward foreigners were soon evident, however. After Louis fled across the dusty Champagne in June 1791, hoping by a bold stroke to recover his lost heritage, the Parisians denounced him for appealing to the foreigner, and the Austrians were removed from the list of the enlightened. After that day whenever popular disturbances or military reverses threatened the safety of the nation, the revolutionists pointed the long finger at foreigners. The government, seeking a scapegoat on whose shoulders to place the blame for disasters due to its own shortcomings, took up the cry and "ended by creating a 'state of mind' and by provoking the vote of the first protective measures against a danger which was constantly denounced, but for which no remedy was advanced." [1]

A remedy was finally sought in the winter of 1793, when the increasing frequency and severity of crises made the position of the government a precarious one. The food riots in Paris in February were instigated by foreigners, according to Robespierre. When the Republican armies fell back from Aldenhoven and Liége in March the agents of Pitt and Coburg were blamed. On 10 March the threat of insurrection disturbed the city, and the presses of the Girondist journalist Gorsas were broken. Some members of the Cordeliers club were recognized among the vandals. The Cordeliers included among its numbers two foreigners, Proli and Guzman. Therefore, it was argued, the foreigner was responsible for the disorders. It was by such curious logic that the revolutionists established the complicity of the "agents of Pitt and Coburg." On 18 March the catastrophic events in the Vendée led the Convention to vote in principle "that all foreigners without occupation shall be expelled from the territory of the Republic." [2]

THE LAW OF 21 MARCH

In accordance with this declaration, Jean Debry on 21 March presented to the Convention a bill setting up conditions which no foreign aristocrat or agent could satisfy, or which would force such a foreigner to risk his life should he attempt to satisfy them. Debry proposed to establish in each commune a committee of twelve members before which every foreigner was to declare his name, age, profession, birthplace, and visible means of support. Failure to register carried with it the penalty of deportation. By this procedure the legislature would safeguard the Republic from outside interference and yet at the same time "protect those whom persecution or the love of free-

---

[1] A. Mathiez, *La Révolution et les étrangers* (Paris, 1918), pp. 121–122. In this book Mathiez presents in considerable detail the series of events responsible for the altered altitude toward foreigners, and the legislation enacted against them.

[2] *Moniteur*, réimpression, XV, 697, 716, 741.

dom has brought here to enjoy the benefits of a regenerated social system."[3]

The extreme decentralization of the Constitution of 1791, to which the Gironde was still faithful, is apparent in the law as enacted. There is no appeal beyond the administrative unit which selected the committee, whether commune or section of commune; nor is there any provision for report to, or instructions from, Paris. Furthermore, the committees were simply recording bodies, destined to receive passively the declarations of any foreigners who chose to appear before them. The right to issue orders to any law-enforcing agency was denied them, and consequently they had no means of seeking out foreigners, or of pursuing those who ignored their decisions. If the activities of the "agents of Pitt and Coburg" were as extensive and as effective as the Convention believed them to be, certainly it had sent a boy to do a man's work.

How can one account for such a feeble piece of legislation? It is impossible to attribute to the Girondist authors of the law a perspicacity which saw through the legend of the foreign plot. They were probably as much the dupes of this overly simple interpretation of the events of 1793 as their colleagues on the Mountain. From the tribune and from their journals they howled at the foreigner with the rest of the pack. Our contention is that the weakness of the committees was a direct result of the insurrection of 9–10 March, an insurrection engineered by a few of the sections of Paris and their committees — secret, revolutionary, or whatever they might be called.

THE INSURRECTION OF 9–10 MARCH

It is unnecessary to recount the long struggle between the Gironde and the Mountain, the provinces and Paris. Their hostility dated from 10 August, and subsequent events intensified it. During the early days of March the disquieting news from the frontiers and rumors of Dumouriez's impending treason produced reactions at Paris similar to those of August 1792, and

[3] For the text of the law, see Appendix II.

the war party, the party of Dumouriez, had to shoulder the blame. In the section assemblies and at the Jacobins, the Girondists were denounced and Desfieux swore that "the people shall enjoy liberty only when the intriguers [the Mountain's term for the Girondists] are exterminated." [4]

Under this prodding, a few sections led by hotheads such as Jean Varlet and Fournier l'Américain attempted to arouse an insurrection which forecast that of 31 May–2 June in organization and purpose — it was based upon the action of the sections and had as its goal the expulsion of the Girondists. On the morning of 9 March the presses of Gorsas and Condorcet were broken.[5] That evening at the Jacobins Desfieux again attacked the Gironde, accusing its members of conspiracy and demanding the renewal of the committees of the Convention which were packed with Girondists — or "counter-revolutionaries," as Desfieux now called them.[6] Some of the Jacobins later adjourned to the Cordeliers and participated in drawing up a petition to the department of Paris. "The department of Paris," it read, "an integral part of the sovereign, is invited to take possession of sovereignty; the electoral body of Paris is authorized to renew the members of the Convention who are traitors to the cause of the people; deputies shall be sent to the committee of insurrection." [7] This declaration was borne off to the Commune, which refused to accept the invitation, and then was presented to a number of the sections. Only five gave the insurrectionists the support they sought, Bonconseil, Lombards, Théâtre Français, Quatre-Nations, and Poissonière, and even here their methods were not above reproach, or so the sections later declared. At Quatre-Nations "an intriguer named Varlet . . . said he was sent by the Cordeliers club and was accompanied by a large number of people who had come with him.

[4] F. A. Aulard, La Société des Jacobins (Paris, 1889–97), V, 73–74.

[5] Moniteur, réimp., XV, 668, 673. Gorsas, impeached on 2 June, was the first member of the Convention to be guillotined. A. Kuscinski, Dictionnaire des Conventionnels (Paris, 1919), p. 300.

[6] Aulard, Jacobins, V, 79–80.

[7] This was the version given by Vergniaud in his speech on 13 March. It does not seem to have been challenged. Moniteur, réimp., XV, 704.

[*sic*] The section has realized that when the proposal for an address was read, they [Varlet's companions] cried 'Put it to a vote' and were the only ones who raised their hands." It took three days for the realization to dawn upon the section.

The insurgents of the section at the same time issued a manifesto to the city. "There is no doubt that the invasion of Belgium (by the enemy) is the work of the unholy faction which paralyzes the Convention. . . . The defenders of the fatherland rise up, but their first glance is towards the chiefs of the conspiracy; when the time to act has come, they will not stop to relate in detail the hateful intrigues of the Rolands, the Brissots, the Gensonnés, the Guadets, the Pétions, the Barbaroux, the Louvets etc.; in the eyes of all free Frenchmen they have been more than unmasked. . . ." [8]

At the section of the Théâtre Français the secretary was later accused of "entering on the register of deliberations on the 9th of this month a seditious deliberation, which had not been passed in the general assembly, but only by fifteen or twenty citizens of that section, and in the middle of the night." [9] To legalize their intended actions as much as possible, the assembly — or the fifteen or twenty insurgents — granted to the section's committee of surveillance the right to issue warrants for arrest. [10]

Nevertheless, despite the heroic efforts of the Enragés and their adherents the sections had refused to start that night. Among the more ardent, however, hope was still alive. Even the Commune was not too certain that the insurrection had finally failed, and on the morning of the 10 March it reported to the Convention only in regard to the riots at the printshops. During that day deputations presented "alarming demands" to the council-general.

At the Jacobins that evening (10 March) action was resumed. Bentabole denounced the Gironde in a hysterical

[8] *Moniteur*, réimp., XV, 704.
[9] *Moniteur*, réimp., XV, 719, 724.
[10] E. Mellié, *Les Sections de Paris pendant la Révolution française* (Paris, 1898), p. 128.

speech. A crowd of recruits, probably a bit drunk, marched around the hall, led by a brass band. Members rushed to the tribunes only to have their voices drowned beneath the excited shouts of the crowd. In the midst of the milling around someone extinguished the lights, increasing the uproar. After half an hour of this confusion the club was adjourned, some members rushing off to the Cordeliers, others to the Convention to watch the Mountain push through the establishment of the Revolutionary tribunal against the wishes of the Gironde.[11]

This act seems to have been the last of the abortive insurrection. It was raining that night and the crowd probably scattered quickly for shelter. Like the episode of 20 June 1792, these March "days" had served only to rehearse the actors for a more serious presentation several months later.

Nevertheless, as an issue in the contest between the Mountain and the Gironde, the movement of 9–10 March led a vigorous existence. Almost daily it was mentioned in debate, and in a speech on 13 March Vergniaud revealed that at last the Gironde understood. He denounced the "conviction that these attacks on property, these acts of violence . . . were patriotic acts." He charged that "a large number of citizens has come to confuse seditious insurrections with the sublime insurrection for liberty, to consider the provocations of brigands the outbursts of energetic souls, and thievery itself a measure of general security. . . . We have seen the development of a strange system of liberty which says to you: You are free; but unless you think as we do on such-and-such a question of political economy, we shall turn you over to the vengeance of the people. You are free; but unless you prostrate yourselves before the idol we worship, we shall turn you over to the vengeance of the people. You are free; but unless you assist us in persecuting men whose honor and learning we fear, we shall single you out with ridiculous names or turn you over to the vengeance of the people."

He continued by attacking the sections of Paris and the

[11] Aulard, *Jacobins,* V, 81–83.

"revolutionary committee" which they had created. "A revolutionary committee alongside the National Convention. But what are its powers?" he asked, "what revolution does it hope to effect? Despotism is no more; does it want to destroy liberty then? There are no more tyrants; does it want to overthrow the representatives of the nation?"

It was a brilliant speech, perhaps Vergniaud's best. If he refused to descend to personalities, to name names, his attack on the violence of the radicals of Paris was no less plain. In his mind, they shared with foreigners and suspects the blame for France's misfortunes, and he did not hesitate to denounce their crimes.[12]

It is not strange, therefore, that when the Girondist Debry presented the bill for the creation of committees of surveillance he should speak not only of foreign agitators but of Frenchmen as well. "We thought," he confessed, "that the principles which influenced us in the decree in regard to foreigners, should also be applied in the Republic to men that no one will take responsibility for: every one owes it to the government to make known his means of existence: if it is his labor which supports him, if it is the product of a vice which corrupts him, or if society has a debt to pay him. Every individual should prove that he is not indebted to the Republic; finally, in a time of troubles, the individual who does not offer a sufficient guarantee of his civic intentions, is justly suspect. . . . Strike down, then, the enemies of the interior and declare without hesitation that the Republic is invincible."

Even when drafting a bill on foreigners, the minds of the Girondists were not far from the enemies of the interior, the demagogues, the anarchists, the *hommes sans aveu*. That double preoccupation is made evident in the law itself.

Its provisions for the control of those not born in France are obvious. But in the preamble there is a vague phrase, applicable to the anarchists as well as to the foreigners. The Convention should "restrain the enemies of the interior from

[12] *Moniteur*, réimp., XV, 700, 702–703.

succeeding in stifling the desires of patriots and in substituting private will for the general will." In view of Debry's remarks about men of no trade, of the inseparability of the interests of all, the remark has a cut to it which could not have escaped the Mountain.

More pointed were the concluding articles, not one of which bears any relation to the preceding ten. Article 11 reads: ". . . when the council-general or the sections of a commune suspend their meetings, they shall indicate upon the register the hour at which the meeting will be resumed." Article 12 declares that any deliberation made between meetings shall be, by that very fact alone, annulled.[13] These two articles made it impossible, legally, for a small group of men, say fifteen or twenty, to adhere to insurrectionary manifestoes and thus bind the entire section, as happened in the section of the Théâtre français on the night of 9–10 March. Article 13, prescribing death for foreigners implicated in riots, strikes directly at Lazowski, Proli, Guzman, and their ilk. Thus, by tacking these three additional articles on to the law, the Gironde believed it had dealt a crippling blow to the more rebellious sections and to those fishers in troubled waters responsible for the violence of 9–10 March.

There were, however, still other enemies in Paris which the Gironde had reason to fear — the committees of surveillance set up in the sections by the Commune in accordance with the law of 11 August 1792. It was their duty to draw up lists of the enemies of the Republic, investigate those who had circulated royalist petitions, receive denunciations, inspect the homes of suspects, and report all their findings to the General Committee of Surveillance at the City Hall. This latter committee the Gironde had crippled, but the committees of the sections had continued to function.

We have already seen the usurpation of the committee of

---

[13] The chance that Article 12 refers to the committees of surveillance is very slight. Logically it follows Article 11. Furthermore, the preceding articles had made no mention of a president or secretary, nor were the committees required to keep a register of deliberations until 7 Fructidor.

the Théâtre français in arrogating to itself the right to make arrests on its own authority. On 13 March the section of Croix-Rouge reorganized its committee in view of the creation of the Revolutionary tribunal. It was to receive "denunciations, signed and secret, from any citizen resident in the section against émigrés and deported priests returned to the Republic, as well as the authors, agents, and accomplices of their residence in France; against the authors, agents, and accomplices of any plot, enterprise, or attack against liberty and the sovereignty of the people, against the unity, indivisibility, and internal and external security of the Republic, of any plot for the reëstablishment of royalty or of any despotic power, of any discourse aiming to bring about or favor counter-revolution, and of any crime relative to the manufacture of false assignats." The president and secretary were empowered to command assistance from the national guard or the *gendarmerie* to make searches at the homes of suspects, accompanied by the justice of the peace or the commissioner of police. The denunciations were to be turned over to those whose duty it was to prosecute the accused.[14]

Such an extension of the powers of these committees of surveillance, and the alacrity with which some of them had joined the insurrectionary movement against the Girondists, made clear to these deputies where the enemy lay. Consequently, the law of 21 March was directed as much against the section committees as against the foreigners. The new law created an institution with a few unimportant duties and no semblance of any power of coercion. To these new committees the Parisian sections were to be assimilated, and they lost as a result the extensive powers once granted to them under the law of 11 August 1792. Obviously the Gironde's purpose was to weaken the committees of the sections by giving them some innocuous task to occupy their time, rather than abolish them completely and risk raising a storm. Their aim was to "defunctionalize" the committees by taking away the substance and allowing the

[14] Mellié, p. 181.

shadow to remain and thus condemn them to long hours of harmless thumb-twiddling. It was a typically Girondist solution, an appeal to legality which for several months seems to have been effective.

In May, however, the "so-called revolutionary committees" of the sections of Unity and of Bonconseil overstepped the bounds and arrested five persons.[15] Vergniaud was quick to recognize the tactics of March, and for two days the Convention occupied itself with the matter. During the debates the Gironde's purpose in the law of 21 March was made clear when Vergniaud on 17 May remarked: "Notice that the warrant for arrest, even had it been issued by the revolutionary committee of the section, would nevertheless have violated the law in another respect, for the law gives the revolutionary committees no power over the liberty of citizens; it subjects only foreigners to their surveillance." Vergniaud was trying to squeeze the committees back into the legal straitjacket prepared for them in March.[16]

The whole matter of these arrests was turned over to the Girondist committee on legislation, which reported on 26 May that "there were no charges against them [the prisoners] save that they had spoken against Robespierre and Marat." The committee, therefore, proposed that the five citizens be released; that the "revolutionary committee" of the Unity section be suppressed, and that the committees of the sections be ordered "to confine themselves to the powers which the law had granted them in regard to foreigners." Despite Marat's protests against the release of one citizen, the decree was passed.

The law of 21 March had operated as the Gironde had planned, and one important weapon of the sections had been rendered impotent for several months at least. Yet laws were not able to withstand the violence of the Paris crowd — in June the Girondists were expelled from the Convention, and

---

[15] *Moniteur*, réimp., XVI, 407.
[16] *Moniteur*, réimp., XVI, 412.

during the succeeding months, when they hid themselves from the world in caves and attics, it must have been bitter for them to realize that the very measure which they had designed to check the lawlessness of Paris had created at the same time those committees of surveillance which were hounding them to their death.

CHAPTER III

THE COMMITTEES IN THE DEPARTMENTS

(MARCH–SEPTEMBER 1793)

THE ELECTED COMMITTEES

THE fundamental weakness of the law of 21 March, and, more especially, of the administration which was called upon to enforce it, is disclosed by the haphazard manner in which it was observed during the spring and summer of 1793. Irregularity in the promulgation and distribution of the laws, and the willfulness of the administration in applying or not applying them, resulted sometimes in the complete nullification of the Convention's orders.[1] As a result the committees established between March and September, according to the law of 21 March, were few in number.[2]

Where the committees were elected the orders of the legislature were not always observed; and this was especially true of the number of votes required for election. According to Article 3 of the law, the candidate must receive as many times a hundred votes as there were thousands of inhabitants — or one vote for each ten inhabitants. Nevertheless, in the department of Morbihan, 12 of 230 voters appeared at Gacilly, at Molac 32, at Bohal 14, at Questembert 21, even though ample notice had been given.[3] At Draguignan (Var) the council-

---

[1] In some cases, the municipality never received official notification of the law, and never bothered to seek it. P. Hémon, *Carhaix et le district de Carhaix pendant la Révolution* (Rennes, 1912), p. 205 note. In the Puy-de-Dôme the law of 21 March was not executed. F. Mège, *Le Puy-de-Dôme en 1793 et le proconsulat de Couthon* (Paris, 1897), p. 217.

[2] In the Calvados, 27 of 268 committees whose records remain were set up before September. In the Seine-Inférieure, 9 of 290 were created during the spring and summer. The Loire-Inférieure had 1, of 48; Alpes Maritimes, none, of 7; Creuse, 1, of 6; Puy-de-Dôme, none, of 10; Sarthe, 1, of 6; Manche, 6, of 27; Doubs, 20, of 83. On the other hand, in the Yonne, 6 of the 13 committees were created before September and in the Nord, 18 of 25.

[3] P. Bliard, "Le Conventionnel Prieur (de la Marne) en mission," *R. H.*, LXXXIII, 227, note 5.

general declared that only 140 voters need be *present* since there were only 1400 voters in the city.[4] Some municipalities made serious efforts to comply with the law. At Palais, on Belle-Île, the primary assembly was adjourned twice for lack of numbers, and when the third assembly also fell short of the required number the municipality held the election in violation of the law.[5]

The voters once gathered, the assembly proceeded to the election of the committee, generally following the involved procedure described below by the committee of Blaringhem (Nord).

Après avoir fait convoqué les citoiens composant cette dite commune, par trois publications différents . . . après examen près de l'article 3 de la dite loi qui exige qu'il faut être le nombre de cent votants par chaque mille âmes existant en chaque commune pour la composition de cette présente assemblée, avons reconnus qu'il y existe le nombre de 17 à 18 cent âmes par consequent atteint au nombre susdit de cent votans pour parvenir à composer cette assemblée — pourquoi nous maire et officiers municipaux notables et procureur de la commune formant ensemble le conseil-general sommes transporté dans ladite église comme dit est, où étant, avons pour donner plus grande connaissance, fait sonner le tocsin le space d'un quart d'heure après ce voyant que l'assemblée, se rendoit nombreuse, notre secrétaire-greffier a fait lecture à haute et intelligible voix les dispositions de la susdite loi et dessuite il a été procedé à la formation du bureau composé d'un president, d'un secrétaire et trois scrutateurs choisis de voix unanime et defferé par l'assemblée au maire, comme président, au secrétaire-greffier de la municipalité comme secrétaire, les officiers municipaux et procureur de la commune en qualité de scrutateur. Après avoir formé ainsi le bureau le président a annoncé aux citoyens tant présent qu' absens que le sujet de cette assemblée consistoit dans l'election de douze citoyens qui composeront le comité de cette commune et que pour satisfaire à la loi concernant cet objet ils auront tous à inscrire douze noms sur une seul billet; à quoi l'assemblée s'étant occupée chaque citoyen s'approcha du Bureau et mis son billet dans le vase à ce destiné et fur à mesur fut inscrit sur une liste joint au présent qui conste que d'après verification faite des billets contenus endit vase, le nombre

[4] M. Patin, "Le Comité de surveillance et la société populaire de Draguignan," *B. Soc. Draguignan*, XVII, 46.

[5] Bliard, *R. H.*, LXXXIII, 227, note 5.

s'est trouvé égale à celui des votans, s'élevant à cent quinze conse-
quemment le scrutin peut être dépouillé conformément à l'article 3
deladite loi. Après avoir fait pluiseurs appelles tant verbales qu'au
son de cloche, personne ne s'étant approchée de plus, il a été operé
au dépouillement dudit scrutin. . . .[6]

Following the election a public announcement giving the
necessary notice to foreigners was issued, a register was pro-
cured, and the committee sat back (literally) and waited for
foreigners.

Then things commenced happening — things which astonish
a twentieth-century mind. To the committees, *étranger* signified
not merely a foreigner, a citizen of another country, but also a
stranger to the community; and the overwhelming majority of
names entered in the registers of the committees are those of
Frenchmen. At Châlons-sur-Marne, the section of Liberty
received fifty-five declarations, of which only one was that of
a foreigner, an Italian.[7] Of 248 declaring at Montivilliers
(Seine-Inférieure) the majority is again French.[8] At Dijon six
persons who had merely changed their residence from the section of Les Halles made declarations of residence before the
committee of the section of Maison Commune.[9]

This misunderstanding became really serious when the committees attempted to apply the penalties provided by the law
— a rare event in itself. Two Frenchmen who had made no
declaration were ordered by the committee of Amplepuis
(Rhône) to leave the commune within twenty-four hours and
France within a week, as ordered by Article 7 of the law.[10]
The committee of Epernay (Marne) tried to expel two Frenchmen for the same offense; but on appeal, the municipality
reversed the decision.[11]

This interpretation of *étranger* was universal — in seaports

[6] Arch. Nord L 10132.
[7] Arch. Marne, Declarations of foreigners, Committee of Section Liberté.
[8] Arch. Seine-Inf. L 5393.
[9] Arch. Côte d'Or, Register of deliberations.
[10] Arch. Rhône CV 10, fo. 6.
[11] Arch. Marne, Register of deliberations.

and mountain villages, in metropolis and hamlet, the committees were unanimous in receiving declarations from French and non-French alike. The misunderstanding is, of course, readily explained, for *étranger* is an ambiguous term, and "stranger" and "foreigner" were one and the same in the eighteenth century. In addition, the legislative assemblies of the Revolution had passed a number of laws requiring declarations of foreigners and travelers; that of 22 July 1791 required all travelers to make declarations concerning their destination, residence, etc.; that of 26 February 1793 ordered landlords to declare the names and quality of foreigners resident with them or in their houses; and it may be possible that the municipality eased some of its own burdens on to the committees.[12]

The committees were exceedingly careless in publishing the lists of all foreigners who had made declarations — or in noting that they had done so, for the mention of such lists is rare.[13] Honfleur was one of the few communes where the names were printed and published, as a result of which practice the president and his committee fell out. President Manoury, while a member of the "permanence," had accepted the declaration of the widow Latour, an Englishwoman, but the committee annulled his action and informed the citizeness she must obtain better evidence of her civism or leave Honfleur within twenty-four hours. Manoury, whose interest may have been only in justice, outplayed the committee by printing and posting a list of his own, which included the name of the "Veuve Latour." [14]

The committees were generally satisfied with the declarations made, and there seem to have been no cases where the members took it upon themselves to verify the facts presented. Having received the declarations of as many "foreigners" as

---

[12] At Ste. Menehould, for example, the committee verified the register of *étrangers* kept in accordance with the law of 22 July 1791. Arch. Marne, Register of deliberations.

[13] The law of 29 March, ordering the landlords in towns of over 10,000 to hand the committees a list of all "foreigners," seems to have been a dead letter. I found no record of any such list among the papers of several hundred committees.

[14] Arch. Calvados, Register of deliberations, 4–19 August 1793.

presented themselves — in short, of those "foreigners" who had a clear conscience and no compromising secrets to conceal — the committees usually collapsed, some after weeks of lingering, others swiftly and definitely, to be revived only in the fall of 1793.[15]

A very few of the committees elected under the law of 21 March had the energy or the effrontery to push themselves into affairs outside their jurisdiction. Finding too few strangers to keep them occupied, the members of the Melun committee petitioned the Committee of General Security for the right to open mail, and in June the Convention granted it the right to arrest suspects.[16]

For similar concern over the activities of suspects the committee of Mirecourt (Vosges) became embroiled with the municipality. On 12 May the committee learned that a list of suspects drawn up by persons unknown was being handed around, and in order to end dissension and fear it called together all its fellow citizens and formed two official lists — one of seventy-three persons considered dangerous, the other of thirty-seven who were merely misled. To the municipality's decision annulling the deliberations, the committee answered on 31 May with a petition to the district in which it expressed a view of the committee's functions probably held by many of its fellows: "In small communes a committee of surveillance which confines its attention to those things relative to strangers would give the impression of a useless, not to say ridiculous institution. It would not fulfill the desires either of its constituents or of the law; it would betray its duties." [17]

Even more aggressive was the committee of Amplepuis

---

[15] At Montivilliers, there were no meetings between 24 July and 29 September (Arch. Seine-Inf. L 5390); at Estaires, five meetings from 18 May to 5 October (Arch. Nord L 10194); Château-Salins, no meeting between 24 May and 12 Frimaire (Arch. Meurthe-et-Moselle L 3171); at Amaye-sur-Seulles, no meetings between 8 April and 22 October (Arch. Calvados, Register of deliberations); at Bussy-le-Grand, two meetings before 30 September (Arch. Côte d'Or L IV a 31). The examples could be repeated indefinitely.

[16] Edmond Campagnac, "Le Comité de surveillance de Melun," A. Révol., I, 469.

[17] L. Schwab, "Les Comités de surveillance dans les Vosges pendant la Révolution," Révol. Vosges, 22e année, pp. 103-106.

(Rhône). Early in May it invited all citizens to make denunciations against suspects; it inspected the mail (21 May),
since it had no faith in the municipality; it asked the department to disarm communes whose leaders were fanatics (that
is, who were still faithful Catholics), or to give the committee
permission to disarm them (16 May); and it interrogated
several patriots as the result of a report that at a sale of
national lands someone had said that both buyers and sellers
were robbers (20–21 May). One of its many suggestions to
the municipality was that, since the concentration in a single
building of arms seized from suspects would be dangerous, the
arms might better be distributed "among the revolutionary
citizens" (20 May). The committee caused several men guilty
of evading the "draft" to be placed in custody (30 May), and
it denounced the committee of Ronne, in which commune many
draft evaders found refuge (31 May). After all this activity,
the committee on 3 June suddenly assumed a more humble
tone to the municipal administration, undoubtedly because
the municipal officers were partisans of the then triumphant
Lyonnais.[18]

Another committee which chafed at the lukewarm attitude
of its administrators was located at Saint-Marcellin (Isère).
Repeatedly it criticized one or another of the governing bodies
for its lax treatment of suspects (25 May, 28 July, 23 August,
20 September). It protested on another occasion against the
large requisitions of wheat made for the Army of the Alps, demands which threatened the lives of its fellow citizens (28 August).[19] Apparently both these committees were simply more
aggressive than their Girondist colleagues in the administration. After September and the purge of the administration,
they failed to justify their early promise.

Admitting the hardihood of some few exceptional committees, the sterility of the average group during the spring and
summer of 1793 would be difficult to exaggerate. The law of
21 March was a complete failure. It created, to quote the

[18] Arch. Rhône CV 10.   [19] Arch. Isère L 904.

committee of Mirecourt once again, "a useless, not to say ridiculous, institution." The committees were given no positive power to seek out foreigners, and were therefore dependent upon the good intentions of the foreigners themselves and the whims of the municipal government and its gendarmes. It is no wonder, then, that the average member soon lost interest in performing a futile task; that attendance at meetings became less regular; and that the committees collapsed from sheer frustration. In consequence, the law of 21 March failed to achieve its avowed purpose, and the committees ferreted out none of the thousands of foreign agents who, according to the myth of the Convention, were lurking in every dark alley, constantly on the alert to seduce honest patriots.

THE APPOINTED COMMITTEES

Infinitely more important than the elected committees were those groups which the local administration and the representatives appointed during the crisis of the spring and summer of 1793. The uprisings in the Vendée and the Lozère resulting from the application of the law on conscription, the defeats in the North, the wave of more or less determined opposition to the dictatorship of Paris, demanded instant and vigorous action. In many departments immediate repression was the answer: the supervision or even arrest of those persons whom the revolutionists believed suspect, either because of previous acts or because of future potentialities. By removing from society influences which they felt were corrupting, they hoped to prevent the spread of revolt and the preaching of counter-revolution.

In their search for citizens to perform this liquidating function, the administrators looked no farther than their own membership, occasionally adding a few representatives of the local Jacobin club. In short, they ordered a few of their colleagues to devote all their time to the pressing business of removing the gangrenous members of the body politic.[20] The repre-

[20] One of the most "bloodthirsty" committees was that of Redon, half of

sentatives on mission followed the same practice — with the usual exceptions. Philippeaux instructed the three administrations at Nantes to name six of their members and two additional citizens from the Club Saint Vincent.[21] The committee for Châteauroux was to be composed of two members from each administration; the Laval committee set up by Sevestre and Billaud-Varenne included twelve members of the municipal council and ten members from the popular society.[22]

These appointed committees, therefore, were simply commissions *ad hoc* of the various administrations, small groups supposed to devote their time exclusively to watching over persons considered counter-revolutionary, controlling their acts in the hope of rendering them harmless. Their creation was a matter of administrative convenience and hardly differed from the allocation of functions to special bureaus as practiced by most administrative bodies. Generally the committees were expected to report to the general council of the administration, which was to approve the action taken and make definitive the provisional decisions of the committee.

Although these appointed committees were generally composed of duly elected public officials, the arrest of suspects during the spring of 1793 was strictly illegal. As early as 15 August 1792 the Legislative Assembly had ordered that all émigrés be confined to their municipalities; in September 1792 the Minister of the Interior had ordered that all suspects at Rouen, Toulouse and certain other cities be conducted fifty leagues farther inland; and the law of 26 March 1793 had ordered the disarmament of suspects; but the compulsory arrest of suspects was ordered only on 2 June.[23]

It has been stated that the law of 11 August 1792 permitted

whose seven members were to be renewed each month! L. Dubreuil, *Le District de Redon (1790–IV)* (Rennes, 1903), pp. 85–86.

[21] A. Lallié, "Le Comité révolutionnaire de Nantes," *R. Bretagne, Anjou*, XXV, 276.

[22] Arch. Indre L 368. See also Abbé F. Gaugain, *Histoire de la Révolution dans la Mayenne, 1ere partie, Histoire politique et religieuse* (Laval, 1918), II, 79.

[23] *Archives parlementaires*, Série I, LXV, 698.

municipalities to arrest suspects as a measure of general security, but the intention of the decree as expressed in Gensonné's report is the arrest of counter-revolutionaries against whom there was concrete evidence and who would be tried by the National Assembly.[24]

Whatever may have been the rights in the matter, some of the committees had prickings of conscience which, however, they soon stilled. By informing the Vendôme committee that "the welfare of the people is the law which authorizes your acts," the department committee at Blois settled its qualms, while at Castelnaudary the committee appealed to the "critical circumstances" even though admitting the illegality of its acts.[25]

Certainly the good *sans-culottes* of Castelnaudary were correct as to their facts — the circumstances were critical, and it was usually in the regions of greatest danger that appointed committees were established. The conscription of 300,000 youths had raised rebellion in many departments, and in the Haute-Garonne (23 March), in Loir-et-Cher (21 March), and at Foix (4 August) the committees were formed with this specific purpose, "to prevent insurrection," and in both cases suspects were arrested.[26] Several weeks later the representatives at Pau set up a committee of surveillance which was to supervise the execution of the laws on conscription as well as watch over suspects.[27] In the Aveyron, Bô and Chabot ordered

[24] This despite Lefebvre, Guyot et Sagnac, *La Révolution française*, p. 123. See also E. Mellié, *Les Sections de Paris*, p. 180. Gensonné's original bill (30 May 1792) indicated that municipalities *could* draw up lists of suspects, prohibit their meeting, "or if there was occasion, disarm them." Even this provision was omitted from the bill as passed on 11 August. *Moniteur*, réimp., XII, 536–537.

[25] H. Blossier, "Le Comité de surveillance du département de Loir-et-Cher et la déchristianisation," *Bulletin historique et philologique du Comité des travaux historiques et scientifiques* (1910), p. 248; Arch. Aude L 2140.

[26] E. Connac, "La Révolution à Toulouse," *R. Pyrénées*, XII, 189; H. Calvet, "Les Rapports du comité de surveillance et des autorités constituées du département de Loir-et-Cher," *A. H. Révol.*, V, 430. G. Arnaud, *Histoire de la Révolution dans le département de l'Ariège* (1904), p. 407.

[27] A. Richard, *Le Gouvernement révolutionnaire dans les Basses Pyrénées* (Paris, 1926), p. 64.

the establishment of committees in each district capital for the purpose of forming lists of those detained on suspicion and of disarming other suspects (9 April).[28]

The threat of the Prussians led the representatives Antoine and Levasseur to suggest a committee of surveillance at Nancy (April 2) which was to receive denunciations and draw up lists of suspects, and the measure was later extended by the department to all communes.[29] On 28 April the decree granted to the committee the right to issue provisional summons to appear and warrants for arrest (*mandats d'amener, mandats d'arrêt*), the committees reporting to the district or the department which was to decide definitely which suspects were to be detained.[30] On 17 April the representatives, the committee, and the three administrative bodies met and continued 32 of 200 arrests, pronounced 43 new arrests, and placed 166 persons under surveillance.[31]

For a few weeks the departmental committee of the Vendée directed the movement against suspects — on 6 April it ordered the district of Les Sables to arrest émigrés and suspects and issued similar orders to other districts and municipalities.[32]

At the other danger spot — the department of the Nord — the municipalities arrested suspects only after the law of 2 June had given them specific authority. At Douai a committee of general security on the 8 and 9 June arrested 79 suspects, the

[28] H. Affre, *Tableau sommaire de la Terreur dans l'Aveyron* (Rodez, 1886), pp. 5, 9.
[29] J. Godchot, "Le Comité de surveillance révolutionnaire de Nancy," *Révol. Fr.*, LXXX, 250. Arch. Meurthe-et-Moselle L 3156.
[30] Arch. Meurthe-et-Moselle L 3421, 76.
[31] Godchot, p. 251.
[32] Arch. Vendée L 1182. The Vendée committees were of little importance during the spring and summer, owing to the occupation of virtually the entire department by the insurgents. There also existed in the Vendée the so-called royalist committees, sometimes referred to as "military councils." The committee of Palluau, "a type of this sort of administration," supplied provisions for the troops, cared for the sick and the prisoners, set up an espionage service, and issued requisitions. E. Waitzen-Necker, "Le Comité royaliste de Palluau," *R. Bas-Poitou*, XIII, 325, 331. They simply replaced the regular administration which generally took to its heels at the approach of the Vendeans, since the officials, as the most loyal Republicans, were the obvious target for brigand vengeance.

majority being lawyers, *rentiers*, and business men.[33] Yet at Cambrai in the same department the council-general itself enforced the law of 2 June until 15 August, when, in view of the imminent siege, the already overburdened municipality created a commission of ten to make arrests, though the municipality itself drew up the lists. A large number of suspects were interrogated and, in conformity with the decree of the representatives of 4 August, were expelled from Cambrai.[34]

Although the surveillance of suspects was the chief concern of the appointed committees, it was not the only one. The departmental committee of Loir-et-Cher was ordered to visa passports (28 April) and the same power was later granted to all the committees of the department.[35] This committee also kept a suspicious eye on the officials of its jurisdiction. In April it dismissed two notaries and the treasurer of the district for irregularities; on 10 May it suspended the municipal officers of Villerbon, and on 16 May removed Salaberry, a municipal officer of Blois.[36] Frequently the committees enjoyed the right of examining the correspondence of suspects at the post office, and it was as a result of this practice that the counter-revolutionary correspondence of Salaberry was revealed.

If the powers and functions of these committees seem chaotic, the boundaries of the jurisdictions over which they exercised their vigilance are also by no means clear-cut. Certain ones had control over the entire department (Rouen, Limoges, Blois); others (Toul, Hazebrouck, and Dijon) were to limit themselves to their communes. The Limoges committee, however, found rivals in the district committees which claimed equal powers, and only on 7 Frimaire did the deputy Lanot definitely subordinate the district committees to that of the department capital.[37]

[33] L. Dechristé, *Douai pendant la Révolution (1789–1802)* (Paris, 1880), pp. 89–92.

[34] A. Pastoors, *Histoire de la ville de Cambrai pendant la Révolution* (Cambrai, 1908), I, 419–20, 422.

[35] Calvet, *A. H. Révol.*, V, 433.

[36] *Ibid.*

[37] Arch. Haute-Vienne L 836.

To add to the confusion, there was still another type of committee, a combination of the two preceding types — a committee of twelve, elected as directed by the law of 21 March, but granted extraordinary powers by the representative or one of the administrations. Collot d'Herbois and Laplanche ordered the department of Nièvre to constitute revolutionary committees, and on 14 April the committees were elected, but their functions included the surveillance and denunciation of suspects and the deliverance of certificates of civism, as well as the surveillance of foreigners. At the same time the representatives were careful to order in each commune a committee of five members of the municipality to receive information from the committee of twelve and take appropriate action, thus preserving a semblance of legality.[38] Similarly, at Ludres (Meurthe-et-Moselle) the power of issuing provisional warrants for arrest, granted to the committees by the representatives, was bestowed on the committee of twelve instead of a committee drawn from the administration and the popular society as was the practice elsewhere in the department.[39] Dubouchet, the deputy on mission in Seine-et-Marne, went even farther and gave the elected committee the right to arrest and "to take whatever measures of general security circumstances may require" (15 September).[40]

Most of these powers, the surveillance and arrest of suspects, the inspection of mail, the issuing of certificates of civism, anticipated some of the duties which the committees were to exercise legally in the fall of 1793. During the summer, however, they were performed simply as a delegation of the power of a superior, and again the problem of legality arises. The deputies' right to grant unlimited powers to subordinates was not denied until 14 Frimaire. As for the rights of the administration, there is no answer. In revolutions, however, with heads and skins at stake, questions of legality arise only for a Robespierre.

[38] P. Meunier, *La Nièvre pendant la Révolution* (Nevers, 1895–98), I, 113–116. [39] Arch. Meurthe-et-Moselle L 3251, 20 May. [40] Campagnac, *A. Révol.*, I, 471.

THE ARREST OF SUSPECTS DURING THE SPRING AND SUMMER

This confusion, this drawing back and going forward which marks the creation of the appointed committees, is reflected in their treatment of suspects. Feverishly the members compiled a list of suspects and rushed the offenders off to prison. Then, after the federalist revolt had been quieted in all save three or four centers, many persons were released, some definitely, some under a theoretical surveillance.

The department committee at Limoges on 23 May revised the list of suspects arrested the previous month and released twenty-four of them. Later, in July, the liberty of many arrested in June was restored to them, the committee declaring that it believed it unjust to hold citizens as suspects "with no proof of the facts or actions which might confirm that suspicion." [41] At Castelnaudary a special committee of safety was organized "to consider the case of those arrested for incivism and aristocracy" (2 July), and during the five days of its existence it reduced the restrictions on all save one of the petitioners.[42] On the northern frontier, merely to satisfy the representatives' clamor for suspects, the committees sent large numbers to Hazebrouck during the closing weeks of August and then ordered their release almost immediately.[43] In the Ain, the department interceded for the suspects arrested at the orders of Amar and Merlino, revoking a number of domiciliary arrests.[44] In short, the laws on the arrest of suspects were applied sporadically.

THE FEDERALIST COMMITTEES

Even as the representatives and the loyal administrations had relied upon special commissions to assume the task of repression, so the so-called federalist departments turned to extraordinary bodies of some kind to organize the resistance to

---

[41] Arch. Haute-Vienne L 837, 22 July.   [42] Arch. Aude L 2140.
[43] G. Lefebvre, *Les Paysans du Nord pendant la Révolution française* (Paris, 1924), p. 816.
[44] E. Dubois, *Histoire de la Révolution dans l'Ain* (Bourg, 1933), III, 88.

Paris. Often a committee was set up within the department administration itself, as at Nîmes, Lons-le-Saunier, Dijon, Toulouse, Nevers, Bordeaux, and Lyon. The direction of the resistance to the Convention, the assembling of military forces, and at Lyon the direction of the siege, were centered in these purely administrative bodies. At Montpellier, however, the departmental committee was chosen by the sections; and at Marseille, a central committee of the sections, which occupied a rather anomalous position between the sections and the administration, was the driving force of the "resistance to oppression." [45]

This central committee of the sections had been set up in April to investigate the conduct of the Jacobin mayor of Marseille, Mouraille. It was constituted by several delegates from the "secret committee" of each section whose duty it was to forward to the central committee any denunciations received against Mouraille.[46]

Boisset and Moïse Bayle, who had withdrawn shortly before from Marseille, on May 2 issued a decree dissolving the secret committees, their central committee, and the popular tribunal which the deputies claimed was assassinating patriots. The sections, however, refused to recognize the decree; on the contrary, at the suggestion of Section 4 they agreed to organize a central committee of general security (5 May). On 10 May two members from each section committee met and organized the general committee of the thirty-two sections, which absorbed the old central secret committee several weeks later.[47]

[45] H. Wallon, *La Révolution du 31 Mai et le fédéralisme* (Paris, 1886), II, 159.

[46] The first record of a "secret committee" is that of Section 7 elected on 10 April. Arch. Bouches-du-Rhône L 1949. This file and L 1950 include a mass of petitions and deliberations of the Central Secret Committee, the *comités secrets des sections* and the General Committee of the sections from which documents one can partially reconstruct the organization and relations of the horde of committees set up at Marseille. There also exists a register for the *Bureau de Surveillance* of the General Committee organized on 23 May, but none exists for either the sections or the committee of the sections, for obvious reasons.

[47] Arch. Bouches-du-Rhône L 1955.

This newly established body formed four bureaux — current affairs, surveillance, correspondence, and execution, probably with a member from each section in each division. The divisions met separately under a president and secretary, save on Thursdays when there was a general assembly of all four divisions.[48]

The bureau of surveillance of this central committee, in addition to the denunciations sent to it by the section committees, inspected suspect mail, received declarations of strangers, and opened its registers to the denunciations of private citizens. The disposition of the case is rarely given, though on 27 May twenty-one depositions were referred to the Popular Tribunal. The guilty were usually denounced for having forced "patriotic contributions" from the wealthy, for arbitrary arrests, for attempted assassination, often simply for being members of the Jacobin club of Marseille.[49]

The denunciations are more informative at Aix, where a similar central committee was organized. In one case it was the popular society, in another the municipality, which had wrung "patriotic contributions" from several citizens. Again there were denunciations against a mob which had broken into the home of a municipal officer of Pertuis the previous summer and cursed and threatened his wife. In the same town a druggist who refused a "contribution" of 3000 *livres* was mistreated and had to take to his bed. At Equilles a *curé* was denounced for saying in his sermon, "Good citizens, don't be discouraged; the time is coming, and you are beginning to realize it already, when the rich will be poor and the poor will take their property and be rich. . . ."[50]

Meanwhile, section committees of seven had been established at Marseille to issue *cartes de sûreté* and keep watch over the activities of strangers (6 May).[51] They were also to receive denunciations and forward them, along with any other

[48] Arch. Bouches-du-Rhône L 1949, L 1955.
[49] Arch. Bouches-du-Rhône L 1951.
[50] Arch. Bouches-du-Rhône L 1903.
[51] Arch. Bouches-du-Rhône L 1950.

information, to the general committee. Until 23 May these committees existed separately from the secret committees, but on that date the general committee asked that the two be combined. There were already enough committees at Marseille.[52] Several months later when the general committee was going through a reorganization, it requested the election of committees of twelve and again ordered the suppression of all other section committees — of public safety, secret, central, and so on. It also prescribed an oath for the members: "I swear to recognize no longer the decrees of the National Convention passed since 31 May last until its membership is completely restored, to have no direct correspondence with it, to obey no longer the orders of the delegates in the departments, to approve the manifesto of Marseille to the republicans of France, to recognize the Popular Tribunal, to see that persons and property are respected, and to coöperate with all my strength in the consolidation of the Republic, one and indivisible, and to maintain liberty and equality." [53]

Central committees of the sections were, in fact, the usual insurrectionary organization devised by the rebels in the Midi.[54] The cities of Louton, Avignon, Tarascon, La Ciotat, Aix, to mention only a few, all set up these coördinating organizations. All of them maintained correspondence with Marseille, and the committees of the department sent the more prominent of their prisoners to Marseille, there to be tried before the Popular Tribunal. The procedure in these cities was the same as at Marseille — denunciations, examination of the suspect's correspondence, the preparation of a case which was bundled off to the Popular Tribunal along with the accused.[55]

At Lyon the role played by the committees during the siege is much clearer, for the registers of some committees, incomplete as they are, still exist.[56] Even before the siege, the Lyon

[52] *Ibid.*　　　　　　　　　　　　　　　　　　　　[53] *Ibid.*
[54] It was also a central committee of the sections of Paris which organized the insurrection of 31 May–2 June.
[55] Arch. Bouches-du-Rhône L 1906.
[56] At Bordeaux the activity of the committees during the federalist period is

committees — not with the same personnel, to be sure — had played a prominent part in the Jacobinizing movement.[57] Technically these pre-revolt organizations were not committees of surveillance. On 28 March the Jacobin municipality had named commissioners from each section to spare it the burden of granting certificates of civism, and speedily increased their powers by authorizing them to arrest nobles, non-salaried priests, and those suspect of incivism, such as *avoués, gens de loi, commis de magasin.* This power of arrest was extended on 5 April to include all suspects. The next duty assigned to the commissioners was the gathering of statistics on the number of weapons in armorers' shops (7 April). Later they were instructed to assist the council-general of the commune in naming the 6400 patriots who were to form the national guard and those to be removed for negligence (14 May); to indicate the names of "speculators, hoarders, and the rich and apathetic capitalists" of their sections (11 May), since a "revolutionary tax" had just been decreed with the tacit approval of Dubois-Crancé and Albitte. Briefly, the committees were considered mere adjuncts of the regular administration.

After the overthrow of the Jacobins on 29 May, new committees were established, and as Dubois-Crancé and his army approached the rebellious city, the general committee of public safety imposed new duties upon them.[58] Two commissioners of *panification* had already been appointed on 4 June and on the following day the Croisette committee asked the department to supply it with flour cards which the section committees ap-

---

unknown. At Caen, the other great center of resistance, the section committees were never organized. F. Guillonet, "Le Comité de surveillance de Caen," *A. Révol.*, I, 572–575.

[57] C. Riffaterre, *Le Mouvement anti-jacobin et anti-parisien à Lyon et dans le Rhône-et-Loire en 1793* (Lyon, 1912), passim.

[58] This committee, which directed the siege, was composed of the three administrations at Lyon and the Popular Commission, the latter formed by delegates from the entire department and set up on 30 June. It had organized and reorganized itself during July and on the 22nd its committee of general security assumed the task of disarming all suspects since the municipality had refused. G. Guigue, *La Commission populaire républicaine et de salut public du Rhône-et-Loire* (Trevoux, 1899), p. 132.

parently were to distribute. On August 9 the committees were asked to track down the cowards who were following the siege from café tables.[59] On the tenth, they made a report on the amount of bread at the bakers.[60] On the 18th the general committee asked for an exact census of all suspects, particularly those whose relatives were believed to have joined the army of Dubois-Crancé — the list to be submitted, if possible, within twenty-four hours.[61] On the 23rd (the bombardment commenced on the 22nd) the committees were to find shelter for those driven from their houses by fire; on the 27th, to examine lofts and remove any firewood found there, and to issue a call for all architects, carpenters, and firemen to appear at city hall; on the 29th to register all masons and carpenters in order that repairing might be done speedily. And for a month these labors went on in much the same way — reports on the food supply, household inspections to discover food and wine, issuance of food cards, collection of bed covers. On 6 September owing to the scarcity of safe buildings the committees were asked to make sure that there was no increase in rent! [62]

All this long recital is simply to demonstrate the one fact that in a crisis the federalist committees were pressed into service to perform any sort of task, the routine work without which the administration could not continue. With their functions doubled and tripled because of the siege, the administration turned to the only other organized, continuous body, the revolutionary committees.

In this, the federalist revolutionary committees agreed with their Jacobin counterparts. Indeed, in most respects political opinions did not influence the character of the activities which the two groups of committees pursued. Both Girondist and Jacobin committees arrested suspects, opened mail, and at need performed countless tasks hardly to be associated with sur-

[59] Guigue, p. 244.
[60] Arch. Rhône CL 48.
[61] Guigue, p. 189.
[62] Guigue, p. 207 et passim.

veillance. Jacobin committees were no greater scoundrels than Girondist, and Girondist principles of toleration and personal freedom did not make the federalist committees less bitter toward their enemies, less violent in the vengeance they visited upon the Jacobins.

To conclude: In the first place, the committees which existed during the spring and summer of 1793 should be clearly distinguished both as to their origin and their function, for the contention that during this period they exceeded their powers results from the failure to make such a distinction. Those elected according to the law of 21 March rarely went beyond the routine duties assigned to them, and played an insignificant role in the events of the summer. The committees to whom either the representatives on mission or the local administration delegated their powers had only that delegation as their justification. But since both the representatives and the administration had been granted vaguely defined powers in regard to general security, the committees seem within their legal rights. If the laws of France did not enjoin actions such as theirs, certainly they did not forbid them. Complaints against the committees were frequent, but such complaints were commonly based on what were said to be arbitrary decisions as to those who were to be detained or to be left at liberty; that is, complainants were concerned with the *application* of the law of general security, not with the committees' *right* to apply it.

In the second place, it is hardly necessary to insist once more upon the irregular and unsystematic character of the committees as an institution. The decentralized national government was incapable of enforcing its own laws. Consequently the provinces, out of control, followed their own inspiration, applied whatever measures they considered necessary, and ignored Paris. The result, seen as a whole, was utter confusion, symptomatic of the crisis which disrupted the entire government of France during this period, and which was only partially eliminated by the reorganization of September and October.

CHAPTER IV

THE LAW OF SUSPECTS

SUSPECTS AND THE CONVENTION

THE activities of the departmental committees of public safety have revealed the existence of another class of enemies more dangerous than the foreigner, the suspects. From the very foundation of the Republic the cry had gone up against those Frenchmen known to be hostile to the Revolution, those whose opinions, if not their acts, endangered the Republic and the lives of its disciples. Their influence was all the more sinister since it was intangible, working quietly and naturally, unaccompanied by any fanfare of oratory. A simple remark, an anecdote maliciously told, the mutual encouragement of a few *Feuillants*, could strengthen the defiance of some or convert into action the passive hostility of others. The revolutionists knew the value of a persistent propaganda in preparing the ground for a sudden stroke, and with what ease century-old institutions fall when the foundations upon which they stood have been cut away. How much more precarious was the position of the year-old Republic, attacked both from within and without by men of influence with resources of intelligence and wealth!

If the Revolution and its victories were to remain, it was necessary either to convert the great majority of Frenchmen to the principles of 1793 or to remove from society those who refused to adapt themselves to the new order of things. The men of '93, realizing the necessity for speed, chose the latter alternative, and, true to their humanitarian principles, determined not upon mass execution but merely upon the detention of those whose actions or even opinions were not "correct."

Yet even a measure as mild as detention was late in arriving.

France had, since 1789, suffered innumerable crises, brought on by persons against whom there seemed well-founded suspicions, yet these people, condemned by public opinion, were hardly interfered with. The deputies had accepted so whole-heartedly the principles of free speech and free thought and the doctrine of trial by jury that they found it difficult to reconcile themselves to imprisonment on mere suspicion. Although the Legislative Assembly had permitted its Committee of Surveillance to arrest persons against whom there were merely suspicions, the permission had been granted only during the crisis of 10 August. The following day the Assembly had attributed to the municipalities the duty of arresting persons against whom there was evidence of being guilty of "crimes which threaten the . . . security of the state, and the trial of which is reserved to the National Assembly" (*dont l'accusation est reservée a l'Assemblée nationale*).

In the stormy days of March 1793 the question of suspects arose again. A delegation from the section of Reunion petitioned the Convention to ratify its decree ordering the disarming of "all nobles, priests, and suspicious men," the latter to be indicated by the denunciation of six citizens. Genissieux proposed that the measure be extended to the entire Republic, and the law was instantly decreed. Again the municipalities were permitted to execute the law, and if they failed, the district, and if the district failed, the department. The municipalities as a result were enabled — for the law was only permissive — to reduce the suspect's ability to harm, but without encroaching upon his physical liberty.[1]

Another crisis, and the Convention passed another law — this time (2 June) ordering the constitutional authorities to arrest "all persons notoriously suspect of aristocracy and incivism or be held personally responsible for the disorders occasioned by their negligence." Again the law was vague, a mere declaration of policy, passed at a moment when it was possible to pass any bill which seemed to promise salvation.[2]

[1] *Arch. parl.*, LX, 581–584. [2] *Arch. parl.*, LXV, 698.

The law was executed fitfully, as we have seen, and the Jacobin element continued to press for more rigorous measures. In August they received reënforcements to assist them in pushing through a decree which was destined to be the final one. During that month there appeared in Paris a new group of *sans-culottes*, the *fédérés* of 10 August, the delegates sent to Paris by the primary assemblies of the Republic to bear witness to the acceptance of the Constitution of 1793. Many "failed to arrive," but those who solemnly acknowledged the Constitution on 10 August were *sans-culottes* of the *sans-culottes*.[3] They were feted at Paris, attended meetings of the Jacobins, and were eager to serve as missionaries of the Mountain. On 12 August a large group elbowed its way on to the floor of the Convention, and the speakers that day addressed their remarks to this crowd of "brothers from the departments." Barère, by this time the official herald of the Committee of Public Safety, tried his best to present the situation of the Republic as not too desperate, but there was news from Lyon, from the Vendée, from Bordeaux, from the northern frontiers, and an intercepted letter which proved that all the bankers of Europe had formed a coalition to destroy the assignat.

Finally, "a citizen, in the name of the delegates sent by the primary assemblies" obtained the floor and proposed "a great example for the universe" which would make "all our enemies bite the dust." He first proposed a *levée en masse* of all patriots. Then, he declared:

> We demand that all suspicious men be placed under arrest, hurry them to the frontiers, followed by the fearful mass of *sans-culottes*; there in the first ranks they shall fight for the liberty which they have outraged for four years, or else they will be slaughtered by the

[3] Pariset estimates that several hundred were "detained" on the way. The Committee of General Security took measures to prevent the arrival of the heterodox, even hiring "Tape-dur" Maillard, of September-massacres fame, to eliminate the less desirable. In theory, there should have been five or six thousand of these delegates. G. Pariset, *La Révolution* (vol. II of Ernest Lavisse, *Histoire de France contemporaine*, Paris, 1920–22), p. 154.

cannon of the tyrants. Women, children, the old and infirm will be protected by the righteousness of France, and will be kept as hostages by the wives and children of the *sans-culottes*.

He ended in that style, and his remarks were turned aside by the platitudes of the president. But Fayol, and Danton after him, demanded the arrest of suspects. "The deputies of the primary assembly," roared the tribune, "have just brought to us the initiative of the Terror against our enemies of the interior; let us satisfy their desires! No! no amnesty to any traitor. . . . Let us announce the vengeance of the people by bringing down the sword of justice upon the conspirators within our gates." Robespierre was also enchanted by the "sword of justice" and proclaimed "the head of Custine, falling beneath the sword of justice, shall be the guarantee of victory." The Convention could do nothing against these tirades and ended by voting "that all suspects should be placed under arrest." [4]

This time, however, the law was not allowed to go out as a bare statement of policy. The Committee on Legislation was entrusted with the task of drafting a law which would assign definitely to some single organization the responsibility for enforcing the measure and prescribe the procedure to be followed. Merlin (of Douai) reported the law in on 31 August, attributing the task of arresting suspects to the committees set up by the law of 21 March, and the Convention after hearing his report ordered its printing. Of discussion or debate there was none, but the printing of a report was sometimes the equivalent of tabling it, and it is possible that once again the Convention had repented at leisure.

Suspects soon came to the fore again, however, for on 5 September when Billaud-Varenne proposed that all aristocrats not in their own communes be arrested, Basire made a pertinent answer. It was not the aristocrats who were the dangerous enemies, he pointed out; most of them were very young or very old. The true enemies were "the *Feuillants*, the *Brissotins*, the hypocrites, the shopkeepers, the big merchants, the

[4] *Moniteur*, réimp., XVII, 387–8.

speculators." He suggested that the Commune of Paris be allowed to renew the revolutionary committees and that the new committees draw up lists of suspects, the same scheme which Merlin had presented on 31 August. Léonard Bourdon tried to halt this step by showing that after the purge operated by the representatives on mission, the administrations, cleared of Girondins, could be entrusted to enforce the law of 12 August. Basire refused to compromise and the debate soon turned to other matters.[5]

The Committee on Legislation continued its work, however, and on 17 September presented a new draft, the result of conferences on the 15th, at which time several changes intended to improve it had been made. With the exception of the *Mercure universel* none of the newspapers printed any discussion. The few remarks printed in the *Mercure* relate to Article 2, which defined suspects:

A member observes that this article is rather arbitrary.

Charlier: It is impossible for it not to be arbitrary. You should take that up with your committee; indeed it is all the better just because the article is not precise.

The article is decreed.[6]

The bill of 17 September incorporated several changes, the most important of which was that increasing the categories of suspects. According to Article 2,

those declared suspect are those who either by their conduct, their relations, their remarks or their writings show themselves to be partisans of tyranny, of federalism or enemies of the people; those who cannot, in the forms prescribed by the law of 21 March last, account for their means of support and the discharge of their civic duties; those to whom certificates of civism have been refused; public officials suspended or removed from their posts either by the National Convention or its agents . . . ; those ex-nobles, together with their husbands, wives, fathers, mothers, sons or daughters, brothers or sisters who have not constantly shown their devotion to the Revolution; those who emigrated in the period between 1 July 1789 and

---

[5] *Moniteur*, réimp., XVII, 584.
[6] *Arch. parl.*, LXXIV, 303. For complete text, see Appendix III.

the publication of the law of 1792, even though they have returned to France within the limits established by that law, or previously.

The vicious character of the law of 17 September has been expounded by historians of the Revolution for a hundred years, and they have always been right. It is not so much in the principle, however, as in its particular application that the Convention sinned. It removed the legal guarantees which the Constitution of 1791 had provided to prevent arbitrary arrest. Yet it did not at the same time substitute for those guarantees any adequate control over the enforcement of a law which by its nature invited injustice. Save for the formal duty of forwarding to the Committee of General Security the charges against suspects and the suspicious papers found among their effects, there was no official, or body of officials, to whom the committees were responsible. But even more serious an omission was the fact that no official was responsible for the committees, or able to check their excesses and make amends for their wrongs. The representatives on mission had the right to replace them, and any citizen had the right to denounce them, but there has always existed a vast difference between the exercise of a right and the performance of a duty. Only by the law of 14 Frimaire did the Convention remedy its error by placing over the committees the surveillance of the national agent of the district.

THE COMMITTEES AND THE SUSPECTS

In the account of the committees during the spring and summer of 1793, it was seen that a considerable number of them, both appointed and elected, arrested suspects on the authority of the deputies and the administration. Frequently liberty was restored to these suspects after the alarms of the moment had passed, with the result that now, even more hostile to the Revolution than before, they could resume their anti-Jacobin activities.

Furthermore, there had been no official definition of the word suspect. Each department, district, or commune, each representative, had a particular version, with "ex-nobles" common to most of them. The law of 17 September was to remedy both these defects. It gave a definition to the word suspect, nebulous as it was, and it declared that suspects were to be detained until peace was declared. Accordingly, the committees established according to the law of 21 March were ordered to arrest as suspects [7] (1) partisans of tyranny and federalism, (2) ex-nobles and their relatives who have not shown their devotion to the republic, (3) dismissed public officials, (4) those to whom certificates of civism had been refused, (5) returned émigrés, and (6) those unable to justify their means of support according to the law of 21 March.[8]

The last four categories were quite definite — an individual either did or did not fall into these classes, and generally the question could be decided on documentary evidence. But under the first two categories the committees could detain virtually any one, for the conduct, the relations, the writings, or the remarks of an individual could be brought forward to testify to his sympathy for tyranny or federalism; while in the case of émigrés' kin, "attachment to the Revolution" was rather difficult of proof. Consequently these two classifications were the most popular.

Perhaps it is for this reason that during the closing months of 1793 the suspects generally fall into the first two classes; perhaps it is simply the stage at which the Revolution had arrived. Whatever the reason, the majority of those detained from October to December belong either to the clergy or to the so-called upper classes, the hated *ci-devants*, the persons in easy circumstances, those who had attempted to strike back at the "anarchists."

[7] Roughly the classes are here listed in descending order of the frequency with which they appear on the registers of the committees.

[8] The committee of Darney (Vosges) on 11 October discussed whether "those" (*ceux*) in the text of the law referred to women as well as men. To avoid any illegality, they determined to arrest no women. Schwab, *Révol. Vosges*, 23e année, p. 110.

The Pursuit of Federalists

The chase for "federalists" was naturally hottest at Lyon, at Bordeaux, and in Provence, but more to supply the guillotine than the houses of detention. At Lyon the section committees received denunciations of those who had borne arms during the siege, and the Temporary Commission almost daily forwarded to the committee of the section of Rue Tupin requests for information on the activities of certain individuals during that troublous period.[9] At Bordeaux, too, one of the committee's chief tasks was keeping the Military Commission well supplied, examining the papers of the Commission of Public Safety, and circularizing the committees of the department for additional evidence against the rebels.[10] In Provence the same methods were employed — the committees examined the registers and documents of the central committees organized by federalists, and reported their findings to the Military Commission. At Marseille the committee was asked to classify the suspects according to their crimes, in order that the Commission could try at one time all those charged with the same offense. In addition, the department and the committees were to supply a list of those who occupied posts in the department during the counter-revolution, those who refused to recognize the authority of the Convention, those who had aided in the organization of armies, had disarmed patriots, had fired on Section 2 (which began the reaction against the Federalists), had occupied positions in the sections, had denounced or testified against patriots, or had ripped down trees of liberty. The committees were to include those who had fled, died, or been killed and the commission would pronounce *en contumace* (22 Pluviôse).[11]

Strangely, the federalists of Caen were rarely dragged to the guillotine — some were arrested as suspects, but the ma-

[9] Arch. Rhône CL 203, CL 184, CL 254, CL 61.

[10] Arch. Gironde, Register of deliberations, 11 October; L 2232.

[11] C. Lourde, *Histoire de la Révolution à Marseille et en Provence* (Marseilles, 1838–39), III, 363–365.

jority managed to enlist in the armies fighting the Vendeans, where they had a better chance for life than before a military commission.[12] The rebels of the Midi had tried the same expedient, but their committees were more persistent than those of Normandy. At Narbonne one of the committees interrogated soldiers of the Army of the Pyrénées Orientales, whose names appeared on lists of *sectionnaires* sent to Narbonne by the committee of Aix.[13]

The charge of federalism was not confined to those districts where the revolt against Paris had taken a violent turn. Throughout France, those who sympathized either openly or secretly with the Girondists were clapped into jail. Frequently the only ostensible grounds for arrest was the excessive wealth of the suspect, for in the minds of most committeemen wealthy egoist and federalist were one and the same. Usually, however, they had the delicacy to find some charge to apply to the rich other than their wealth — "federalist," "speculator," "hoarder" — these could be applied with a certain amount of justice to any man of fortune.

The committee of Nantes, however, admitted freely its attack on the wealthy as such. In their apologia, *Account rendered by the Members of the revolutionary committee of Nantes to their Brothers in the District administration of the aforesaid place,* they declared: "To this cursed federalism, our fine gentlemen added monopoly on all kinds of merchandise of primary necessity. . . . We were unable to await material proof of denunciations before acting. . . . We do not fear to say it, it is to the imprisonment of the *ci-devants* and all persons of means that the people is indebted for the success of opening warehouses and putting into effect the beneficent law of the maximum." [14] The committee was not boasting; 300,000 pounds of flour was found in the warehouses of the Thionet brothers after they had been declared suspect.[15]

---

[12] F. Guillonet, "Le Comité de surveillance de Caen," *A. Révol.,* I, 574.

[13] Arch. Aude L 2221, 8 Ventôse et seq.

[14] Quoted by A. Duchatellier in *Histoire de la Révolution en Bretagne* (Nantes, 1836), IV, 76–77.

[15] G. Martin, *Carrier et sa mission à Nantes* (Paris, 1924), pp. 184–185.

The members at Bordeaux were as frank in their attack on businessmen. On 8th Frimaire the committee recently (2 Frimaire) established by Ysabeau and Tallien ordered the arrest of eighty *négociants* and took elaborate precautions in serving the warrants, yet at least twelve managed to escape. The committee hoped to break up a huge "mercantile plot" intended to starve the people by hoarding and refusing to continue business operations. The records of all the merchants were seized as evidence, but they failed to reveal the threads of any such plot.[16]

THE COMMITTEES IN THE WEST

In the West, the Vendée war and the Chouans complicated the committees' task, for hundreds of persons were detained solely for having become involved with the rebels, which meant virtually the entire population. Indeed, in Maine-et-Loire and in Mayenne whole towns were arrested for their guilty relations with the brigands.[17] As a consequence, in the jails of the cities of the West the greater number of prisoners detained were captives of war or their families, sent back from the theatre of operations to be tried by the military commissions set up by the representatives. Many never came to trial, for at a time when food was scarce and prison space limited thousands were drowned or shot either by the committees themselves, as at Nantes, or with their coöperation, as at Angers.

Amid all the charges and counter-charges in regard to the responsibility of Carrier and the committee of Nantes in the drownings which took place there, this much is clear: that there were drownings at Nantes (according to Lallié, eleven mass drownings with 4860 victims, of whom 148 were priests; A. Velasque gives 3003; while G. Martin believes there were only seven *noyades* with 2000 incontestable victims);[18] that

---

[16] Arch. Gironde L 2164.

[17] E. Bourcier, "Essai sur la Terreur en Anjou," *R. Anjou*, VII (1872), 50; Gaugain, I, 467–469.

[18] A. Lallié, *Les Noyades de Nantes* (Nantes, 1879); A. Velasque, "Du nombre des victimes de la Terreur à Nantes," *R. H. Révol.*, XIV, 174; Martin, p. 279.

the number of "pure" suspects, if any, must have been few (Martin reports that arrests of suspects from October to Frimaire, when the drownings commenced, were approximately 300, including the 132 sent to Paris; after Frimaire arrests of Nantais were rare, save for some who violated the maximum, or other economic orders, while of those condemned by the military commission, some prostitutes, pickpockets, and common criminals were sentenced, but the majority sentenced were "brigands"); [19] that the committee managed the *noyades* (the minutes of the committee show an order for a lighter for the "deportation of suspects," and it gave orders for ships to be prepared); [20] and that Carrier had knowledge of them, even though he did not order them.[21]

The only extenuation for these acts lies in the abominable prison conditions which all authorities agree upon. The committee pled with the municipality to supply more and healthier prisons, but that body debated interminably and ended by writing to the district. Six days after the committee on its own initiative had obtained new quarters and had transferred the prisoners to them, the reply from the district was received, and several district commissioners arrived to inspect the alleged conditions at the old prison! [22]

The committee also found it necessary to provide for cleaning the streets, and turned over to the commission of public health for this purpose considerable sums of money, part of the proceeds of its tax on the wealthy. It spent other sums combating the plague. It also bore the responsibility and expense of establishing new prisons, and on one occasion at least ordered the commandant of engineers to send some of his men to clear out the prison of the Entrepôt.[23]

[19] Martin, pp. 156–158, 261.

[20] A. Lallié, "Episode de la Terreur à Nantes," *R. Bretagne, Anjou,* III, 419; Lallié, *Noyades,* p. 18; and the testimony of many witnesses at the committee's trial.

[21] Lallié declares that Carrier participated in preparations for the drowning of 19 Frimaire (*Noyades,* p. 17).

[22] Lallié, *Noyades,* p. 150.

[23] Lallié, "Le Comité révolutionnaire," *R. Bretagne, Anjou,* XXV, 350;

These were duties for which the administrations were responsible, but as the municipal officer Lamarie himself confessed, "the municipal government was simply a nonentity compared with the revolutionary committee which directed everything." [24] Whether the committee's enterprise was the cause or the effect of this administrative inactivity is problematical; nevertheless, the committee did make an effort, a bit too heroic in the case of the drownings, to dispel the double danger of famine and disease.

At Angers similar circumstances gave rise to similar remedies. The committee there worked hand in glove with the military commission. Members aided in questioning the brigands, especially the women, and were present at the shootings.[25] For example, the committee on one occasion sent two members to assist the commission and also to "supervise their [the brigands'] burial so that it is done in such a manner as to spare the commune of Angers any danger from the bad air which might result." [26] Crowded prisons also added to the committee's worries, and after the horrors of filth and disease had been brought to its attention, it swallowed its revolutionary principles long enough to send out nuns to bring about more healthful conditions.[27]

As was the case with some of their predecessors during the summer of 1793, the committees of the West assumed powers not their own. Yet in both cases it is possible to recognize, without being guilty of special pleading, that in a large measure their hands were forced. The rebellion in the West disrupted normal government and created problems so numerous and so formidable that the regular administration, still new to its task, was unable to cope with them. These are the facts which

---

XXVI, 136–138; Lallié, "Les Prisons de Nantes pendant la Révolution," *R. Bretagne, Vendée*, LIV, 214.

[24] Quoted by Lallié, "Episode de la Terreur à Nantes," *R. Bretagne, Anjou*, III, 431.

[25] F. Uzureau, "Les Victimes de la Terreur en Anjou," *Anjou Hist.*, IV (1903–04), 279, 282.

[26] "Correspondance du comité révolutionnaire d'Angers," *Anjou Hist.*, XXVI (1926), 42–43. [27] Uzureau, "Victimes . . . ," *Anjou Hist.*, IV, 295.

explain the usurpations of which the committees were guilty, usurpations unequaled in other parts of France. Consequently unless one is willing to admit that these circumstances were ultimately responsible for the drownings and shootings, one is forced to assume that the Frenchmen of the western departments were more vicious, more bloodthirsty, than those in the other sections of the Republic — which is absurd on the face of it.

To base a characterization of the arrests during the Terror upon the relatively fragmentary evidence we have collected may be unjustified. Yet in any extensive study it is necessary to work from materials which, though not exhaustive, are at least representative. In this manner it is possible to arrive at conclusions which can be depended upon if they do not clash too violently with other observations.

The conclusion seems to be that the majority of suspects detained, as opposed to persons guillotined, were of the upper classes: ex-nobles, émigrés, lawyers, men of letters, discredited members of the administration. Priests, too, must be included, for those arrested were the non-jurors, who, if not of upper-class origin, often shared the opinions and aspirations of that class. Inevitably there were members of the lower class detained; nothing shows this better than the committees' embarrassment in their efforts to provide food for them. Often these suspects were the servants of the well-to-do, persons whose loyalty exceeded their discretion. Others were simply the grumblers, persons constitutionally opposed to any act of government, the café statesmen from whom no nation is free. For counter-revolutionary remarks they were put in prison, where a more appreciative audience awaited them. The fanatics, those guilty of violating the maximum, of hoarding, or of making false declarations of their grain, usually belonged to the lower classes. Their numbers were not overwhelming, for the rural areas, where the majority of these people lived, generally escaped the surveillance of the committees.

The question of the chronology of arrests, the significance of the increasing severity or moderation of the committees, is virtually insoluble on any general basis. Inevitably there were reactions to events in Paris, but the necessary modifications to be made in any broad statement indicate that Paris did not impose upon the departments any universal regularity. It would be more accurate to say that the events which affected Paris frequently exercised a similar influence on the departments, but that local events and the temper of the local terrorists could alter the nature of the departments' reaction.

For example, the history of Julien *fils* and his Terror at Bordeaux commencing in Prairial forms a contrast to a tendency toward a decrease in arrests elsewhere in France during the spring of the Year II. Poitiers arrested sixty-six in Germinal, but only fourteen in Floréal and eleven in Prairial. Troyes saw a steady falling off from the month of Ventôse, arresting only four in Floréal and Prairial. Toul had arrested thirty-seven in Ventôse, but during the spring months it arrested only eleven. In the departments visited the same phenomenon was noticed. Douai released four in the first *décade* of Prairial after approval of the representative; in the second *décade*, eighteen; in the third, twenty-one. At Caen the removal of the committee set up in the fall ended what little Terror that city had seen. The committee of Fontenay in La Vendée, after a moment of energy in Germinal, relapsed into routine in the following month.

This falling off in arrests is presented as a tendency and is not substantiated by any complicated system of charts. It is submitted merely as an observation resulting from the study of the documents of many committees, and no finality is claimed for it. It should not be accepted as a sign of moderation, for the reactions of the majority of the committees to the fall of Robespierre point to a confirmed faith in Terrorism as the only solution for the problems of the Republic. That arrests were fewer may possibly be interpreted as meaning that, with the likely subjects already imprisoned — the nobles, the federalists and their associates — the rest of the population became more circumspect and refrained from acts which might arouse the suspicions of the committee. According to this interpretation, the committees had indeed achieved the goal set for them; but like the Convention after the death of the Dantonists, the citizens of France had lost the freedom of thought and action for which the Revolution had been fought.

CHAPTER V

THE ORGANIZATION OF THE COMMITTEES
(September–October 1793)

Establishment of the Committees by the Representatives

The promulgation in the departments of the new law of suspects, voted on 17 September, coincided roughly with the arrival of the second great mission of representatives (September and October 1793). Both these events brought about a profound change in the organization and activity of the committees.

This new mission of representatives had been decreed not only to put into execution the law on conscription voted on 23 August, but also to purge the various administrations of their moderate and Girondist elements. Often coöperating with the local popular society, or again as at Orléans assembling all good citizens to pass on the political character of the local officialdom, the deputies ordered wholesale dismissals and replacements to the applause of the *sans-culottes*.

The renewal of the committees was made imperative by the fact that those previously set up had been composed almost exclusively of administrators elected in November and December 1792 and by now suspect because of Girondist sympathies. Members who were not "equal to the occasion" were replaced by *sans-culottes* indicated to the representative by persons upon whom he relied. The machine was being organized, and those not believed capable of fulfilling the exacting requirements of revolutionizing the departments were sent beyond the pale.

The representatives on mission, furthermore, did not limit themselves to changing the personnel of the committees of surveillance by purge. Armed with unlimited powers, these new *intendants* not infrequently forcibly revived the committees, altering their organization to enable them to handle better the difficulties of the local situations or sometimes merely to put into execution the personal views of the representative. The perpetuation of the old system of appointed committees, each with its own type of organization and its own functions, was the result.

Fouché's acts in the Nièvre indicate to what extent the personal views of the representatives influenced the character of the committees' functions. According to Fouché's instructions, the committees, aided by the Republican guard, were to collect from the rich the revolutionary taxes necessary to finance their operations and to provide a dole for the unfortunate. They were also to carry out the decree ordering all proprietors to surrender their excess wheat and all manufacturers to continue the exploitation of their establishments.[1] Fouché's championing of the poor *sans-culottes* is obvious. Frequently the representatives ordered the committee to collect the revolutionary taxes which they had levied on the wealthy or the suspects. Taillefer at Villefranche (Aveyron) set up a committee which in addition to arresting suspects and officials and seizing arms and silverware was to levy taxes and other contributions to indemnify the republic and pay the expenses of the local revolutionary army.[2] At Nancy, Saint Just and Lebas created a special committee to levy and collect a revolutionary tax on the wealthy, the proceeds to be used in financing several new battalions for the Eastern frontier.[3] Laplanche at Caen entrusted to the committee, in addition to its official duties, the surveillance of hospitals, prisons, and houses of detention, the inspection of mail, and the performance of frequent inspections in both the city and the country to seek out arms, munitions, and food.[4] The committee at Bordeaux was ordered by Ysabeau and Tallien to conform to all laws and orders of the Convention

---

[1] Meunier, pp. 265–266.
[2] J. B. Serres, *Histoire de la Révolution en Auvergne* (Mauriac, 1895–99), VIII, 102–103.
[3] Godchot, *Révol. Fr.*, LXXX, 256.
[4] Arch. Calvados, Register of deliberations, 16 Frimaire.

and to an instruction drawn up by the representatives them-selves.[5]

If the committee had received no specific instructions, aside from the laws of the Convention, it frequently applied to its superiors, asking for "the course it was to follow." Especially in the case of the committees in the department and district capitals, it was again to the representatives that they turned, although another committee or the administration was some-times queried.

The Committee of Langon (Gironde) on 5 October sent Ysabeau a list of ten questions which troubled it. Some of the answers are as enlightening as the questions: First, "Can the committee call before it the poor who have been won over only by silver or assignats and for whom a good dressing down would be enough to make them yield and confess perhaps the identity of the agents or agitators?" To this Ysabeau replied, "Repri-mand and instruction for the poor, and close surveillance over their contacts and the means used to corrupt them." Second, "Can the committee extend its surveillance and issue warrants in communes which are neighboring and part of the canton, which from feebleness or inexperience leave unmolested their former lords who still scatter money around at their chateaux and receive there the agents of their lords . . .?" Ysabeau: "The surveillance of committees established in a canton capi-tal extends over all the canton. Besides, it doesn't matter who performs the job, provided it is done." [6]

The representatives were quite often responsible for the extension of the committees' geographical jurisdiction, that is,

---

[5] According to this instruction the committee was to report daily to the representatives; to enter and sign all deliberations in a register; to issue no warrants for arrests with less than seven signatures, no summons with less than two, and no order for release (subject to the representatives' approval) with less than seven; to keep four registers, one for orders and deliberations, one for denunciations, one for suspects arrested, and one for those brought up for trial; to inspect the prisons every three days in coöperation with the municipal-ity; and to publish a list of detained in the newspapers each *décade*. P. J. O'Reilly, *Histoire de Bordeaux* (Bordeaux, 1863), I, 536, 537.

[6] Arch. Gironde L 2229.

for granting complete authority over an entire district or department to a committee instead of to a commune or section of a commune as provided in the law of 21 March. The motives for this action are obvious. The representatives both at Paris and on mission had discovered the advantages of centralization, and during these very months the Convention was preparing the death of the decentralized constitution of 1791.

An example of a centralized committee is found in the Loir-et-Cher, where the committee of Blois had at its orders "revolutionary agencies" of three members at each district capital, and in the cantons individual "revolutionary supervisors." The latter merely sent reports to Blois, while the "agencies" could arrest only in cases of extreme emergency.[7] At Nîmes the committee attempted to subordinate the other committees of the departments to its orders, forbidding those not authorized by the Convention or the representatives to make arrests. The committees, however, ignored these instructions, and the department council was forced to issue a decree supporting the instructions of the central committee.[8]

An even more pertinent argument for centralizing the system of surveillance was the lack of suitable men in the smaller communes. Even in as populous a section as the four departments of Pas-de-Calais, Nord, Aisne, and Somme, the representatives Elie Lacoste and Peyraud had in their decree limited the committees to communes of more than 1000 inhabitants, and specified that there be at least seven members on each (22 September).[9] Lebon on 10 Frimaire suspended this decree of his colleagues and ordered the committee of Arras to watch all twenty-two communes of its district, declaring that in the country communes it was impossible to find "seven good republicans free from the influence of the rich and the *fer-*

[7] E. Campagnac, "Le Comité révolutionnaire de Blois et l'affaire de la Guerche," *A. Révol.*, V, 206–207.
[8] Arch. Gard 1 L 3, 10, 257.
[9] F. J. Darsy, *Amiens et le département de la Somme pendant la Révolution* (Amiens, 1878–93), I, 271.

miers." [10] Couthon in the Puy-de-Dôme experienced the same difficulty in finding capable men in the country communes, and created, therefore, a temporary "roving commission of general surveillance" to supplement the efforts of the committees he had set up in each district capital. Couthon's problem was made even more difficult by the flight of many potential suspects to the country to escape the too close surveillance of the city *sans-culottes*.[11] The Beauvais committee explained similar difficulties to André Dumont: "For a long time those who fear our surveillance have fled to the country where they conspire at their ease. . . . Unbind our hands, give us jurisdiction over the district, and we shall answer with our heads for purging it of all those scoundrels." [12]

The role of the representatives in this national reorganization was by far the predominant one. The countless changes in personnel, in function, and in jurisdiction resulted from their initiative; sometimes the enforcement of the law of 17 September itself was undertaken only after their arrival in the department. If they themselves did not establish the committees, it was as a result of their orders that their delegates or the local politicians in the popular societies and the administration acted.[13] Since they assumed the responsibility for establishing the committees, the representatives also assumed a tutelage over them, directing their attention to ends which the deputies considered desirable, suggesting that they ignore one problem and concentrate their attention on another. The committees, in short, were used to execute the personal policy of the representatives, a policy which was sometimes more extreme, sometimes more moderate, than the views of the dominant party at Paris. By the end of the winter, however, the centralizing in-

---

[10] L. Jacob, *Joseph Lebon 1765–1795* (Paris, 1934), I, 271–272; A. J. Paris, *La Terreur dans le Pas-de-Calais et dans le Nord* (Arras, 1864), p. 97.

[11] Mège, pp. 301–302, 572–573.

[12] H. Baumont, "Le département de l'Oise pendant la Révolution," *B. Soc. Oise*, VI, 66.

[13] During the fall of 1793 the election of committees by the popular assemblies, as provided by the law of 21 March, was almost unknown save in the country communes.

fluence represented by the Committee of Public Safety had eliminated that independence, and both the representatives and the committees were checked.

THE COMPOSITION OF THE COMMITTEES

The difficulties experienced by the representatives in assembling a group of committeemen "equal to the circumstances" have already been hinted at, but a closer investigation, revealing their social position and their talents, if any, is almost imperative if we are to understand the chaos and confusion which characterized their activities in the fall of 1793.

They were, of course, *sans-culottes*. In the cities the vast majority were artisans and workingmen — their civil condition was usually indicated by one of the *-ier* words — *fripier, limonadier, perruquier, meunier, charpentier*, and so on. Occasionally one finds a "man of law," but the term is always ambiguous. Priests, despite the specific ban on them, are occasionally encountered. But a few sample lists would be more enlightening.

The famous drowning committee at Nantes had as members two masons, two nailmakers, a lawyer, a bankrupt shopkeeper, a basketmaker, a building-contractor, a clockmaker, a pinmaker, a *maître d'armes* (an ex-gentleman, pardoned for two murders committed before the Revolution, according to Wallon), and two men without known profession.[14] At Bayonne the committee was composed of only eight members: an actor, a dancing master, a tailor, a locksmith, a clockmaker, an ex-priest, a Spanish lawyer, and a German.[15] That of Sancoins (Cher) was composed of an administrator, two teachers, one ex-soldier, a farmer, a surgeon, an ex-priest, a saddler, a baker, a merchant, a former employee of the salt warehouse, and a tailor.[16] Three professions which recur frequently are those

[14] H. Wallon, *Histoire du tribunal révolutionnaire* (Paris, 1880–82), V, 327; Lallié, "Le Comité révolutionnaire," *R. Bretagne, Anjou*, XXV, 279 note.

[15] R. Cuzacq, "Le Comité révolutionnaire de Bayonne," *B. Soc. Bayonne*, 1929, pp. 26–27.

[16] "Le Comité révolutionnaire de Sancoins (Cher)," *A. Révol.*, V, 178, 492.

of barber, innkeeper, and saloonkeeper — citizens who were well placed to hear the latest gossip and pass it along to the committee.

In the district and canton capitals most committee members were literate although generally they had a better ear than eye, for the orthography is often fantastic.[17] As for their patriotism, it was irreproachable. They had been hand-picked by the deputies on mission, often with the aid of the Jacobin club, and they were consequently most steadfast partisans of the new regime. Their moral character has been too often damned by opponents of the Revolution. Certainly many of them were scoundrels. Undoubtedly they were responsible for many petty vexations of the kind which French bureaucrats still enjoy manufacturing. But familiarity with their daily work and their less sensational proceedings reveals many examples of generosity and sympathy, and goes far to weaken the old legend of their effrontery and insolence.

In the country communes the members were, of course, farmers — landowners, tenants, sharecroppers, laborers. The representatives and the *sans-culottes* of the cities distrusted them — and justly so, for the registers of the country committees are virtual blanks. They met perfunctorily to reëlect a president and secretary, declared they had seen nothing contrary to the laws, and then retired. Indeed, the national agent of Dinan told the Committee of General Security that most of the country communes established committees simply in order to escape surveillance.[18] Most of the peasants probably had no love for the Revolution. To some of them it had given land, but it had taken their sons from the fields to fight "the crowned tyrants of Europe"; it had driven off their priests; it had told them at what price they were to sell their grain,

---

[17] For example, the register of the Quimper (Finistère) committee is headed "ce caet apartien à la surveillance de Quimper-Odet." J. Trévédy, "Histoire du comité révolutionnaire de Quimper," *R. H. Ouest*, XII, 297. The committee of Aix-en-Provence once wrote a letter to "Jambon" Saint-André. Arch. Bouches-du-Rhône L 1712, 19 Fructidor.

[18] L. Dubreuil, *Le Régime révolutionnaire dans le district de Dinan* (Paris, 1912), p. 65.

and if they refused to sell, had deprived them of it by force.

The charge that most of these rural committees of surveillance were under the influence of Girondins, that is, of the larger landowners, is probably accurate. The economic and social life of a small agricultural village of several hundred is far too compact for a handful of malcontents to denounce their fellow citizens. The testimony of Lebon sustains this view:

> Circumstances are such that the wholesale establishment of committees of surveillance in the country would harm, rather than help, the Republic.
>
> Our brothers in the small communes have been so degraded by the old regime that they are not at present sufficiently enlightened in regard to the new to succeed in foiling the plots of the malicious and the intriguers.
>
> Whom to put on the committees? The rich? The big farmers? That would be putting the wolf in the sheepfold, making victims of the unfortunate. Should we put the poor on, then? That would be performing an almost useless task, for the latter would hardly have the courage to attack the men of fortune under whose dominance they are held by their poverty. We have had that experience in setting up the majority of the municipalities.[19]

Book-learning was rare among the peasants and even the educated had their limitations. "Nous ne comprennions lins truxions des decrest [sic] de la Convention," confessed the committee of Meulle.[20] But the worst blunder seems to have been at Saint-Memmie (Marne) where on 14 Thermidor the committee received a denunciation against the "veuve Nicaise . . . soupçonnée d'avoir eu un enfant." Solemnly the twelve members of the committee gathered the local municipal officer, the national agent, and the health officer, and in a body (clad in their official scarves, one hopes) they proceeded to the home of the *suspecte* and after a very complete examination by the health officer drew up a *procès-verbal* which omitted no detail. It seemed the suspicions were not unfounded.[21]

---

[19] Quoted by Paris, pp. 154–155.
[20] Arch. Calvados, Register of deliberations, 1 Frimaire.
[21] Arch. Marne, Register of deliberations, 14 Thermidor.

The whole situation was probably best summed up by two committees of the Bouches-du-Rhône. At Cassis the secretary reported: "On ne peut pas choisir des membres qui reunissent tallent et patriotismes. nous sommes tous ignorans." Or more succinctly at Roquefort: "Le nombres des personnes à tallans sont très rares ches nous comme étant que des paysans, si ce trouve quelqu'un chez nous, nous doutons de leur civisme pour cela." [22]

As a result of this scarcity of talent the law in some cases was simply ignored and the committees were composed of fewer than twelve members. The representative Roux-Fazillac explained the situation to the Committee of Public Safety in a letter written 27 September: "The committees of public safety which I have established in each district capital [of the department of the Charente] are composed of only six or eight members. . . . I could not increase all the committees to twelve members without taking the risk of transforming the character of many of them, for in some places men of truly revolutionary opinions are very rare. . . ." [23]

In other places it was necessary to draft men to serve. Taine quotes a citizen of Aignay (Côte d'Or) who declared to his fellow citizens: "I was put on the committee of surveillance by force and installed by force." If there was any disagreement, "it was always threats. . . . Always trembling, always afraid — that is the way I passed eight months in that miserable post." [24] In the Vendée in Floréal the representatives included in their decree naming nine members to form the committee of Les Sables d'Olonne the provision that "all citizens called to fill the above functions cannot refuse them on any pretext under penalty of being considered suspect." [25]

[22] Arch. Bouches-du-Rhône L 1011, 25 Pluviôse, 7 Ventôse.
[23] A. Aulard, *Recueil des actes du Comité de Salut Public* (Paris, 1889–1925), VII, 93–94.
[24] H. Taine, *The French Revolution* (New York, 1885), Book VII, ch. iii (vol. III, p. 249).
[25] Arch. Vendée L 1257, 15 Floréal.

THE DISTRIBUTION OF LAWS

The chaotic condition of French administration during 1793 is revealed by the repeated complaints of the committees that they had no copies of the laws they were expected to enforce. On 13 September, more or less as an afterthought, the Convention decreed "that the laws relative to general security, the execution of which is entrusted to the revolutionary committees, shall be sent to these committees throughout the territory of the Republic." Conforming with this order, Paré, minister of the Interior, circularized the departments, asking them to compile lists of the committees to whom a copy of such laws would be forwarded. Under date of 29 September an epitome of these laws was printed, containing not only the decrees which related to the committees, but also a large number of so-called revolutionary laws, all passed previous to 13 September.[26] The circular itself declared "everything pertaining to general security, hoarding, foodstuffs, requisitions, speculation, the removal of symbols of royalty and feudalism, measures to prevent and punish corruption in regard to national property, is a part of the functions of these Committees." [27] The vast majority of these laws had not been attributed to the committees by the Convention, but Paré, as minister of the Interior charged with their execution, had anticipated the law of 14 Frimaire in calling upon the committees to aid in enforcing them.

Despite this effort of the government the decrees were late in arriving. On the 20th day of the first month Dieppe declared in regard to the sixteen committees of its district that "the citizens who belong to them for the most part are not familiar with the laws whose enforcement is entrusted to them." It was not until 1 Nivôse, however, that the department of Seine-Inférieure circularized the districts for the names of

[26] The list included such decrees as that dissolving the *Caisse d'Escompte*; the rate of indemnity for those caring for abandoned children; the laws against hoarding, refusing assignats, and so on. Arch. Seine-Inf. L 220.
[27] *Ibid.*

committees to which the minister's list should be sent, even though it had received the request from Paris on 5 Brumaire.

Only on 11 Pluviôse did the committee of Saint-Saens receive this list of laws passed before 13 September together with a copy of the law of 17 September, but while acknowledging receipt to the department, it suggested that it would be convenient to have copies of the decrees passed *since* 17 September.[28]

This tardiness was not peculiar to the Seine-Inférieure, however. The activities of one of the section committees at Narbonne were constantly hampered by its ignorance of the laws. The national agent had forwarded a denunciation on 17 Nivôse, to which the committee replied that it would be very glad to punish the citizen according to the law of 29 September (the maximum), if the national agent would be so good as to send the committee a copy of the law of 29 September.[29] The district of Fontenay (Vendée), discovering that some of the committees in its jurisdiction possessed no copies of the laws of 21 March, 12 August, and 17 September, had additional ones printed and dispatched on 19 Pluviôse. Yet on 20 Ventôse the committee of Chaille (organized on 16 Frimaire), one of the canton capitals of the district, reported that it had no laws or instructions concerning its functions.[30] It was in the same class as the Laval committee whose secretary confessed that "all the laws were unknown to us, save the law of the people, the supreme law." [31]

SALARIES

Perhaps the most persistently pursued of the committees' activities was their constant petitioning for their salaries. By the law of 5 September 1793, passed on the motion of Billaud-Varenne, "the members of the revolutionary committees who devote their days and nights to public service [will] receive

---

[28] Arch. Seine-Inf. L 220.
[29] Arch. Aude L 2223.
[30] Arch. Vendée L 1258, L 1246.
[31] Gaugain, II, 81.

an indemnity, and this indemnity shall be fixed at the same amount as that of the electors." [32]

The law as printed read: "An indemnity of 3 *livres* a day shall be granted to members of the committees of public safety." A revolutionary tax, levied on the rich, was to provide the funds. Upon this decree the committees set up according to the law of 21 March and those set up later by the representatives, based the claims to payment which they pressed upon the administration and the representatives. [33]

In some cases where they had been authorized by the representatives to levy revolutionary taxes, the members were able to withhold a certain amount of the proceeds to meet their salaries and expenses. At L'Aigle (Orne), 7,000 of the 14,000 *livres* were retained by the committee, while Orléans was given 6,225 *livres*, 10 s from the "revolutionary treasury." [34]

In other cases, where proceeds from revolutionary taxes were not available, the committees appealed to the administration or to the representatives. The district of Draguignan instructed its committee to levy a tax on those on the rolls of the forced loan, and the department of the Oise advanced the committee of Senlis their 3 *livres* a day until the taxes on the rich were levied. [35] Other administrations were not so helpful. The municipality of Le Havre confessed it had no funds to fulfill the claims, and the department of the Meurthe gave a similar answer, suggesting that the committee of Nancy apply to the representative. The Quimper committee had more success. One appeal had netted it 1500 *livres*. Needing more money, it appealed to the representative without result, then to the

[32] *Moniteur*, réimp., XVII, 586.

[33] The members can hardly be condemned as grasping, for as most of them pointed out in their appeals, "all being artisans and men with families, they cannot provide for their families without having a salary which repays them for their time, which they devote entirely to the public welfare." A. Denis, *Le Comité de surveillance révolutionnaire de Toul* (Toul, 1911), p. 114 note.

[34] D. Lottin, *Recherches historiques sur la ville d'Orléans* (Orléans, 1834), 2e partie, III, 129. Previously one of the members had paid the expenses! Arch. Loiret L 1179, 8 Prairial.

[35] Patin, *B. Soc. Draguignan*, XVII, 118. Baumont, *B. Soc. Oise*, V, 261.

district, which replied that there were no wealthy in Quimper to tax. Nevertheless, to end the importunate demands of the committee, it ordered the department to pay 2400 *livres* from funds set aside for the repression of disorders! [36]

Certain committees limited their demands simply to expenses, although they are, of course, the exceptions.[37] It was the practice to honor these requests, and the amounts paid show that the expenses were only office expenses.

From this brief account of the subject which was never far from the minds of the committees it can be seen that there existed no universal practice in regard to the payment of the members. Their fortune, good or ill, depended upon the financial condition of the local administration or the generosity of the representatives. Nevertheless, they persisted in their demands, and after Thermidor the Convention turned its attention to the subject.

Cambon, speaking for the Committee of Finances, reported on the matter on 6 Frimaire III. He claimed that the law of 5 September referred only to the committees of public safety set up in the departments by the representatives; that is, the committees which we have referred to in our account of the committees during the spring and summer as the "appointed committees." He therefore proposed the payment of such of those committees as were maintained by the decree of 4 June 1793 (the Jacobin, as opposed to the Girondist committees), the committees set up according to the law of 7 Fructidor, and those committees set up by a decree of the representatives, allotting all of them this indemnity. Payment was to be made on the basis of actual days for which the members could furnish proof of attendance. Cambon personally was opposed to paying any committees save those set up by the law of 5 September; indeed, on the 14 Brumaire III he had admitted that the Committee of Finances "considers itself fortunate in having,

---

[36] Trévédy, *R. H. Ouest*, XII, 612–614.
[37] Ceyreste and La Penne, Arch. Bouches-du-Rhône L 1011, 6 Floréal, 15 Prairial.

as a result of its inertia, saved 591,000,000 *livres* for the public treasury," but a contract was a contract and the Committee's proposal was embodied in the law of 13 Frimaire III.[38]

Frankly, the revolutionary committees had been cheated. While it is true that by a law of 26 May 1793 committees of surveillance were forbidden to call themselves "revolutionary committees" (the term reported in the newspapers for the law of 5 September), and that on 20 September Jeanbon Saint-André speaks of committees of surveillance and committees of public safety as two different institutions, yet on 1 Pluviôse the Convention replied to a petition of the committee of surveillance of Belleville for compensation by passing to the order of the day "motivated on the fact that the law of 5 September which regulates the amount and manner of paying committees of surveillance, is applicable to all the communes of the Republic." [39]

One member pointed out that the committees had paid themselves, referring to the accusations of theft and extortion brought after Thermidor, but as even Cambon admitted, a contract was a contract.[40]

[38] *Moniteur*, réimp., XXII, 426, 734, 742.
[39] *Journal des débats*, Pluviôse II, p. 3.
[40] *Moniteur*, réimp., XXII, 425.

CHAPTER VI

THE MACHINERY OF DETENTION

DENUNCIATIONS

To DECIDE who was suspect and who was not presented no problem to the committees. Undoubtedly the good *sans-culottes* already had many marked for detention, men and women whose reactions to the events of the Revolution had given concrete evidence of their hostility. As a result, the first meetings were generally spent in naming the more obvious individuals, sometimes with no indication of their "crime," or with only a stereotyped remark such as "incivic remarks," "aristocrat," "has shown no attachment to the revolution," "fanatic," "counter-revolutionary," "indifferent," or, often, with specific remarks attributed to the suspect, mentions of his failure to accept the constitution of 1793, and so on.[1]

Denunciations soon came to the committees to assist them in their task, and a call to all good patriots to denounce the enemies of liberty was usually among the first of a committee's acts.[2] The Angers committee proclaimed to its fellow citizens that "denunciations, which were hateful under the old regime because they served tyranny, have now become legitimate because today they are intended for the good of all. The committee therefore invites all good citizens to come and declare to it all they know which may be contrary to the interests of the Republic."[3]

[1] The council-general of Dijon listed many simply as *arrestocrate et suspect* (Arch. Côte d'Or L IV a 47 h/2, fo. 70), and at Blaringhem a person was denounced for *arrestocratie* (Arch. Nord L 10132), terms more aptly to be applied to the committees themselves. One young girl confessed she preferred talking like the "brigands" to being raped. She was charged with uttering a *propos contre-révolutionnaire*. Blossier, *B. Com. Hist.* 1910, 251.

[2] At Poitiers a box outside the door for denunciations provided 24-hour service. E. Salliard, *La Terreur à Poitiers* (Paris, 1912), p. 50.

[3] F. Uzureau, "L'Arrestation des fédéralistes angevins," *Révol. Fr.*, LXVII, 235.

Generally the citizens were not backward about presenting to the committees all the gossip they had heard, for many of the charges are simply a mass of *on dits*. But it is impossible to generalize about the denunciations. Some were ridiculous, for example that of a citizen of Blaringhem who declared a widow and her three children were suspects, because they had not been in his house since the time they learned that he loved the Republic and had bought their farm.[4] Some were as amusing as this one against a member of the battalion from the district of Gray (Haute-Saône):

Jean Baptiste Buvard l'ainé a dit, que hier, environ les huit heures du soir vingt quatre nivôse courant, étant au domicile du citoyen françois Fontaine aubergiste public à Valay, où il venait d'opiner sur un arbitrage, le citoyen Lambert y entra, et après plusieurs paroles inconséquentes que proféra celui-ci, il se répandit abondamment en envectives et propos indécents, disant: qu'il se foutoit de toutes les autorités constituées, qu'il ne reconnoissoit que les autorités militaires, qu'il se foutoit et contrefoutoit de la municipalité de Valay aussi bien que du comité de surveillance de cette commune; que la municipalité lui avait fait une requisition pour rejoindre, qu'il se foutoit de sa requisition comme d'elle; et montrant la copie de ladite requisition dit: Voilà pour faire un torche-cul.[5]

Fortunately the committees generally had the good sense to realize that many of the denunciations were not worth their attention, that many of the persons denounced had perhaps talked a bit extravagantly when in their cups. The members usually ignored charges of this kind or else undertook an investigation to corroborate the facts alleged. Constantly there comes up evidence that the denunciations were not always taken at their face value and that cases were examined with a certain amount of care before arrests were made. The committee of the Center section of Dijon and the committee of Dieppe usually made a preliminary examination of the papers of the suspect, and if no documentary evidence of guilt was

[4] Arch. Nord L 10132.
[5] P. Maréchal, *La Révolution dans la Haute-Saône* (Paris, 1903), pp. 369–370.

discovered the affair was closed.[6] The committee established at Bordeaux on 11 Brumaire released a number of persons after a fruitless inspection of their papers, and its successor on 17 Frimaire permitted a citizen to obtain documents from his home to prove his innocence. The denouncer was sternly rebuked by the president, and a similar case on the same day led the president to request the members "to make an investigation in regard to the denouncer who appears to have been a bit irresponsible."[7]

In some places one even sees a bit of crude detective work. A close examination of a "journeyman joiner's" hands by one committee revealed them to be much too tender for one following that profession, and the gentleman was shipped off to the house of detention.[8] At Limoges the committee called in expert opinion to decide upon the guilt of a volunteer, Gabriel David. The case was conducted as follows:

> Est comparu pardevant nous, en conformité du mandat d'amener decerné contre lui, Gabriel David, qui a été interrogé ainsi qu'il suit:
> As-tu écrit "Merde pour la nation" sur ton congé?
> Répond que non, qu'il ne sait comment les mots infâmes s'y trouvent, et ignore quelle est la sacrilège main qui les a tracés; qu'il a été étrangement surpris lorsque le commissaire des guerres les lui a fait lire, qu'il jure de nouveau ne point en être l'auteur et appelle en témoignage de son innocence la parfaite securité où il étoit que ce congé ne contenoit rien d'incivique, rien qui peut être à sa charge, que s'il en eut été autrement il ne l'auroit pas presenté au commissaire des guerres mais bien livré aux flammes. . . .

The committee took little stock of his protestations and "in view of the urgency of this inquiry" asked two writing-masters to come immediately. Both compared specimens of David's handwriting with the *mots infâmes* on the leave and pronounced them the product of the same hand. Still protesting, David was escorted off to the house of detention.[9]

[6] Arch. Côte d'Or L IV a/47a passim; Arch. Seine-Inf. L 5215 passim.
[7] Arch. Gironde L 2164.
[8] Salliard, p. 53.
[9] Arch. Haute-Vienne L 843, 28 Messidor.

OTHER SOURCES OF INFORMATION

When the committee came to the end of its inspiration, it was always possible to seek assistance from other official or semi-official bodies — the administration, the representatives, the sections, or the popular societies. Only rarely was the requested information refused; in most cases those asked were only too happy to send along lists of enemies of the people.

There were still other methods which the committees employed. We have told how the committees in the federalist centers examined the registers and miscellaneous documents of their predecessors to ferret out *sectionnaires* and denouncers. Elsewhere similar compromising documents were resorted to. At Sedan and Dijon, the committees made use of the membership list of the suppressed counter-revolutionary clubs. A counter-revolutionary address to the *veuve Capet*, at that time Queen of France, was unearthed by the committee at Montargis (Loiret) and the signers were tracked down.[10]

Failing all these, the committee could put the town through a purge, as at Péronne (Somme) and Mattaincourt (Vosges), or search the streets for suspects, as at Tours, Bordeaux, and Aix.[11] Another method was to send missions into the countryside, which usually harbored some who had fled the cities in time to escape the warrants of the committees.[12]

These inquiries and investigations, these requests for official lists, repeated hundreds of times over, lead one to the conclusion that the arrest of suspects was by no means as irresponsible as it has sometimes been described. The precautions taken, while not conforming to the high principles of Wigmore, safeguarded citizens from too flagrant injustice. That there were injustices, that some arrests were made simply

---

[10] Arch. Loiret L 1174, Floréal.

[11] G. Ramon, *La Révolution à Péronne* (Péronne, 1886), pp. 44–45; Schwab, *Révol. Vosges,* 23e année p. 42; Arch. Gironde L 2175, 26 Prairial; Arch. Bouches-du-Rhône L 1712, 6 Germinal.

[12] At Les Sables, Arch. Vendée L 1215, 15 Floréal; at Aurillac, Serres, IX, 32–33.

to satisfy personal spite, that the committees' standards of guilt often varied according to the wealth and political dispositions of the accused, it is impossible to deny. But from a revolutionary point of view, the unpredictability of the committees' acts was a strength, since it forced opponents of the Revolution to avoid even the very suspicion of evil.

ARRESTS

To effect an arrest, the committees were generally dependent upon the local gendarmerie or the National Guard, although in large cities the committee occasionally retained special agents.[13] To the gendarme or agent was handed a warrant similar to the one written on the outside cover of the register of Grenoble's committee of 21:

> De par les loix. Nous membre du comité central de surveillance, établi dans la ville de Grenoble en exécution de la loi du 21 Mars dernier, et organisé le 29 8bre par l'arrêté du représentant du peuple Petitjean; mandons et ordonnons à tous gendarmes nationaux dépositaire de la force publique de conduire dans la maison d'arrêt de cette ville les citoyens —— pour avoir fait rebellion à la loix; ordonnons au concierge de ladite maison de les recevoir et des les retenir jusqu'à ce qu'il en soit autrement ordonné. Fait à Grenoble —— [14]

Sometimes a *procès-verbal* of the arrest was drawn up; as frequently it was not. The committee of Angers, for example, reported that suspects had been "sent to the city by the fifties and the hundreds without any *procès-verbal*, without denunciations, without even lists of names," so that a large number of those concerned were sent back to their communes.[15]

The *procès-verbal* was simply a report of the arrest or of the reason no arrest was made, of the applying of seals to prevent the extraction of damaging papers, and of any other acts

---

[13] Nantes used the Compagnie Marat for this purpose; Bordeaux on 11 Frimaire retained six special agents. A. Lallié, "La Compagnie Marat et autres auxiliaires du comité révolutionnaire," *R. H. Ouest*, XIII, 305–306; Arch. Gironde L 2164.

[14] Arch. Isère L 870.

[15] Bourcier, *R. Anjou*, VI, 128.

of the arresting officer. The following is an example, typical of the verbose, legalistic style affected by the committees:

4e jour du 2e mois, l'an 2e

Ce jourd'huy 4e jour des second mois l'an 2e de la République française une et indivisible.

Je soussigné Nicholas Abraham Blot, commissaire du comité de surveillance établi en cette ville de Rouen en Exécution d'un mandat d'arrêt à moi remis cejourd'hui décerné contre la citoyenne Caquerau Cavelier, femme Boisgrisel demeurante ordinairement à Neufchâtel & actuellement à Rouen, Rue de l'Aumône no 126, auquel dernier domicile Je me suis transporté accompagné du citoyen françois dumomhel adjutant de le garde nationale de Neufchâtel et parlant à la personne de la citoyenne Cavelier femme Boisgrisel je lui a notiffié le mandat d'arrêt dont j'étais porteur lui déclarant devoir la conduire en la maison d'arrêt de St. Lo à quoi elle a obéi sans aucune resistance; perquisition faite dans tous les aistres de la demeure ainsi que dans les meubles & effets, je ni ay trouvé rien de suspect, sur lesquels j'ai apposé le scellé d'une bande de papier cacheté du cire rouge sur lesquels est Empreint le cachet dont j'ai accoutumé de me servir dans l'exercice de mes functions. Après quoy j'ai conduit ladite cityonne Cavelier femme Caqueray Boisgrisel en la maison d'arrêt de Saint Lo où elle est restée à la garde & charge du concierge de ladite maison & le scellé mis sur les meubles et effets de la citoyenne Cavelier femme Boisgrisel ainsi que les clefs de sa demeure ont été remis à la garde de la citoyenne Thérèse Paturel femme Fautrois demeurant même rue de l'aumone no 2 qui a consenti s'en charger à l'exception d'un lit fourni dans son entier ainsi que linge & hardes à l'usage de la dite citoyenne femme Caqueray de Boisgrisel qui sont restés en sa disposition et de tout ce que dessus j'ai fait et redigé le present procès-verbal pour ainsi que le mandat d'arrêt être déposé au comité de surveillance pour sur le tout être requis et ordonné ce qu'il appartiendra lecture faite et ont avec nous signé le présent procès-verbal: Nicholas Abraham Blot; du Momhel (avec paraphe.)[16]

On the occasion of mass arrests, such as occurred during the early weeks of the committees' existence, or during the visits of the representatives, more elaborate preparations were usu-

---

[16] Arch. Seine-Inf. L 5403. A *paraphe* was a complex scrawl of lines whose intricacies were known only to the individual making them. It was a sign of genuineness, preventing the duplication of documents since the *paraphe* was harder to forge than a signature. Some of the registers were numbered and *paraphé* to prevent the insertion or extraction of sheets. This practice was specifically ordered by the law of 7 Fructidor.

ally made. For two days, 8–9 Frimaire, the committee of Bordeaux deliberated on the procedure to be followed in the arrest of 80 business men accused of hatching a "mercantile plot." Finally the committee arrived at a formula: First, seals were to be placed in the offices of the business men; second, copies of all letters were to be transferred to the committee's offices; third, the suspects were to be removed to the Seminary under guard, and two cannons were to be set up there to protect the house of detention; fourth, two *sans-culottes* were to be left at each office to guard the seals; and fifth, 1200 men were to be requested from General Brune, divided into sixteen detachments, with a committeeman or agent leading each. Brune agreed to supply the necessary (?) men and the committee instructed him to place three groups of 400 each at strategic points at eleven o'clock that evening. Meanwhile two members were sent to the City Hall to procure another house of detention and chose the convent of the Benedictines, which after a few repairs would "still hold a great number if circumstances require it." At the same time the guard at the Séminaire St. Raphael was doubled. The lists were then divided into groups and assigned to members and their agents (including the brother of Ysabeau), and the party went into action. But apparently the raid was too long in preparing, for of the eighty named twenty-three managed to escape, and since several who were ill were left at their homes the convent of the Benedictines was not necessary. The papers of the eighty were seized, however, and at the same time seals were applied to the papers of such foreign consuls as were engaged in trade.[17]

There were other localities where the committees went to less trouble to gather in the suspects. The Central committee of Haute-Vienne on 11 September drew up a list of suspects and indicated the house of detention where each was to be confined. Then the suspects were invited to surrender themselves at the house indicated.[18] At Amiens, at Toulouse, and at Bourg

[17] Arch. Gironde L 2164.
[18] A. Fray-Fournier, *Le Département de la Haute-Vienne pendant la Révolution* (Limoges, 1909), II, 98.

(Ain) the same course was taken on several occasions. One order was worded: "The central committee also places under arrest Citizen Chossat Monthburon, with the request that he go immediately to the Clorists." [19]

PRISONS

Another of the myths for which the unsavory history of the Nantes committee is perhaps responsible is the long tale of horrible prison conditions, of filth and vermin, of frightful mortality. These conditions did exist in the prisons of Nantes, Saumur, and other centers of concentration for prisoners of war, where hundreds arrived daily and where the physical equipment to care for the captives was simply not available. Elsewhere it is an entirely different story.

In the first place, a sharp distinction was usually made between prisons where common-law criminals were confined and houses of detention reserved exclusively for suspects. Here again the West was exceptional — suspects were sometimes mixed with Vendée brigands and Chouans. At Les Sables the committee sent several of its members to the houses of detention to discover whether such conditions existed. On finding several brigands there, the committee made arrangements with the municipality to transfer them elsewhere.[20] The houses of detention were usually *maisons nationales*, that is, the *hôtels* of émigrés, chateaus, schools, or convents.[21] The advantages of these buildings were obvious. They were generally well supplied with large rooms, spacious eating halls, and well-enclosed

[19] Darsy, I, 283; Connac, *R. Pyrénées*, XII, 416; P. Le Duc, *Histoire de la Révolution dans l'Ain* (Bourg, 1879–94), IV, 50–51, 76.

[20] Incidentally, this committee was probably the only Vendée committee which employed the term "brigands" — elsewhere, and especially at Fontenay, they were particular about calling them "rebels." Arch. Vendée L 1215, 14 Floréal.

[21] The Châlons committee might almost be accused of arresting suspects to get additional houses of detention. On 19 October it was instructed by the department to use the home of an émigré's wife who had recently been arrested. On 24 Brumaire it arrested her sister and immediately ordered that *her* home should be used as a house of detention. Arch. Marne, Committee of the Section République, Register of deliberations.

gardens where the suspects could take their constitutionals. The great disadvantage from the committees' point of view lay in the fact that there were no special safeguards to prevent escape, so that reports of missing suspects were not infrequent.

Until the decision of the Commission of Civil Administration, Police and Courts, of 21 Thermidor II, which attributed the supervision of houses of detention to the municipal governments, there was no universal rule on the matter of responsibility for the management of these buildings. Boisset ordered the department directory of the Gard to continue to exercise its control over houses of detention and hospitals, since "the surveillance given by the law of 14 Frimaire" to the committees "has nothing to do with the surveillance of houses of detention. . . ." [22] Other committees distinctly stated that the administration of such houses was not part of their functions, while Fontenay and Cambrai raised no objections to allowing the municipality to take the responsibility. [23] Coöperation between the two bodies was the usual solution; and at Issoudun (Indre) it was the only solution possible, since the committee and the municipality each attempted to pass the burden to the other. [24]

Whether the municipality managed the houses or whether it fell to the lot of the committee to add this to its cares, the general principles of management were the same. Restrictions were placed upon the contacts of the suspects with the outside world, and letters to and from them were examined by the *concierge*, the committee, or the municipality before delivery. Certain committees prohibited the entry of any visitors, while Dieuze permitted mothers, fathers, husbands, wives, and children of suspects to visit them from seven o'clock in the morn-

[22] Arch. Gard 1, L 6, 3.
[23] Le Havre, Arch. Seine-Inf. L 5327, 12 September; and Rouen, F. Clérembray, "La Terreur à Rouen," *La Normandie*, XIV, 517; G. Gaillard, "La Loi des suspects à Fontenay," *Société d'émulation de la Vendée* (1915–1922), p. 102; Pastoors, p. 480.
[24] Arch. Indre L 1552, 28–30 Frimaire.

ing until seven at night.[25] The committee of twenty-one at Grenoble frowned on such laxness and was quite angry when those detained at Sainte Marie d'en Haut, managed by the committee, petitioned for transfer to the Oratoire, which was under the control of the municipality and where the "detained received visits and enjoyed greater liberty."[26] At Melun friends and business agents as well as relatives were permitted to see the detained, and such reliable journals as the *Moniteur* and the *Journal des débats* could be read.[27]

Living conditions seem to have been not too severe. The suspect was permitted to bring the necessary articles from his home to furnish the room assigned to him. If there was not sufficient space, the suspect might be forced to share his bed with another unfortunate.[28] At some places the wealthy suspects even had servants to perform their menial tasks. Those at Saint-Brieuc, once in the house of detention, had to remain, while at Dieuze they were only to remain long enough to serve the food they had brought.[29] The Pau committee, on the contrary, forbade servants unless permission was obtained from the committee or the representatives.[30] The whole practice was quite counter-revolutionary, according to the Limoges committee, which worked up great indignation and on 11 Floréal summarily ordered all servants to leave the prisons and hinted they might more profitably be cultivating the fields or the arts than "serving stinking aristocrats."[31]

It is not surprising that both the committees and the de-

[25] Arch. Meurthe-et-Moselle L 3191, 3 Ventôse.
[26] Arch. Isère L 871, 24 Frimaire.
[27] Campagnac, *A. Révol.*, II, 550–551.
[28] E. Galmiche, "Quelques documents sur le comité de surveillance de Saint Brieuc," *A. Bretagne*, XXVIII (1912–13), 588. Bernard ordered two in a bed at Beaune — one rich and one poor; P. de Barbuat, "Le Comité de surveillance révolutionnaire de Beaune," *M. Soc. Beaune* (1911), p. 172. Lebon at Arras ordered that men and women be separated, for he refused to "allow the enemies of liberty to multiply"; Paris, p. 197.
[29] Galmiche, *A. Bretagne*, XXVIII, 590; Arch. Meurthe-et-Moselle L 3191, 3 Ventôse.
[30] F. Rivarès, "Pau et les Basses-Pyrénées pendant la Révolution," *B. Soc. Pau*, 2e série, IV (1874–75), 501.
[31] Arch. Haute-Vienne L 840.

tained were unanimous in complaining of the *concierges*; the French *concierge* is hardly beloved by his fellow citizens. Charges of bribery, of habitual drunkenness, of insults and cruelty appear in the registers of the committees. The charges of the detained at Limoges were readily believed by the committee, and on 1 Thermidor the *concierge* was dismissed.[32] The *concierge* at Fontenay was reprimanded severely by the committee for failing to turn over property to those indicated by the condemned, and the committee of Bordeaux was forced to dismiss several of its *concierges* who, while no disciples of Babeuf, were no great believers in the difference between "mine" and "thine." [33]

These cares — enforcing regulations, hiring guards, making frequent inspections, and hearing complaints — might seem enough to trouble these workingmen, entrusted with duties for which they had no preparation. But they had a duty more onerous than any of these, that of providing food for the suspects. During the fall, the detained had usually been permitted to have their meals brought from their homes, with the result that the well-to-do ate well and the poor ate poorly or not at all. The committee of Les Sables sought to simplify its problem by refusing to receive into its house of detention suspects from other communes, unless they were accompanied by eight bushels of wheat. Several meetings later the keys of one suspect's barn were sent off in order that the necessary grain might be removed.[34] Other committees tried pooling all the food and serving it at a common table, but not infrequently the late-comers found that their prison mates had cleaned the table.[35]

None of these expedients was very successful and with the increase in the numbers of the poorer suspects, confined for fanaticism or for violations of the economic legislation of the Terror, the problem of providing for them became acute. The

[32] Arch. Haute-Vienne L 843.
[33] Arch. Vendée L 1186, 6 Germinal; Arch. Gironde L 2175, 14 Prairial.
[34] Arch. Vendée L 1215, 21, 25 Brumaire.
[35] Denis, pp. 195–196, 98–99.

committees in most communes, therefore, fell back upon the law of 26 Brumaire which ordered that all political prisoners should be fed the same type of food, that the suspects should eat at a common table, and most important of all, that the rich should pay the expenses of the poor. This was true of all expenses, for the salaries of guards and *concierge* were to be paid by the suspects — which meant, in practice, by the rich.

In consequence, catering was added to the functions of the *concierge*, often with restrictions on the type and quantity of food he could supply since frugality was one of the stipulations of the law.[36] These instructions were violated, of course, and it was for supplying sumptuous meals to certain of the suspects that the *concierge* at Limoges was dismissed by the committee.[37] The expenses incurred by the *concierge* for the purchase of food, and often for the general maintenance of the house of detention as well, were assigned by the committees to the wealthy suspects in proportion to their presumed income or to the amount of taxes paid. The rich protested loudly against this in many places, failing to realize that they were at the mercy of the committee and the administration. At Draguignan (Var), where twenty-three wealthy suspects were called upon to pay the expenses of sixty-five of their prison mates as well as their own, those assessed stubbornly refused to pay. The committee replied by ordering that, to prevent communication with the outside, bars would be placed before "certain" windows.[38] In similar circumstances at Les Sables the suspects were told to pay up or their property would be sold to meet their assessments, but at Allauch the committee was in a quandary, for the property and revenue of the detained had already been confiscated.[39] At Quimper, where the

[36] At Châteauroux the menu was to consist of soup, meat, poultry, and salad or a vegetable. Arch. Indre L 1538, 3 Nivôse. In the department of the Ain each suspect was to receive $1\frac{1}{2}$ pounds of bread, 1 pound of meat, a bottle of wine, and a plate of vegetables, herbs, or roots. Le Duc, IV, 102.

[37] Arch. Haute-Vienne L 843, 29 Pluviôse.

[38] Patin, *B. Soc. Draguignan*, XVII, 70–71.

[39] C. L. Chassin, *La Vendée patriote* (Paris, 1893–95), IV, 29; Arch. Bouches-du-Rhône L 1011, 29 Ventôse.

district allotted only ten sous a day for nourishment, the committee had a trying time with the nuns it had arrested. On 9 Frimaire the members protested and then threatened to release the nuns, "for we cannot keep women in custody to starve them to death." The protest was repeated several times in Pluviôse. Then on 8 Ventôse the committee had to send several members to the house of detention to break up the religious fast the nuns were observing (perhaps making a virtue of necessity) by forcing them to eat.[40]

But despite these annoyances, some of which were probably magnified into "affairs" by the bored suspects who welcomed any new diversion, life in the houses of detention was not the appalling ordeal often imagined.[41] Social life developed there, the suspects "played the violin, composed verses, spent their time on coquettish toilets and paid ceremonious party calls," according to an Englishwoman detained in the Somme.[42] One of the suspects detained at Pau amused himself and annoyed the committee by writing the following poem in its honor:

Barranquet, de Toulouse, au comité de surveillance

Pester, jurer, sacrer mieux qu'aux bords de la Seine
    Ne fit jamais le bon père Duchêne
Ne servirait de rien: Serais-je moins reclus?
Quel remède à cela? Courage et patience
Mais comment occuper la triste désoeuvrance
Où je languis depuis deux mois et plus?
    Du comité de surveillance
Sur ma lyre je vais célébrer les vertus.
Fort beau projet! Et de sa vigilance
    Je ne puis dire que du bien,
    Mais de sa bienfaisance
Oh, par ma foi, je n'en sais rien.
Et puis, comment chanter quand on n'est pas content?
    Comment chanter en si vilaine cage,
        À mon âge?

[40] Trévédy, *R. H. Ouest*, XII, 448, 705–708.
[41] The committee at St. Malo did its best to relieve the monotony, for it decided to set up a library in the house of detention. Arch. Communales LL 151 (S. 8).
[42] Quoted by Ramon, p. 33 note.

Mettez donc au bas du présent:
Citoyen videz-nous le champ,
Et sur les bords de la Garonne
Avec l'aide du Tout-Puissant,
Je m'en irai, toujours chantant
Votre âme bonne et belle.
Comptez sur l'exposant.[43]

In certain houses of detention conditions went beyond simply being comfortable. The popular society of Nîmes was confident that the prisons of the city were houses of pleasure; and at Laval, an agent of the Executive Council was horrified to discover that the Benedictines was a "house of prostitution and debauch." To prevent too much gayety of this kind, the committee of Saint-Brieuc (Côtes-du-Nord) found it necessary to inaugurate a ten-o'clock curfew.[44] The suspects of Châlons led "a scandalous life, indulging themselves in the excesses of the table, in gambling and pleasures of the flesh, receiving the visits of all sorts of strangers and procuring through them both obscene and incivic writings, and correspondence and secret and dangerous intelligence from the enemies of the nation." The committee, therefore, issued new regulations which included the hour of rising and retiring, the admittance of approved barbers and doctors, and so on.[45] Cases are not lacking to indicate even more strongly the truth of the conclusion that the houses of detention were not unbearable. The mother of two daughters asked the committee of Aix if she might bring them to prison since there was no one to care for them save their blind grandmother, and at Quimper a suspect made the request that his wife and child might live with him at the house of detention.[46]

[43] Barranquet could hardly have been dying of cholera. F. Rivarès, "Pau et les Basses-Pyrénées pendant la Révolution," *B. Soc. Pau*, 2e série, IV, 511.

[44] F. Rouvière, *Histoire de la Révolution dans le Gard* (Nîmes, 1887–89), IV, 159; Gaugain, I, 471; Galmiche, "Quelques documents," *A. Bretagne*, XXVIII, 592. The same regulation prohibited the detained from keeping firearms in the prison!

[45] Arch. Marne, Register of deliberations, 8 Thermidor.

[46] Trévédy, *R. H. Ouest*, XII, 703; Arch. Bouches-du-Rhône L 1728.

Nevertheless, the discomforts of detention, despite our efforts at minimizing them, were certainly not negligible. But they were less physical than spiritual. Physical conditions were generally all that could be expected of the eighteenth century, for filthy and squalid prisons are not peculiar to revolutions.

The terrifying aspect of these prisons was the enforced idleness, the stupefying monotony imposed upon persons of a fine temperament. Here was the cause of their coquetting and their dissipation, the drunkenness of the *concierge* and the gluttony of the suspects. It was not the native frivolity of the aristocrat nor the perversity of scoundrels which drove them to a reckless life, it was a sincere effort to preserve their minds, if not their bodies, from corruption.

PETITIONS

Once in jail, the first problem for the suspect was to get out again, and consequently the committees were besieged with petitions protesting the civism of the authors, reciting the proofs they had given of their devotion to the Republic, promising an exemplary conduct if only they might be released. Some of these petitions are amusing: — the petitioner thunders about being *père de famille*, left a widower with seven children, and usually ends groveling; others recite the woes suffered by the petitioner for the past ten years, and so on and on. One of the most amusing and at the same time most pitiful is that written by a young man of Avesnes (Nord) detained by the committee for evading the draft:

Au Citoiens

Au citoiens manbre du comité de survilliance ge te pris de prandre mes afaire de plutos pousible car voilas disuite gour que ge suis au Vainay biens ynosans quoy ÿnosans maitez moÿ plutot a la tete de larmay que de mes tenir enfermé dans un prison comme ge suis quoy que ge nes sois pas de la Regisicion je prefere etre a la tete de l'armaÿ que d etre aux Vainaÿ dans un prison comme ge suis cis tu crois que ge suis de la Regisicion mesnvoÿ a la tete de l'armay mes ge tasure foÿ de Republiquain que ge ne suis pas de la Regisicion cis gavet été de la Regisicion gauray partie un de premier comme un bon

Republiquain comme ge suis ge nauray fait de Resistanse et gaurait partie un de premier mais comme ge naité pas de la Regision ge nai pas partie mais sis tui gnore de moÿ mais moÿ a la tete de larmaÿ et mais tiens pas au Vernaÿ comme ge suis parce que ge suis biens miserable. . . .

> faite á Vaine le douze thermidor
> faite a la maison dure a Vaine
> Pierre Joseph Moine [47]

To halt the flood of petitions which poured down upon them from both suspects and their friends and relatives, the committees took steps which have brought down upon their heads the censure of historians. As usual, Nantes is singled out as the worst offender, for on 24 Frimaire the committee announced that all who interceded in behalf of those detained would be declared suspect. One of the members at his trial swore that the decree should have read "Those who intercede at the homes of the committee members . . ." and that on several copies he had written that qualifying phrase.[48] This expedient was not peculiar to Nantes, however. Over the door of the committee of Poitiers was written, "It is forbidden to intercede on behalf of those detained under penalty of being declared suspect"; and Lebon had written over his door, "Those who enter here to beg the release of those detained will go out of here only to be placed in custody themselves."[49] The committee at Bordeaux followed the example already set by the deputies and forbade all personal solicitation, providing a box at the entrance to their offices for the deposit of petitions.[50] The usual practice, however, was merely to forbid any solicitation outside office hours, especially at the homes of the members.

For the suspects, drawing up petitions was a serious and difficult business, for they had no way of knowing the charges on which they had been arrested. During the first months of their service a few committees, on their own initiative, had

[47] Arch. Nord L 10121.
[48] G. Lenôtre, Les Noyades de Nantes (Paris, 1912), p. 165 note 1.
[49] Salliard, p. xii; Paris, p. 190.
[50] Arch. Gironde L 2164, 11 Frimaire.

presented the prisoners with copies of the *procès-verbal*, but they were exceptional, the greatest number either refusing to deliver copies or ignoring the question. As a result, the suspect, in submitting his appeal, was at a loss to know what to protest against and was careful not to defend himself against too much lest he give the committee additional grounds for detaining him.

Under the pretense of increasing the efficiency of the Committee of General Security, Lecointre (of Versailles) on 18 October persuaded the Convention to order that the suspects be given a copy of the charges levied against them by the arresting committee, and that these should also be entered in the prison ledger. The decree repeated the provision of 17 September which instructed the committees to forward copies of the charges to Paris.

The Convention had allowed Lecointre to play upon its feelings with his picture of distressed patriots clamoring for justice, unable to answer their accusers. Six days later (3rd day of the second month), Louis (of Bas-Rhin) and Robespierre restored the Convention to the correct position of revolutionary severity by requesting the repeal of the law. Lecointre and Philippeaux had been able to hold their ground against Louis, so Robespierre intervened in the discussion. He pointed out that the red tape of charges and *procès-verbaux* would discourage citizens, and ended pointedly: "When public notoriety accuses a citizen of crimes whose proof is not written, but lies in the hearts of all indignant citizens, is not the Convention becoming over-judicial in the first decree? . . . This is not the time to paralyze the energy of the nation." The law of 18 October was repealed. Not until the fall of Robespierre were copies of the charges delivered to the suspects.[51]

RELEASES

Overwhelmed as they were with these pleas, the committees once more found themselves in a situation concerning which

[51] *Moniteur*, réimp., XVIII, 160, 216.

the laws were silent. "Arrest!" the Convention said, but there was nothing about release until the peace, which was a long way off. But if a person could prove to them that they had been misinformed, and he was not suspect, by arguing that they were to arrest only suspects the members could convince themselves they were justified in setting at liberty those whom a short while before they had arrested. However they argued, the committees during the fall of 1793 did, from time to time, liberate some of those detained.

Those who were not fortunate or clever enough to establish, as far as the committee was concerned, their civism, often followed up their initial effort with a more modest request — to be simply confined in their homes. Illness was the usual excuse, and at times it seemed as though a plague had hit the town. At Aix the disease revealed itself in Floréal, but reached full intensity only after the fall of Robespierre. During the first decade of Vendémiaire III almost sixty were sent home to be cured. The committee, perhaps with its tongue in its cheek, expressed to the representative at Marseille its perplexity over the great number of petitions it was receiving.[52] The members at Aurillac (Cantal) were more perspicacious, for they established a special infirmary in the house of detention, where the majority of cures were no doubt phenomenal in their speed.[53] The national agent at Troyes also refused to be taken in by transparent excuses, and on 2 Prairial he ordered that all suspects who were at home because of illness were to return immediately to their respective houses of detention.[54]

Business was also used as grounds for either temporary or permanent confinement at one's home, and when the committee considered that the interests of the Republic were involved, the suspect's petition was usually granted. Some were released

---

[52] Arch. Bouches-du-Rhône L 1712.
[53] J. Delmas, *Régistre du comité révolutionnaire du Cantal* (Aurillac, 1897), pp. 82–83.
[54] A. Babeau, *Histoire de Troyes pendant la Révolution* (Paris, 1874), II, 293 note 2. The committee of Bordeaux, declaring such a practice struck at equality, issued similar orders. Arch. Gironde L 2164, 14 Frimaire.

at Châlons-sur-Marne during Nivôse in order to prepare their papers for declarations in regard to the forced loan.[55] At Montargis (Loiret), Citizen Triquet was permitted to leave the house of detention two or three times a *décade* to inspect his workshop, and at Limoges a citizen was permitted to stay at home under arrest "to follow his trade of dyer."[56] On several occasions arrest interfered seriously with the life of the municipality, and the committee had to take steps. At Vienne (Isère), the local chandler was released for a *décade* because the town's supply of candles had been exhausted; at Bourg (Ain), the postmaster was released under surveillance so that he could resume his very necessary functions.[57]

The vigilant eye of two *sans-culottes* kept watch over the daily lives of those who were fortunate enough to win the privilege of remaining in their own homes. By preference men with families and fathers of soldiers were chosen to fill these positions of trust, though at Troyes the guards were neither the one nor the other, which led to much grumbling.[58] It was an easy way to earn a living and an easy way for the local Jacobin party to care for its needy members, for the guards received from the suspects one and a half times the prevailing wage in the community.[59]

Complaints against the guards were frequent in Bordeaux, and on 12 Frimaire the committee ruled that they were entitled only to "pay, wood to keep warm and candles," and threatened dismissal if they demanded more.[60] The guards at Aix seem to have been as presumptuous, for a farmer wrote to the committee, informing it that the "good *sans-culottes*" had set his house on fire once and asking that the committee request more discretion of the guards to prevent the repetition of the "same

[55] Arch. Marne, Register of deliberations, Committee of Section Égalité.
[56] Arch. Haute-Vienne L 843, 15 Pluviôse.
[57] *Procès-verbaux du comité. . . . de Vienne*, p. 45; Le Duc, IV, 51.
[58] Babeau, II, 300.
[59] The Bordeaux committee, however, doubled the legal number of guards and cared for twice as many *sans-culottes*. Arch. Gironde L 2164, Brumaire, Frimaire passim.
[60] Arch. Gironde L 2164.

unfortunate accident." He also asked the committee to instruct the guards

> to be a bit discreet and reasonable about a small supply of white and muscatel wine which they found in a demi-john, although thus far they have preferred the muscatel. I beg them to spare me the little bit which remains and give their preference to the white wine, which is at their service. . . .[61]

Abuses such as this cannot have been infrequent, for the presumption of guilt was always against the suspect, and as a result complaints would be infrequent.

The right to release, which the committees had claimed and exercised during the fall of 1793, was denied to them by the law of 14 Frimaire. Only the Convention, the Committee of Public Safety, the Committee of General Security, the representatives on mission, and the courts were qualified to release suspects. As far as the committees were concerned this law was generally observed, and in many cases it was no doubt a welcome release. Nevertheless, there arose from time to time exceptional circumstances under which the committees felt themselves justified in granting freedom on their own authority.

At Péronne during Ventôse a number of suspects were released, with the excuse that they were not noble and therefore had been arrested unjustly during the execution of the decree of St. Just and Lebas ordering the imprisonment of all former nobles in the four departments of the Aisne, Somme, Nord, and Pas-de-Calais (16 Pluviôse).[62] The Angers committee, having been reproved by the representative Francastel for a number of releases, excused itself as follows:

> You must also believe that during the first revolutionary movement it was possible for the committee to be deceived and to arrest some innocent persons; but always just in the performance of its duty, the committee has never been ashamed to correct an error. It owed liberty to innocent persons, it has given it to them. There

---

[61] Arch. Bouches-du-Rhône L 1728.
[62] Ramon, p. 177.

were others whom, due to lack of proof and contagious diseases, we were forced to set at liberty provisionally. . . .[63]

RELEASES BY REPRESENTATIVES

Since the committees themselves were not permitted to release the persons they had arrested, the suspects turned immediately to the deputy on mission in their department as the closest agency which could authorize releases. The result was a complication of the procedure through which petitions passed. Some were addressed to the deputy himself, and many of these were referred to the committees for approval. Together with any petitions handed to the committees, these were then returned to him with an appropriate endorsement, indicating the charges and the committee's recommendation. The final decision rested with the representative and the committee released only on definite notification from him.[64]

During the visits which the representatives paid to the towns of their jurisdiction the consideration of petitions naturally increased. During the first two *décades* of Pluviôse, the committees of Châlons were busy making recommendations, and on the 13th of the month the houses of detention of the section of the Republic were reduced from three to one.[65] Wholesale deliveries such as this were not unusual. Lebon, for example, released in Nivôse all those included on a list of 139 submitted to him by the committee of Saint-Pol (Pas-de-Calais).[66]

Not infrequently the representatives created special commissions outside of the committee to hear petitions and report on their merits. Boisset set up a commission of eight, two from the popular society, two from each of the three administrations (department, district, and municipality), "to relieve

---

[63] Bourcier, *R. Anjou*, VI, 131.

[64] The deputies rarely gave the committees authority to release on their own initiative, although in the Vendée, where mass arrests were made by the army, Ingrand permitted the Fontenay committee to release those against whom there were no written charges. Arch. Vendée L 1186, 12 Messidor.

[65] Arch. Marne, Registers of deliberations, Committees of Section République,. and Section Liberté.

[66] Jacob, I, 285–286.

those who tremble because of the warrants issued by the former committee of surveillance of Nismes as the result of injudicious arbitrariness or hatred." [67]

A commission of three was established at Bordeaux on 16 Pluviôse by Ysabeau and Tallien, composed of a justice of the peace, a member of the Libourne committee, and the national agent of Bordeaux. It was to question those detained as to the causes of their arrest, and report to the local committee which would then forward the information and some of its own to the deputies.[68]

The law of 17 September had simply instructed the revolutionary committees to arrest suspects, which seemed a simple operation. Nevertheless, this superficially simple operation forced the committee to assume administrative functions certainly not foreseen by the Convention. To procure buildings and provide for their maintenance and inspection, to allocate the expenses to the wealthy suspects, and in some cases to procure food for the less fortunate detained were duties which rightly belonged to the municipal government. Yet in the majority of cases the latter were only too willing to renounce a part, or all, of their responsibility and permit the committees to assume tasks which were at best tedious. Strictly these activities were usurpations, but considering that they were made in most cases with the tacit approval of the regular administration, the committees can hardly be charged with forcing themselves into a jurisdiction which was not theirs.

[67] Arch. Gard 1, L 6, 13, No. 97.
[68] Arch. Gironde L 438.

CHAPTER VII

THE COMMITTEES CONTROL THE LIFE OF THE COMMUNE

CENSORSHIP OF THE MAILS

To COMPLETE the surveillance which the committees were charged with exercising, they either were granted or assumed the duty of censoring the mail received in their communes. The Committee of Public Safety had already ordered that all letters from abroad be opened, and the Minister of the Interior had duly forwarded the decision to the various administrations.[1] During the summer the examination of such mail and often of letters addressed to suspects was made by one or another of the local governing bodies.

When in the fall the committees became the guardians of the suspects' thoughts as well as their persons, the daily visit to the post office generally became one of their functions. In some localities the committees were conceded this right by the municipality or the department; elsewhere they simply assumed this function as an extension of their unchallenged authority to censor any communication with the detained.

Inevitably, indignant citizens complained of this interference with their private business, and the acts of some committees justified the protests. The municipal committee of Dijon was accused of being so negligent in opening registered letters that the sums enclosed never arrived at their destinations. In fact, all the letters at Dijon were handled in such an irregular manner that the post-Thermidor committee confessed that "it is impossible to obtain any information concerning the fate of the letters and of the property they may have contained." [2] The committee of Blaye complained to that of Landerneau that considerable sums were being removed from post offices to

[1] Aulard, *Comité de Salut Public*, III, 506–507.
[2] Arch. Côte d'Or L IV a 47 h/2, fo. 90.

the considerable damage of the merchants of Blaye. Landerneau promised an investigation.[3]

Legally, of course, the committees' rights extended only to those letters written to the detained, but their zeal and their curiosity overcame their scruples on more than one occasion. The deputy Laurent wrote to the Committee of Public Safety on 22 Frimaire: "The committees of surveillance no longer spare our letters. They open them just like those of suspects. Imagine how alarming this measure can be and the cruel advantage our enemies will take of it." [4]

Through some strange quirk of revolutionary jurisprudence, the recipient of a letter expressing counter-revolutionary sentiments was considered suspect, whether the letter was unsolicited or not. According to its critics, the committee of Aurillac took advantage of this custom by counterfeiting letters from émigrés to residents of their commune, imitating the postmark, and so on. If slightly unethical, it certainly shows an enterprising spirit.[5] Still more strangely, it seemed to be against the rules — at Dijon, at least — to examine letters mailed in the committee's commune.[6] Furthermore, only two committees were found, those at Carcassonne and Beaune, which took the trouble to inform the committee of the writer's commune concerning the suspicious nature of his correspondence with residents of their towns. Joseph Lebon, however, worked on this principle, and, discovering 50,000 letters bound for England, proceeded to spread them all over France, returning them to the committees of the writers' communes.[7]

The nuisance value of committees exercising this power of inspecting all the mail which arrived in the commune can readily be imagined. Opponents of the existing regime were circumspect in their correspondence, hesitating to commit to

[3] A. Duchatellier, *Brest et le Finistère sous la Terreur* (Brest, 1858), p. 51.
[4] Aulard, *Comité de Salut Public*, IX, 356–357.
[5] Serres, IX, 102.
[6] Arch. Côte d'Or L IV a 47 h/2, fo. 64.
[7] Paris, p. 106. Acknowledgment of the receipt of the letters was found in the papers of the committees of Neufchatel, Arch. Seine-Inf. L 5401, 14 Messidor; Caen, Arch. Calvados, Register of deliberations, 28 Ventôse; Orléans, Arch. Loiret L 1179, 13 Germinal.

writing any save the most innocent remarks; and thus another avenue of communication was closed to the counter-revolutionaries.

PASSPORTS

The putting of visas to passports was another part of the committees' daily routine which was either granted them by the municipality or usurped with the latter's approval. The duty of actually issuing the passports generally remained with the communal government, which perhaps sought the advice of the committee before granting the application, as was done at Caen.[8]

The purpose of the visa, of course, was to keep a check on the movement of persons considered suspect. Generally passports were visaed by the committee of the traveler's commune, and the traveler's destination indicated. This simple visa was honored at the gates of the towns along the way by the guards posted there. Nevertheless, it was not unusual for the local postmaster, acting on orders from the committee, to refuse a new relay of horses to travelers unless they visited the committee's offices.[9] At Aix-les-Bains, where this system was in effect, quite a scandal shook the town when it was discovered that the committee's *concierge* was giving visas and registering passports. He explained that he had been ordered to do so since it was too much trouble for him and for the members to go chasing around town in search of someone else to grant the visa.[10] To avoid such inconvenience the committee of Douai appointed ten citizens to examine passports at the gates of the city, and at Angers there existed a special committee whose only duty was to visa passports and receive the declarations of strangers.[11]

[8] Arch. Calvados, Register of deliberations, 23 Brumaire.

[9] Châteauroux, Arch. Indre L 368; Quimper, Trévédy, *R. H. Ouest*, XII, 526.

[10] F. Vermale et A. Rochet, "Registre des délibérations du comité révolutionnaire d'Aix-les-Bains," *M. Soc. Savoisienne*, XLV (1907), 4e fascicule, 65, 71.

[11] Arch. Nord L 10144, 15; "Comptes décadaires du comité d'Angers," *Anjou Hist.*, VII, 267.

CERTIFICATES OF CIVISM

The last of the routine functions which occupied so much of the committees' time was granting visas for certificates of civism. The cards, by the law of 2–10–24 August 1792, were required of all citizens, yet in a number of communes only public officials not elected by the people were forced to carry them. They were issued by the municipality or the sections, though in rare cases (Dijon, Redon, and Blainville) the committees issued them.[12] The certificates had then to be visaed by the district and department, and according to the law of 29–30 January 1793 no reasons for refusals need be given.

The Committee of Public Safety, however, had no firm trust in the administrations, and on 20 September Jeanbon Saint-André proposed that these two visas be supplemented by a third visa, that of the committees of surveillance. "The committees of surveillance and of public safety established by your agents," he explained, "are everywhere composed of *sans-culottes* and energetic patriots, for gentlemen disdain to enter subaltern administrations which exercise no other authority than that of surveillance and which are known only through their devotion to the public welfare." The measure was passed, with the proviso that, failing a committee, a special commission of six citizens would be chosen for this duty by the popular society.[13]

The certificate of civism as employed by the committees became one of the most versatile instruments of the Terror. Non-elective public officials whose cards were not visaed lost their posts. At Caen, the committee refused to put its stamp of approval on the certificates of those whose taxes were in arrears, while Landerneau ordered the treasurer not to pay the salaries of public officials unless their certificates had been

[12] Arch. Côte d'Or L IV a 47/a, 19 Floréal; L. Dubreuil, *Le District de Redon 1790–IV* (Rennes, 1903), p. 129; Arch. Meurthe-et-Moselle L 3155, 1 Sept.

[13] *Moniteur,* réimp., XVII, 711. At Fortunade (Corrèze) a citizen organized a popular society solely to visa his certificate. *B. Soc. Corrèze (Tulle),* IX, 143–144.

visaed.[14] Elsewhere the committee's precious visa was used in raising money. The Aurillac committee announced on 19 Brumaire "that all certificates of civism which have been granted to those who have been released are revoked without regard to the contributions they have made, and it shall be the same with the certificates of those who have made contributions to avoid imprisonment." [15] The Saint-Malo committee also used its visa to speed up its campaign for patriotic contributions, one citizen placing 75,000 *livres* down with his certificate. If the offer was not high enough, they told the applicant that they had a little list from Carpentier (the representative to whom the committee proudly related these achievements), and the little list indicated those from whom no contributions could be received. In consequence, the committee confessed, "we tantalize them and we believe that five will become ten." [16]

There were other committees less open about the sums they received, for the proceeds usually went into the pockets of the members. Indeed, this is usually one of the stock charges brought against the committees during the Thermidorian reaction — Nantes, Quimper, Beaune, almost any committee taken at random, is accused of lining its pockets in this fashion.

These three functions, together with the power to arrest suspects, completed the machinery by which the committees controlled their communes. Spiritually as well as physically every citizen was subject to the scrutiny of twelve of the firmest Jacobins in town who, by scanning every opinion written or spoken, and by regulating every movement made, erected as effective a despotism as France had ever seen. Their only justification was that they did it in the name of liberty.

---

[14] Arch. Calvados, Register of deliberations, 16 Nivôse; Duchatellier, *Brest,* p. 35.

[15] Delmas, pp. 56–57.

[16] E. Herpin, "Histoire d'un comité de surveillance," *A. Soc. Saint-Malo* (1910), pp. 14–16. One day its civic exhortations were so heroic the victim is said to have died of fright. *Ibid.,* p. 17.

THE COMMITTEES AND THE CHURCH

An attempt to outline in general terms the vagaries of the religious problem of the Revolution, the strong irreligion in one place, the loyalty to Catholicism in another, would be open to a thousand methodological objections and would in the end prove very little. Is the committee which arrests ten "fanatics" more irreligious than one which arrests fifteen nuns who have refused to take an oath? Are ten arrests in Brumaire the equivalent of ten in Prairial? The safest remark to make is that the committees, like every other organization of the time, were deeply involved in the whole bewildering situation and that the course which each committee took was dictated less by the laws of the Convention than by the sentiments of its members and their fellow citizens.

Within a single department one can find striking contradictions. During Prairial the committee of Draguignan, capital of the Var, indulged in a mild priest chase; on 11 Messidor the committee of Tourves, a canton capital, confessed that it had been forced to revoke its orders to remove the church bells and halt public services on orders of a member of the district administration.[17] In the Côte d'Or, the committee of Beaune found it necessary to issue warrants for fanatics at Bligny-sur-Beaune and Pommard where masses were still celebrated (Floréal); while at St. Jean-de-Losne, in the same district, all six of the persons detained were charged with fanaticism.[18] In the Meurthe the committee of Blamont, a district capital, after ordering that the bells be no longer rung to summon to mass, was forced to apologize to the district, declaring it never intended to attack the celebrating of the mass (23 Frimaire). Two weeks later the committee of Nancy in the same department arrested several priests for celebrating Christmas mass.[19]

[17] Patin, *B. Soc. Draguignan*, XVII, 95–97; Arch. nationales F 7, 3822.
[18] Barbuat, *M. Soc. Beaune* (1911), p. 176 and note; Belloni, *Comité de Sûreté Générale*, p. 353 note 1.
[19] Arch. Meurthe-et-Moselle L 3160, 23 Frimaire; Godchot, *Révol. Fr.*, LXXX, 258.

In Finistère the committees of Quimper and Brest made raids on homes suspected of harboring priests; at Carhaix, also a district capital, the *curé* continued the practices of the Catholic church, used incense, wore ecclesiastical garb on all occasions, and preached against divorce and the marriage of priests.[20] At Monthelon (Marne) the committee, knowing no law against it, supported the petition of many of the citizens that on the following Sunday the doors of the Temple of Reason be left open, since the citizens would like to perform the ordinary functions of the Catholic religion there.[21] The Committee of Belmont (Aveyron) succinctly reported the situation in its commune as follows: "Dans ce pais il n'existe que des fanatiques; quand à des ennemis de la Révolution, le comité n'en connoit pas."[22]

In certain of the smaller communes, in Brittany especially, where the committees included what few Jacobins there were in town, their power was used to force attendance at the mass of the constitutional priest.[23] The practice was not peculiar to these two departments, however, for at Angers the committee released a mother and her daughter who had been arrested for not attending the constitutional mass, and at Woltz (Haut-Rhin) the district ordered the committee to resign for having used its power in the same manner, releasing the "fanatics" only if they promised to attend constitutional mass.[24]

Robespierre's speeches on freedom of worship at the Jacobins on 1 Frimaire and in the Convention on 6 Frimaire led to a decree on religious toleration which had a certain mitigating effect in the departments. At Grasse a speech regretting the

---

[20] Duchatellier, *Brest*, p. 129; Hemon, p. 272.

[21] Arch. Marne, Register of deliberations, 1 Nivôse.

[22] Affre, p. 81.

[23] At St. Brieuc, Lamballe, and Lannion; H. Pommeret, *L'Esprit public dans le département des Côtes-du-Nord pendant la Révolution* (Paris, 1921), pp. 243–244. At Bazouges-la-Pérouse (Ille-et-Vilaine); La Grimaudière, *La Commission Brutus Magnier à Rennes* (Nantes, 1879), p. 62.

[24] Bourcier, *R. Anjou*, VII, 65; Arne Ording, "Bureau de Police du Comité de Salut Public," *Skrifter utgitt av Videnskaps-Akademi i Oslo 1930, II Historisk-Filosofisk Klasse*, vol. II, no. 6, p. 70.

closing of the churches brought about the arrest of the speaker, but when the "fanatic" declared he had found those principles in Rousseau and Robespierre, the committee released him.[25] About the same time the department of Landes criticized severely the committee of Dax for "locking up farmers and poor countrywomen for fanaticism, actions which create it by persecution instead of trying to destroy it by ignoring it." [26] Even before Robespierre had plumped for toleration, when a *curé* of Troyes was threatened with arrest for violating the revolutionary committee's orders not to celebrate the mass, his parishioners quoted the constitution and he was not molested (27 Brumaire).[27]

Despite the official acceptance of toleration, during Frimaire and the early days of Nivôse, a number of priests at the urging of the committees handed in their letters of nomination and ordination to indicate their abdication and their recognition of the fundamental error of Catholicism. There was no great wave of renunciations, however, and after Nivôse passed, they were rare. In Loir-et-Cher the central committee directed an exceptionally persistent drive on Christianity. During Frimaire it had made a series of household inspections to ferret out counter-revolutionary writings. On the 15th of the month it had issued a dechristianizing manifesto and ordered the arrest of all constitutional priests who had not abdicated, but the effect was slight and only 12 of the 300 legally recognized priests abdicated.[28]

To what extent the abdications were observed is problematical, for in several cases at least the committees later discovered that priests who had resigned a short while before were still celebrating the mass. A priest at Issoudun (Indre) was arrested by the committee for this breach of faith, but at Darney (Vosges) the committee deliberated at length and then wrote

[25] J. Combet, "Les Comités de surveillance du district de Grasse," *Révol. Fr.*, LVII, 350.

[26] A. Richard, "Le Comité de surveillance et les suspects de Dax," *A. H. Révol.*, VII, 29.   [27] Babeau, II, 139.

[28] Blossier, *B. Com. Hist.*, 1910, p. 254 *et seq.*, pp. 271–272.

a long preamble of *considérants* before dumping the case into the laps of the district committee.[29]

Further grist for the committees' mill was furnished by the Convention on 9 Nivôse, when it ordered the arrest of all nuns who refused to take the oath to uphold the constitution. Since August 18, 1792, all congregations had been suppressed, but ex-nuns had been permitted to continue their teaching and nursing as private individuals.[30] Occupying the positions they did, they were a dangerous influence in the lives of the people, and during Brumaire and Frimaire some had already been removed. The committee of Angers as early as 7 September had asked the municipality to replace the sisters at the hospitals with patriots, and had to repeat its request on 1 October.[31] At Fontenay (Vendée) the committee of the Section of the Hospital arrested nine sisters at the hospital as suspects in view of their dangerous contacts with their patients, whose loyalty to the new government they would be able to undermine.

The new law was generally enforced without any noticeable pressure from the administration, an early indication of the fact that the efforts of the representatives and of the completely "regenerated" administration were restoring a bit of order in the tangled red tape of revolutionary government. The majority of the nuns refused to take the oath and were therefore placed under arrest. No sooner had this operation been completed than trouble commenced, trouble best expressed by the committee of Blamont when it said that the new nurses were less experienced, less efficient, and less serious than the sisters, and that "there was good reason for regretting the old nurses." In consequence, the Sisters of Saint-Charles were invited to return, not under their former title, but simply as "nurses." [32] Angers, when its request for a purge of the sisters was finally granted, made the same discovery, and since the new nurses

---

[29] Arch. Indre L 1552, 1 Nivôse; Schwab, *Révol. Vosges*, 23e année, p. 115.
[30] C. D. Hazen, *The French Revolution* (New York, 1932), II, 552.
[31] Correspondance," *Anjou Hist.*, XXVI, 38–39.
[32] Arch. Meurthe-et-Moselle L 3160, 17 Frimaire.

made the patriots who were ill suffer even more, the committee asked for the release of several nurses held at Beaumont.[33] At Quimper it was so difficult to replace the sisters that the committee ordered that three of them should be considered under arrest at the hospital (1 Prairial).[34] Expedients of this kind were not unusual, and a number of committees were forced to forget their principles in order to provide competent care for the sick.

A large proportion of committees attempted to enforce the observance of *décadi* instead of "ex-Sunday." There were, however, members who were guilty themselves of this violation of Republican principles. The revolutionary committee of Grenoble learned that several members of the Beaucroissant committee were guilty of this practice, but limited themselves to a warning as "brothers and friends."[35] Some committees took stronger steps, however. Citizen Deffès, who had indulged in a subterfuge to remain idle Sunday, was ordered by the committee of Mirande (Gers) to remain on his property and not leave it for one month without the written permission of his municipality, and the committee of Château-Salins arrested one citizen for refusing to observe the revolutionary day of rest.[36] The citizens of Loriol, however, showed no partiality and rested on both *décadi* and Sunday, which the committee could only explain by saying that they liked it, for all the idlers loved the Republic and had made sacrifices. The lamentable part of the situation was that it aggravated the labor shortage, and it is not improbable that some committees were as interested in this aspect of the problem as in the ideological attitude.[37]

[33] "Correspondance," *Anjou Hist.*, XXVI, 41.
[34] Trévédy, *R. H. Ouest*, XIII, 24.
[35] Arch. Isère L 871, 2 Messidor.
[36] *Revue de Gascogne*, XIII, 303; Arch. Meurthe-et-Moselle L 3171, 3 Messidor.
[37] D. Faucher, "Le Comité de surveillance révolutionnaire de Loriol," *Comité des travaux historiques et scientifiques, Section d'histoire moderne et contemporaine. Notices, Inventaires et Documents*, VII: *Etudes et Documents Divers*, p. 142.

It hardly seems necessary to repeat once more the observation that the attitude of the committees toward the religious problems of the Revolution is impossible of generalization. The prejudices of the members, of their fellow townsmen, and of the deputies on mission varied so widely from month to month and from place to place that one hesitates to commit oneself. Yet, putting one's faith in the grain of salt, it is possible to say, first, that the committees in the larger communes attempted to enforce at least the externals of worship according to the new constitutional church, and second, that in the fall of 1793 the activities of many of them reflect the dechristianizing, Hebertist temper of Paris. Beyond that it would be dangerous to go.

CHAPTER VIII

THE PURSUIT OF WEALTH

The Search for Precious Metals

PERHAPS because it was possible to make a dishonest penny, the committees were zealous in their search for gold, silver, and other useful metals — copper especially. Several laws had already ordered the confiscation of all gold and silver plate in the churches (29 September 1789 and 10–12 September 1792) and on 23 July 1793 the Convention had decreed that all save one of the bells in each commune were to be melted down to be used in fabricating cannon. The Convention extended this policy on 23 Brumaire by directing that all gold and silver, coined and uncoined, diamonds, jewels, epaulettes, etc., buried in the ground, hidden in caves, inside walls, roofs, floors, or pavements, were to be confiscated by the Republic. It was a measure directed both at the speculators and the wealthy, amounting virtually to confiscation, and provided the Republic with hard cash for its purchases abroad.[1]

The committees in the fall of 1793 renewed the campaign, with this difference, however, that what had once been simply a patriotic measure, inspired by zeal in the defense of the nation, had now partly assumed the character of an attack on the church. It was part and parcel of the dechristianizing movement which swept France during those months, and in this movement the committees often took part officially.

The initiative in this campaign frequently came from the representatives, who on their own authority extended the laws of the Convention. Taillefer wrote the Committee of Public Safety from Castel-sarrasin (Tarn-et-Garonne) on 9 October. "All the committees of public safety which I have

---

[1] *Moniteur*, réimp., XVIII, 416.

installed are careful to deposit in the district treasury, as suspect property, the gold, the silver, and the plate of those
detained, those confined, those under surveillance, monopolists,
hoarders, speculators, egoists, and those who are indifferent in
regard to the Revolution." [2] An agent of the Committee of
Public Safety, Rousselin, on 25 Brumaire ordered that all
silver and precious objects from the churches of Troyes were
to be deposited with the central committee, and on 12 Frimaire
the committee commenced its *visites domiciliaires* to take
declarations of metal currency.

The Church was often the object of this pillaging — illegally,
of course, unless the ornaments were hidden; but the wave of
dechristianization which struck France in the fall of 1793 was
not to be halted by legality. The Beaune committee, commencing on 27 Brumaire, took a leading part in the spoliation of
the churches and chased down persons believed hiding other
religious paraphernalia.[3] Saumur organized an auto-da-fé of
chaplets and of feudal titles; the jewels and metal of the
former were carefully put aside.[4] The municipality and committee of Thouaré (Loire-Inférieure) in Germinal drew up an
inventory of the metal ornaments in the "ex-church," after
having previously removed "all those statues of fanaticism
of which we now recognize the error." [5]

The committee of twenty-one at Grenoble found the monas-
tery of the Grande Chartreuse a veritable treasure mine. On
18 Brumaire the committee, desiring the nation "to have everything which belongs to it," named five commissioners to go
where necessary and draw up *procès-verbaux* of what they
found. (The order written in the register was as vague as that.)
On 20 Brumaire the committee reported triumphantly to the
Committee of General Security that they had found fifty-nine

---

[2] Aulard, *Comité de Salut Public*, VII, 335.

[3] Barbuat, *M. Soc. Beaune*, 1911, p. 175.

[4] Desmé de Chavigny, "Histoire de Saumur pendant la Révolution," *R. H. Ouest*, VIII, 469–470.

[5] J. S. de la Londe, "Notes sur l'histoire de Thouaré," *B. Soc. Arch. Nantes*, XXXII, 179–180.

chests of precious objects at the Grande Chartreuse! Nor was that all, for several of the fathers had carried some property away and on 18 Brumaire three of them had been caught with "stolen" goods in their possession.[6] Elsewhere the same story is repeated, sometimes indicated only by the formal remark that there has been deposited with the district such and such an amount of silver, "with and without coats-of-arms," "from the sacristy," or from "the ex-church."

When once the churches were emptied of their precious objects the committees turned to private sources and sought to ferret out gold and silver which the aristocrats had hidden away. Again, they might seize it as the property of émigrés or of those who had "died judicially," or yet again simply as "the removal of symbols of royalty and feudalism."

Citizen Camberlin, member of the committee of Villers-Cotterêts (Aisne), presented to the Convention on 22 Frimaire 112 *marcs*, 4 ounces, 4 *gros* of silver plate (about 55 pounds), a cross, 4 silver-plated candelabra, and 3 dozen silver table knives, the property of citizeness Mazancour, émigré, all of which was found in a house located in a quarry one league from the commune.[7] At Orléans, the municipal committee simply ordered all the goldsmiths in town to deposit whatever had been left with them for sale, and the goldsmiths duly obeyed. This measure was so successful that the watchmakers were next summoned and deposited whatever objects they had which "should be converted to the profit of the Republic." [8] A young girl of Poitiers indicated to the committee a place where she was certain some silverware was hidden, and the raid netted the committee 80 to 90 covers of silver, 24 to 30 tablespoons, 25 silver plates, and 27 bags of gold and silver, containing 13,000 to 14,000 *livres*.[9] At Lyon the silver-confiscating business was so fruitful that a special Central Commission for Deposits was set up and the committees were

[6] Arch. Isère L 870.
[7] *Arch. Parl.*, LXXXI, 387.
[8] Arch. Loiret L 1178, 11–12 and 18–19 Floréal.
[9] Salliard, pp. 84–85.

instructed to transfer to its office all the gold, silver, and assignats — generally the property of rebels and émigrés —
which was previously kept at the rooms of the committees.[10]
To prevent any silver being overlooked the representatives on
11 Frimaire had forbidden its removal from the city, and the
committees were busy during Frimaire putting a halt to smug-
gling.[11]

The supreme silver thieves, however, were the members of
the Bordeaux committees set up on 11 Brumaire and 2 Frimaire. Special *visites domiciliaires* were sometimes made for
this sole purpose; at other times the silverware was found by
members while making arrests.[12] On 3 Frimaire, for example,
the following entry was made in the committee's register:

Citizen Lafargue has been conducted to Fort du Ha, in virtue of a
warrant issued for his arrest, and there were seized at his home:

> 2 tablespoons
> 12 teaspoons
> 14 forks
> 3 coffee spoons
> 815 *livres* in silver
> 8 flasks

One citizen jumped before he was pushed. Citizen Dupuch
contributed twelve covers of silver, five coffee spoons, two
tablespoons and 521 *livres* in gold and silver, on 1 Frimaire.
The committee applauded his patriotism, even more remarkable
since he was an aristocrat, and granted him "the favor of the
law which leaves at liberty those who have constantly given" —
not silverware, but — "proofs of civism." [13]

Some of this silver bore coats-of-arms, which was the ostensible purpose of seizing it — "to remove signs of feudalism";
some of it did not. The silverware of seven Bordelais citizens
was caught just in the nick of time on 10 Frimaire, for the gold-
smith was about to remove the objectionable signs, and the

---

[10] Arch. Rhône CL 185, 26 Frimaire.
[11] Arch. Rhône CL 185, 11 Frimaire, CL 203 passim, CL 152.
[12] Arch. Gironde L 2164 passim.
[13] Arch. Gironde L 2164.

committee would have been baulked! Profiting by this experience, on 13 Frimaire it ordered an inspection of all goldsmiths
to discover what of interest was on deposit in their shops. This
move no doubt brought unfavorable publicity, for toward the
end of Frimaire the deposits came to an end. During Nivôse
they were resumed, but not to the same extent as before.

The spoil, on several occasions borne into the committee's
offices in large baskets, was turned over to the treasurer, whose
bond of 20,000 *livres* bears witness to the importance of the
committee's operations. From time to time the treasurer presented receipts given him at the Mint for deposits made with
him, which seemed to make everything legal.[14] But Dorgeuil,
who took the lead in these expeditions, was accused after
Thermidor of being careless in drawing up his *procès-verbaux*,
and when the silver was weighed at the Mint it was all spilled
in together so that no record of his contribution could be made
for purposes of verification.[15]

ASSIGNATS

During the crisis of the spring of 1793, the Convention decreed the forced circulation of the assignat and forbade the use
of coined money (11 April); and on 1 August it repeated its
order, setting a penalty of twenty years' imprisonment for
refusing assignats, or for accepting them at less than their
face value. This order was included among the "revolutionary
laws" of Paré's circular, and the committees were expected to
aid in enforcing it.

Of actual assignat business, however, the committees in
general had little. Fouché in the Nièvre, Pinet, Monestier and
their colleagues in the Landes and Basses-Pyrénées, strengthened the orders of the Convention, but only rarely do the committees seem to have been aggressive.[16] Occasionally a person
was arrested for speaking against the assignats or for dis-

[14] Arch. Gironde L 2164.
[15] A. Vivie, *Histoire de la Terreur à Bordeaux* (Bordeaux, 1877), II, 122.
[16] Meunier, I, 268–269; Richard, *A. Révol.*, VII, 27; Cuzacq, *B. Soc. Bayonne*,
1929, p. 28.

tributing false ones.[17] A soldier from Beaune sent his father Republican assignats signed by the rebels in order to give them currency in the districts in insurrection. Since they were outlawed by the representatives they could be had cheaply, and the son sent them home for his father to pass, confident that the representatives' decree would be unknown at Beaune. The committee, however, discovered both the assignats and the letter of explanation in the course of their inspection of the mail, and informed the Committee of General Security.[18]

Near the frontiers of the North, across which the flow of false assignats seems to have been plentiful, the committee of Dunkirk was on the alert for counterfeit notes. Everyone entering the commune was conducted to the offices of the committee and there required to show all his assignats. They were inspected by an expert, the good being separated from those which seemed false, and the latter were sent to the inspector-in-chief who returned the good ones. The same procedure was followed in shops and at the post office. But these efforts, no matter how persistent, were of little avail against the millions of counterfeit assignats poured out by the factories of the Coalition, and the committee tried to interest its colleagues along the frontier in adopting similar measures. But neither in the other cities of the Nord, nor in the Meurthe and the Côte d'Or, on the East, did the committees adopt Dunkirk's suggestion, despite the circular it sent out on 4 Ventôse. A month later it issued another circular, this time revealing that the inhabitants of frontier districts were trading with the enemy, giving coined money for false assignats, which sounds rather fantastic. It again asked for coöperation, but once more the other committees were unmoved.[19]

[17] At Limoges, Arch. Haute-Vienne L 843, 4 Pluviôse; at Roquebrussanne, E. Poupé, "Le Comité de surveillance de la Roquebrussanne (Var)," *Bulletin historique et philologique du Comité des travaux historiques et scientifiques*, 1907, p. 297; L. Chapuis, *La Révolution à Hautvillers*, reviewed in *A. H. Révol.*, VI, 319.

[18] Barbuat, *M. Soc. Beaune*, 1911, pp. 236–237.

[19] Arch. Nord L 10187, 2. Strangely, the question of assignats seems never to have arisen in the Vendée committees, for Republican, royal, and counterfeit

CONFISCATED PROPERTY

Although the seizure of gold and silver was a lucrative enterprise indeed, the profits of the Republic from confiscating the property of émigrés and of those condemned to the guillotine were so high that the accomplishments of the committees shrink in comparison to petty larceny. In the pursuit of movable property, especially gold and silver, we have seen that the committees were indispensable, but in the confiscation and administration of national lands, officially a function of the districts, they had little share.

Occasionally the district would request from a committee the names of those who had escaped its warrants, for after absence of two months without cause an individual was legally an émigré and his property subject to confiscation. In the Bouches-du-Rhône the committees were to furnish tables of those who had fled after the defeat of the sections.[20] Occasionally the committees would volunteer information, as at Marseille and La Ciotat, where the district was informed of "an inheritance in which the nation should share."[21]

Actual participation in the confiscation was usually limited to applying the seals which were to prevent any removal of property until such time as the district could make an inventory and arrange for its sale. At Estaires, a member of the committee was ordered to coöperate with the municipality in the confiscation and sale of émigré property; while the municipality of Salon ordered the committee to apply the seals to the property of the parents of deserters.[22] In several departments the committees were assigned the duty of confiscating and administering the property of suspects. Fouché at Moulins, bent on assuring the happiness of mankind, ordered the committee to

---

assignats abounded there. But the Vendée committees, with the possible exception of that of Les Sables, were never eager to appear too conspicuous.

[20] Arch. Bouches-du-Rhône L 1011, 14 Ventôse.

[21] Arch. Bouches-du-Rhône L 1011, 17 Nivôse, 19 Pluviôse.

[22] Arch. Nord L 10194, 17 Brumaire; Arch. Bouches-du-Rhône L 1873, 27 Thermidor.

sell the movable property of suspects and to farm out the landed property to a good *sans-culotte*, the revenue to be collected by the treasury.[23] In the Haute-Vienne the same expedient was resorted to, though the arrangement seems not to have been as strict as in the Allier, for after Thermidor one of the guardians was authorized to deliver some wheat to the owner.[24] This practice was, however, exceptional.

The committees of Lyon also formed an exception, for here the administration entrusted to the thirty-two committees the confiscation and supervision of the property of all rebels and counter-revolutionaries, ordered by the representatives on the 2nd day of the 2nd month.[25]

As a result, application of the seals on homes and warehouses was commenced by the committee of the Rue Juiverie on the 9th day of the 2nd month.[26] Couthon, however, halted the confiscation of suspects' property, and it was not until the arrival of Collot d'Herbois on 14 Brumaire that the operation was resumed. On 18 Brumaire the municipality requested the committees to forward "a list of all wealthy citizens whose property had not been confiscated; a duplicate of the 4-columned list of the citizens you have arrested or should arrest, being careful to indicate by a cross those you have arrested; and a general list of those you have been unable to arrest, also of four columns." [27] The sequestrations were resumed; the committees applied their seals to the doors and windows of the buildings and appointed a *sans-culotte* as guardian. They were to draw up *procès-verbaux* to include an inventory of the contents and report to the municipality.[28]

On 23 Nivôse the committees were ordered to send the mu-

---

[23] L. Biernawski, *Un Département sous la Révolution française, L'Allier de 1789 à III* (Moulins, 1909), p. 288.

[24] Arch. Haute-Vienne L 836, L 844, 26 Fructidor.

[25] Arch. Rhône CL 203, 4 Frimaire. Barère on the 28th of the 1st month announced that the representatives had ordered confiscation. *Moniteur*, réimp., XVIII, 167.

[26] Arch. Rhône CL 122.

[27] Arch. Rhône CL 261.

[28] Arch. Rhône CL 185, 27 Brumaire, 18, 27 Pluviôse; CL 163.

nicipality a list of all absent citizens, the cause of their absence, when they left, the state of the property, if it was confiscated, whether they participated in the rebellion, and if they were wealthy. Another circular on 11 Pluviôse asked for the names and addresses of all "capitalists, *rentiers*, rich merchants, whose property has not been confiscated." [29]

By this time the Temporary Commission seemed to have covered everything, but in order to make a clean sweep of the confiscation the Central Bureau of the committees ordered on 28 Brumaire that all persons in the service of those recognized as suspect were to be arrested and questioned in regard to hoarding of movable property, "such as silver plate and metal currency. And [the committees] will tell them that rewards will be given by the representatives of the people to those who are instrumental in making discoveries of value to the nation . . . they will tell them that the procurer of the commune already has information and well-founded suspicions on the complicity of these individuals with their former masters in regard to the hiding of these objects." The procurer also announced that he had asked the representatives for "extraordinary rewards for those committees which showed the greatest zeal in their operations." [30]

The members were not such innocents as to need instructions in third-degree methods, as can be seen from the long complaint which Laporte, one of the representatives at Lyon, wrote Couthon on 24 Germinal. The disillusioned deputy reported a great amount of dishonesty and corruption at Lyon, which some blamed on the revolutionary army brought down from Paris. But he observes that "it is the revolutionary committees who have applied the seals, who have the keys to confiscated homes and stores, who have placed there guardians in their service, who have made no inventories, who have not called the interested parties to witness their acts, who chased women, children and servants from their homes in order to have no

[29] Arch. Rhône CL 261.
[30] Arch. Rhône CL 261.

witnesses, who in short have done all they desired. . . ." Even after the representatives ordered that no seals be removed without their approval, "would you believe that two men, agents of the committee, broke into a store and were starting to loot it when they were caught red-handed? Everyone swore they were patriots and they had to be released." Another member set himself up in a millionaire's home and there he and his fellow members, accompanied by some women friends, indulged in the pleasures of the flesh. It was impossible to protest, according to Laporte, or people would cry that patriots were being oppressed.[31]

The Temporary Commission, however, did protest once, and declared that it learned with regret that "various committees have treated with a severity of which the law disapproves women and children whose fathers and husbands have been justly punished for their crime. The property of those condemned is indeed national property, but the law grants their widows and children those things which they need most urgently, that is, their clothes and even their beds and bedclothing and other linen which they need. . . . The said property is also granted the wives and children of fugitives, suspects and even counter-revolutionaries, as well as the wives of those under arrest."[32]

To put an end to these "irregularities" a special Commission for Confiscated Property was created and on 12 Pluviôse it informed the committees that they were forbidden to remove the protecting seals without an agent of the commission. On 17 Ventôse the district hopefully asked for a table of confiscated houses and merchandise, the seals on which had been removed without the approval of the representatives and the participation of the district. As far as it is possible to discover, the district never got their lists.[33]

If we have dwelt overlong on these exploits of the committees

---

[31] *Papiers inédits trouvés chez Robespierre, Saint-Just* [etc.] . . . *supprimés ou omis par Courtois* (Paris, 1828), III, 82–85.
[32] Arch. Rhône CL 185, 7 Nivôse.
[33] Arch. Rhône CL 261.

of Lyon, it is only to compare them with the much defamed committee of Nantes. The latter and its accomplices, the Compagnie de Marat, indulged in looting which in comparison seems the work of amateurs. As for the drownings, the victims would have ended under the guillotine or in front of a ditch, facing a firing squad. Nantes, too, had made honest efforts to prevent a plague from sweeping the town. But at Lyon the "friends of Chalier," good patriots all, the men who were to found the Republic of Virtue — these *sans-culottes* just thieved.

REVOLUTIONARY TAXES

Removing silver, raiding churches, and digging in château gardens were at best unmethodical. The so-called revolutionary taxes, however, were comprehensive and as systematic as it was possible for anything to be in the fall of 1793. These extraordinary levies were generally decreed by the representatives on mission, and struck at groups which varied in accordance with the representative's views. Often the tax was imposed on all the wealthy of the district and was proportionate to the regular tax-assessments.[34] At Nancy this was true in theory, but in the list drawn up by the first committee eight Jews were assessed for a total of 3,000,000 *livres*. (The whole amount of the tax was 5,000,000 *livres*.) [35] This committee was dismissed before collections commenced, and on the new list one paid according to one's status. Four groups were created: those wealthy before the Revolution; hoarders and egoists; those who had made their fortune during the Revolution; and rich of the proscribed classes.[36] The taxes levied in the Nièvre on orders from Fouché were also aimed at "enemies of the people." The assessments did not correspond to the

[34] Arch. Gironde L 2268, L 2229; "Le Comité de Sancoins," *A. Révol.*, V, 505–507; Arnaud, p. 424.
[35] Arch. Meurthe-et-Moselle L 3360. Nancy was anti-Semitic. The popular society asked the Convention to expel the Jews from the Republic, and the committee itself refused them passports. Godchot, *Révol. Fr.*, LXXX, 254.
[36] Arch. Meurthe-et-Moselle L 3360.

land tax paid, and before the Terror ended most of those who bore the tax were arrested as suspects. The list indicated that a certain citizen was being taxed as an egoist, another as the father of three émigrés, a third as a selfish bachelor, and so on, but patriots were exempted from the list.[37]

At Perigueux it was the incivic wealthy who paid and in the Lozère, Aveyron, and Cantal the "malevolent" — "the supporters of royalism, superstition, and federalism, the monopolists, profiteers, egoists, and indifferent."[38] At Toul, on the contrary, only the detained were taxed, although it was suggested to other wealthy persons that a "voluntary" contribution immediately might spare them the pain of paying a tax later.[39] Hints of this type were not unusual, and a large part of the money extracted from the wealthy by committees all over France was officially considered "voluntary."

The purposes for which this money was raised varied as widely as the methods of raising it. At Dax (Landes) the 150,000 *livres* was to care for the poor during the coming winter.[40] At Belfort and in the Meurthe the proceeds were used to defray the expenses of raising and equipping the local battalions and to care for their parents or their wives and children, while at Melun the tax served to support the needy parents of the soldiers.[41] At Sancoins (Cher) the 301,799 *livres* gathered financed the committee, paid all the expenses of the house of detention and its guards, paid for equipping the national guardsmen, gave their wives pensions, and paid for charity workshops, poor and sick relief, the maintenance of a hospital, several revolutionary festivals, repairs to the hall of the local Jacobins, and repairs for the town clock.[42] In the Ariège the money was used partly for feeding the poor, while the remainder went to the committee of Pamiers for expenses.[43]

---

[37] Meunier, I, 270, 273, 309.
[38] Aulard, *Comité de Salut Public*, XI, 147; Delmas, pp. 43–46.
[39] Denis, pp. 34–35.
[40] Richard, "Dax," *A. H. Révol.*, VIII, 26.
[41] *Arch. parl.*, LXXX, 379–380; Arch. Meurthe-et-Moselle L 3259; Denis, pp. 32–34; Campagnac, *A. Révol.*, I, 471.
[42] Arch. Cher L 929, fo. 4.   [43] Arnaud, p. 424 note.

Troyes and Bourg retained part of the proceeds for their salary, a practice which was not usual, despite the law of 5 September.[44] The Convention seems to have nullified that law when by the law of 14 Frimaire it forbade the levy of any special tax, unless ordered by a decree of the Convention (Section III, 20), which made it impossible for the committees to collect their salary if they had not already done so. Two days later even the fortunate few who had gathered their funds were deprived of their stipend, for on Simond's motion the Convention ordered that "levies made upon citizens throughout the Republic by revolutionary committees or committees calling themselves such, or by any incompetent authority, will be deposited in the National Treasury by the district administrations."[45]

What was spent was beyond the hands of the Treasury, but in some cases a remaining portion was sent to Paris. Some of the 1,674,000 *livres* collected at Troyes was sent to Paris, the committee itself retaining only 42,633 *livres*.[46] In the Orne, the committee of l'Aigle was forced by the Treasury on 28 Messidor to disgorge 7,000 of the 14,000 *livres* it had collected.[47] This was the reason for the incessant petitioning of the committees for salaries of which we have already spoken. They had, in effect, been cheated by the government. If they themselves cheated the suspects and the wealthy who were to pay their expenses according to the law of 5 September, their acts, by a bit of casuistry, can be justified.

POOR RELIEF

In certain localities, a portion at least of the revolutionary taxes was devoted to charitable purposes. At Sancoins (Cher) the poor, under the supervision of the committee of surveillance, were set to work upon the roads. In the neighboring department of the Indre, the committee of Châteauroux ordered

---

[44] Babeau, II, 172; Le Duc, IV, 77.

[45] *Arch. parl.*, LXXXI, 16. But see above, the case of the committee of Belleville, p. 66.

[46] Babeau, pp. 159, 172.   [47] *Moniteur*, réimp., XXIV, 720.

the opening of a subscription for the needy parents of soldiers with the openly expressed threat that if contributions were not proportional to wealth, a revolutionary tax would be levied.[48] The central committee of the Haute-Vienne ordered the district committees to distribute 70,000 *livres* to the needy parents of soldiers (Frimaire). Possibly this was part of the revolutionary tax levied in the department, amounting to 97,022 *livres* 13 *sous*.[49]

Lyon is again exceptional, for the committees and the *amis de Chalier* could hardly be restrained in their clamors for the spoils of their triumph. As early as 23 October, two weeks after the triumphant entry into the city of the Republican army, the committee of Rue Tupin drew up a list of its needy, 461 of them, evidently on the orders of the administration.[50] The arrival of Fouché with his sentimental communism stimulated this interest in the welfare of the unfortunate, and on 24 Brumaire he issued his decree declaring that the "infirm, the aged, orphans and the needy will be lodged at the expense of the canton." [51] The accepted procedure seems to have been to oust from their homes the suspects and rebels of Lyon, for on 23 Ventôse the committee of Rue Tupin was informed by the municipality that its decisions ordering the removal of aristocrats of its jurisdiction to lodge the *sans-culottes* of the Bourgneuf quarter "must be limited to dislodging only those against whom there is a denunciation" — a condition which the committee could probably satisfy with no great difficulty.[52]

To assist those "oppressed, tortured or imprisoned" during the siege, the newly established Temporary Commission of 4 Frimaire asked the committees for lists of their names, the type of losses and probable indemnities.[53] Nor were these the only benefits; the committee of Gourguillon on 26 Frimaire drew up a list of thirteen citizens not yet employed; probably

---

[48] "Le Comité de Sancoins," *A. Révol.*, V, 508; Arch. Indre L 1538, 26 Brumaire.

[49] Fray-Fournier, II, 118–120; Arch. Haute-Vienne L 836.

[50] Arch. Rhône CL 60.

[51] L. Madelin, *Fouché* (Paris, 1900), I, 132.

[52] Arch. Rhône CL 61.

[53] *Ibid.*, CL 185.

they were later placed as guards of the property sequestrated by the committees.[54] The same committee had a register of unemployed, their trade, and the indemnity they were given by the municipality.[55] At the time of the sale of confiscated property (15 Ventôse), the committees received from the district cards to be distributed among the poor to permit them to buy at a reduced amount, though only in small quantities.[56] The offices of the Lyon committees, probably the busiest places in their sections, had become poor-relief agencies and employment bureaux, distributing a patronage which was not inconsiderable. With the majority of committees, however, concern with the administration of charity is rare, which would indicate that they left to the municipalities and the popular societies the always unwelcome task of caring for the needy.

PATRIOTIC CONTRIBUTIONS

As intended by the Convention the patriotic contributions collected all over the Republic were to be in kind — shirts, shoes, and so on, for the army. Duquesnoy, returning from the frontier, reported the deplorable conditions there and asked that all who had six shirts be instructed to send one of them to the army, as well as shoes and stockings. Romme proposed that the order be limited to an invitation, and despite Duquesnoy's protests, the decree was passed as worded by Romme. Chabot, however, shared Duquesnoy's low opinion of the wealthier citizens, and the Convention accepted his amendment that "the invitation should be extended to the aristocrats' (apparently only aristocrats had six shirts) by the revolutionary committees in person. "And," shouted Duquesnoy, "those who don't contribute should be arrested as suspects"; but his motion was cried down.[57] However, the law of 19 Brumaire was enforced in that manner. The deputies had realized what power of coercion rested in the hands of those small groups of *sans-culottes*, scattered all over France,

[54] *Ibid.*, CL 203.
[55] *Ibid.*, CL 121.
[56] *Ibid.*, CL 161, 14 Ventôse; CL 261, 14 Ventôse.
[57] *Moniteur*, réimp., XVIII, 385.

and again had succumbed to the temptation to compel, to force things violently into the framework of ideas they had envisaged.

The committees acted as had been expected and often admitted quite frankly that they were applying pressure. We have already cited the case of the committee at Saint-Malo: "No patriotic contribution, no visa on your certificate of civism." In the Puy-de-Dôme a *sieur* was released when he contributed 50,000 *livres* and offered 1,000 *livres* to each of fifteen soldiers who would distinguish themselves for bravery.[58] A citizen of Nantes arrested "for neglecting to aid the Republic in proportion to his fortune and the uncertainty of his civism," was released when his wife repaired his omission by "contributing" 50,000 *livres*.[59] By similar tactics and by their seizures of precious metal and property the committee was able to gather, according to Lallié's careful investigation, 586,918 *livres*, all "voluntary" gifts to the Republic, for in Floréal when the district asked the committee for an accounting as required by the laws of 16 Frimaire and 15 Nivôse the members replied they had "never raised loans, levies, nor forced contributions"! [60]

Elsewhere the contributions were what the Convention had intended them to be — contributions of clothing of all kinds. The committee of Toul led, perhaps, in the quantities of shoes and socks and what-not it gathered, for here the compelling influence of Prussian troops seconded the patriotic exhortations of the committee. Its final account submitted on 26 Floréal shows:

2670 shirts	43 pair gaiters	3 caps
139 bed-covers	20 collars	3 haversacks
494 pairs of socks	96 pairs of shoes	20 petticoats
28 suits	7 pair boots	27 tablecloths
87 pair breeches	28 lbs. leather	20 napkins
29 pair trousers	4 hats	18 remnants of

cloth, thread, etc., 7344 *livres*, 5 *sous*, and 53 pounds of prunes! [61]

[58] Mège, p. 313 note.
[59] Lallié, "Le comité . . . de Nantes," *R. Bretagne, Anjou*, XXVI, 7.
[60] *Ibid.*, pp. 67, 71–72.   [61] Denis, pp. 42–44.

Almost without exception the committees opened registers in which to inscribe the donations presented by patriotic citizens. Save in the larger centers, where the committee members seem to have been more artful than their country contemporaries, the contributions were largely confined to clothing and perhaps a small sum of money.

To form an estimate of the committees' role in the expropriation of the wealthy, it is sufficient to realize that actions such as those described were taking place all over France. Revolutionary taxes of staggering proportions were levied in many departments, simply upon the authority of the representatives on mission; patriotic contributions were squeezed out by any method which seemed effective; any gold or silver upon which the committees could place their hands was carried off to the Treasury.

In the majority of cases, these confiscations were simply based on the conviction of the representatives that the Republic needed the money more than the wealthy, and if in some cases the representatives appealed to the law of 5 September, ordering a tax on the wealthy to defray the expenses of the committees, we have seen that the proceeds were rarely used for that purpose. Battalions of troops were raised, free theatres financed, the poor relieved by the money that poured in; and while these are laudable enterprises, they were clearly financed through arbitrary expropriation.

This "soak the rich" campaign is only one symptom of the contempt, if not hatred, which the *sans-culottes*, as represented by the committees, felt toward the wealthy. In their registers the terms used in speaking of the wealthy citizens are always disparaging, and if it is ever possible to recapture from inanimate documents the spiritual phenomena of a time long past, it is possible to read in the registers of the committees the enmity and the envy of the dispossessed. If ever a class policy was pursued, it was at this time, when to be rich was to be suspect and to be poor was to be nature's greatest achievement, a good *sans-culotte*. To assume with Mathiez that there was no class hatred during the Terror because the Mountain was composed of bourgeois lawyers "allied with the proletarians" is to forget that the Revolution took place outside the Salle du Manège.

CHAPTER IX

THE LAW OF 14 FRIMAIRE

The Establishment of Revolutionary Government

AFTER the fall of the monarchy the administration of France sustained a succession of profound shocks, for political events made imperative the organization and reorganization of the institutions which governed France. Not only were the ostensible heads of the administration removed, but it was found necessary to replace the hirelings, the permanent secretariat which gives to every government stability and continuity. Although governments and ministers rise and fall, under normal conditions the experience of these men in actual situations permits them to handle new tasks with relative ease and apply an old solution to a new problem.

In Republican France the old royal administration was suspect. Consequently, it was replaced by the elections of November 1792, and the lesser posts were filled with officials of Girondist leanings. From the time of their election France was in turmoil. The struggle between the Mountain and the Gironde had already begun, and with the arrival of a new year, military reverses and civil war put the administrations through an exhausting ordeal. It is impossible to say whether it was the inexperience of the new administrators or the essential weakness of the Constitution of 1791 which made them as inefficient, hesitant, and self-willed as we have seen them. It is certain that the solution to the problems raised by their vacillations could not be found within the limits of that Constitution.

The Convention therefore sent into the departments a host of representatives, armed with unlimited powers to organize the mass levy of troops, to purge the administration, and to take any other steps which would impart to the local governments of the nation the energy the circumstances demanded. During September and October the representatives swept through France, removing, replacing, haranguing the local officials, instilling in many of them ideas and methods which led them beyond the limits conceived by the Convention. The deputies themselves levied revolutionary taxes, confiscated gold and silver, instituted revolutionary armies to scour the countryside for suspects and for food; they often gave the signal for a savage attack upon the Church. In much of this activity, the committees, subject to no control, free-lances as it were, were persuaded to be accomplices.

It was then that the leaders of the Convention decided that they had had enough of energy, that this radicalism must come to an end. At Paris these extreme policies, for convenience referred to as Hebertist, had roused opposition. Especially had the assault against the Church alarmed the Committee of Public Safety; it was difficult enough to feed the importunate Parisians without having the peasantry in revolt. Robespierre therefore came to the defense of religion at the Jacobins on 1 Frimaire, attacking the attackers of fanaticism, and throwing suspicion upon the acts of Proli, a Hebertist, whose schemes, declared Robespierre, were aimed at the overthrow of the Republic.[1]

A month later, in his report on revolutionary government, he denounced in his vague way "the inventors of false systems." "In indicating the duties of the revolutionary government we have pointed out the shoals. The greater its power and the swifter its action, the more its actions must be dictated by good faith. The day when it falls into impure and faithless hands, liberty will be lost; its name will become the pretext and the excuse for even counter-revolution." Again anonymously, he attacked Cloots: "Nothing more resembles the apostle of federalism than the ill-timed preaching of the Republic one and universal. The fanatic clad in his scapulary and the fanatic who preaches atheism have much in common.

[1] *Moniteur*, réimp., XVIII, 507–509.

. . . We have seen Englishmen and Prussians (Paine and Cloots, who were excluded from the Convention the next day) chasing through the cities and villages announcing, in the name of the National Convention, an extravagant doctrine. . . ." Certainly the Hebertism which swept France during the fall of 1793 was out of favor with the spokesman of the Committee of Public Safety.

In his campaign against the extremists, he was aided by Danton and the party later to be damned contemptuously as the Indulgents. On 2 Frimaire Danton had reënforced Robespierre's plea for freedom of worship and on 13 Frimaire he found welcome Robespierre's aid in extricating himself from a difficult situation at the Jacobins. The Hebertists' star was waning.[2]

The law of 14 Frimaire was, therefore, an attempt at correcting sins of commission as well as sins of omission, to restrain as well as to constrain the administration. It was to check the waywardness of certain representatives, for it forbade the delegation of unlimited powers to agents; it forbade the levying of revolutionary taxes; it dissolved the revolutionary armies; it forbade the representatives to oppose or suspend the administrative orders of the Committee of Public Safety; and ordered them to report every ten days to the same committee. In short, it tore down an entire system of proconsulship improvised by the representatives during the preceding months and substituted for it a centralized administration whose keystone was the national agent of the district, a less embarrassing assistant than the representative since he was an employee, not a colleague — an employee who could be controlled, severely reprimanded, even removed without creating a political battle at Paris.

To these national agents the committees of surveillance were subjected, as were all administrative bodies of the departments. No longer were they the autonomous units of the fall, enforcing or ignoring the laws as they chose, answerable to no one but

[2] Mathiez, *La Révolution française* (Paris, 1922–27), III, 120–121.

themselves and to an occasional representative whose unfamiliarity with local politics made him the dupe of the first party which gained his ear. They also were to report every ten days to their new supervisor and give him an accounting of their errors and shortcomings. He was to reprimand them for their faults and denounce them if their crimes were too great.[3]

This, at least, was the theory; but the experience of the preceding nine months could not inspire confidence or even hope that this new law would be better observed than its predecessor. The Committee of Public Safety consequently strove with all means at its hands to impose upon the provinces this new system of government which was to end the reigning confusion.

By a flood of circulars which poured out to the departments the Committee impressed upon the administration the urgency of the new organic law, declared that upon its enforcement depended the safety of the Republic and the preservation of the benefits of the Revolution. To the representatives, to the department administration, to the district, to the communes, to the national agents, to the committees, to the generals, to the courts, criminal, revolutionary, and military, these instructions were issued. Then, in Nivôse, the Committee followed up these exhortations with a questionnaire of twenty-six sections, demanding of the districts a report on the execution of revolutionary laws. The Committee sought precise information on the functioning of the revolutionary committees: were they properly chosen? had they enforced the law of 17 September? were any of the arrests due to spite and the spirit of revenge? It asked if the maximum was enforced, if there was difficulty in filling requisitions, whether the farmers had adopted the new methods of cultivation. In short, the districts were catechized.[4]

[3] Those sections of the law of 14 Frimaire relating to the committees of surveillance are reprinted verbatim in Appendix IV.

[4] P. Mautouchet, in his *Le Gouvernement révolutionnaire* (Paris, 1912), prints long extracts from all these circulars, pages 243–255. One of the questionnaires

To explain to the committees their new functions and to urge them to even greater activity the Committee of Public Safety in Nivôse dispatched one of the circulars already mentioned in which the members were hailed as "Sentinels of liberty" and in the same sentence were told that "the fatherland places in your hands new weapons against its enemies"! Each of the organizations of the state was declared necessary to its perfect functioning, but it was equally necessary that each part should understand its role so that conflicts and usurpations might not destroy the balance. Revolutionary law was analyzed, revealing three parts: first, the law itself, for which the Convention was responsible; second, the supervision of the law, divided into superior surveillance exercised by the two great Committees and the representatives, and simple surveillance, the duty of the districts; and third, the application of the law, the function of municipalities and committees. "Thus," said the Committee, "the action which emerges from the Convention comes to its completion in you; you are like the hands of the body politic of which it [the Convention] is the head, and ourselves the eyes; through you the will of the nation strikes as soon as it decides." It is an attractive picture, but unfortunately the body politic was not without dirty hands, as the Committee recognized, for its next sentence is an exhortation to vigilance, honesty, and dignity.

Briefly it outlined the specific duties of the committees, inveighed against usurpations and the dangers of federalism, and ended in that hyperbolical style so dear to the revolutionists: "This Revolutionary organization, which pours terror in torrents upon the hydra of conspirators, must bring virtue and consequently yourselves into port while the tempest thunders down upon the head of the guilty and crushes them." The opinion of Dorgeuil, the Bordeaux silver thief, and that of the drowning dozen of Nantes in regard to this promise of salvation for the virtuous, and consequently themselves, are not recorded.

and the answers forwarded to the Committee are reprinted in the same book, pages 302–308.

Nevertheless, for the majority of the *sans-culottes* to whom it was addressed it must have been invigorating and at the same time satisfying. Most of them were not very big frogs in rather small puddles and were trying to puff themselves up to make more nearly equal the size of the frog and the size of the puddle. To discover this, it is only necessary to examine their records, read their sometimes ludicrous efforts to write in the fervid style of the day, witness their jealousy of their rights and their petty tyrannies designed to impress their fellow citizens.

Much of this was pretense, of course, and there was another side to these *sans-culottes*. For they displayed to an infinite degree a willingness and an ability to undergo punishing toil, to endure privation and even downright misery, in order to bring to fruition the ideals of the Revolution. Their lot frequently was endless hours of work, without financial assistance from the government, enforcing laws which made them at least unpopular if not hated; yet they persisted in it with constancy and devotion, justified by the cause they believed they were serving — the freedom of mankind and the attainment of social justice.

REORGANIZATION OF THE COMMITTEES

The law of 14 Frimaire was promulgated in the departments during the month of Nivôse, and as a result of the strenuous efforts of the Committee of Public Safety and the representatives most committees conformed readily to the new instruction.

Of the provisions of the law of 14 Frimaire, by far the simplest to observe was that requiring the reëlection of president and secretary every fifteen days. A few of the committees had anticipated the Convention and determined upon a monthly renewal of officers principally to share the burdens of office among all the members.[5] These and other committees generally conformed, and although the officers might occasionally serve

---

[5] E. Pionnier, *Essai sur la Révolution à Verdun* (Nancy, 1905), p. 379 note; Bayeux, Arch. Calvados, Register of deliberations, 9 of 2nd month.

a few days more or less than the statutory fifteen, the general practice of alternation was assured.[6]

Many committees, especially those in the country, often had little other business than the reëlection of new officers. Their registers are comparable to that of Blesmes (Marne), which held only eleven meetings from Nivôse to Prairial (six months) and which, after inscribing the election of the president and secretary, announced that "n'ayant rien vu ni reconnu contre les lois ce quatre pluviôse, le comité se retire." [7]

The exclusion of all members of the administration from the committees was a more difficult operation. The committee which did not include among its members at least one administrator was rare indeed, and frequently the majority of the members were occupying other official positions. Persons in such circumstances were required to opt within twenty-four hours for the position which they wished to retain. With startling unanimity they bade farewell to the committees, undoubtedly because it relieved them of an unpopular task which gave no financial rewards. Of the hundreds of cases examined, there was only one where a committeeman chose to stay on, and that is hardly clear-cut — the commander of the national guard of Romans (Drôme) resigned his military functions.[8]

After the officials had indicated their decision, the committees were often sadly depleted. At Le Havre ten of the members resigned and the committee appealed to the representatives for replacements.[9] At Les Sables the committee declared itself suspended, since all were administrators, but on appeal to the representative Laignelot they were ordered to continue their functions until otherwise ordered.[10] The representatives at Rouen, however, were forced to reconstitute the committees of the entire department, since all those they had previously

---

[6] There are always the inevitable exceptions. Donzé-Bastien, the "boss of Toul," monopolized the presidency until the first *sans-culottide*, year II.

[7] Arch. Marne, Register of deliberations.

[8] U. Chevalier, *Le Comité de surveillance révolutionnaire et la société républico-populaire de Romans en 1793 et 1794* (Romans, 1890), p. 38.

[9] Arch. Seine-Inf. L 5327, 22 Nivôse.

[10] Chassin, *Vendée patriote*, IV, 107.

established were "composed, in the greater part, of public officials" who chose to retain their positions in the regular administration.[11]

It was generally to the representatives that the committees
appealed for replacements. In some cases, knowing the city,
the deputies themselves appointed new members, in others
they referred the matter to one of the administrations or
the popular society. On rare occasions the popular assembly
was convoked, as at La Tour-du-Pin (Isère) and La Penne
(Bouches-du-Rhône), where virtually an entire new committee
was elected.[12]

Simultaneous with this operation was the elimination from
the committees of all those between whom there was relationship to the fourth degree. On 7 Frimaire Thuriot had proposed,
and the Convention had passed, this regulation. Its effect on
the smaller communes can be imagined, but an even clearer idea
is given by the fact that the committee of Blaringhem spent
two meetings wrangling over who married whom and how many
children they had.[13] At Saint-Nicholas-les-Arras (Pas-de-
Calais) the committee was "composed of almost a single family"
and Lebon on 25 Nivôse dismissed it.[14]

GEOGRAPHICAL JURISDICTION OF THE COMMITTEES

A large number of the committees set up by the representatives and the administration during 1793 were to extend their
surveillance not only over their communes, but over their district or even their department as well. According to the new
organization outlined in the law of 14 Frimaire these committees were to be dissolved, since, as "congresses and central
assemblies," they "tended toward federalism" (the Convention
underlined this phrase).[15] More strictly, these two clauses
were aimed at central assemblies such as that organized by

[11] Aulard, *Comité de Salut Public*, IX, 641.
[12] Arch. Isère, Register of permanence, 26 Frimaire; Arch. Bouches-du-
Rhône L 1011, 3 Ventôse.
[13] Arch. Nord L 10132.
[14] Jacob, I, 316.   [15] Section III, Articles 16 and 17.

the revolting departments at Caen in the summer of 1793, or the joint meetings of department, district, and municipal administrations such as that held at Bordeaux during the same period.

Notwithstanding, a certain number of the central committees resigned as a result of the new order. That of Bourg was replaced on 25 Frimaire, and on the same date the central committee of the Haute-Vienne declared itself dissolved, and a new committee for the commune of Limoges was named by the popular society.[16]

Nevertheless, it is by no means certain that these central committees were required to resign. They were not, save in a few cases, delegates of other committees, nor were they "extending the exercise of their powers beyond the territory assigned to them" (Section II, Article 15), since the representatives or the administrations creating them had specifically indicated to them the territory over which their powers extended. This ambiguity in the law was appreciated by a number of central (or to be precise, departmental, or district) committees, and instead of stepping down immediately they appealed to the representative for a decision. The committee of Bordeaux on 5 Nivôse queried Ysabeau and Tallien, who at first maintained the committee's jurisdiction over the entire department.[17] Only on 16 Pluviôse was the committee dissolved (theoretically, for abusing its powers), and a new committee set up with its powers limited to the commune of Bordeaux.[18] Even then the committee was extending its jurisdiction beyond the limits set by the law, for at Bordeaux, as in all other communes divided into sections, there should have been a committee for each district of the city. Nevertheless, similar committees existed in other large cities of France, and the practice was so widespread as to be virtually the rule.[19]

Though these committees were violating the letter of the

[16] Le Duc, IV, 201–202; Arch. Haute-Vienne L 836; L 843, 23 Nivôse.
[17] Arch. Gironde L 2164, 5 Nivôse; L 442, 17 Nivôse.
[18] Arch. Gironde L 438.
[19] Toul, Marseille, Aix, Rouen, Caen, Limoges, Dijon, Nîmes, Carcassonne

law of 14 Frimaire, they were rarely interfered with. To a government which had so recently devised a system of extreme centralization, the advantages of a single center of action were obvious, and in appealed cases the great Committees generally continued the existence of these central committees. The representatives as well recognized that one committee for an entire commune was preferable and coupled this sentiment with a continued distrust of sections in general. Consequently, to increase the committees' efficiency the representatives usually permitted the central committees to exist and even suppressed section committees and set up a single committee for an entire city.[20]

The deputies reveal the same attitude in dealing with the country committees. Conditions in the country had not changed since 1793, educated men were still few, and those few were not always to be trusted. The Convention, indeed, would have done better when reorganizing the government if it had suppressed entirely all committees save those in canton, district, and department capitals and had granted to the former rights of surveillance over the entire canton. The representatives on mission attempted to remedy this defect and continued their practice of creating country committees with jurisdiction over more than a single commune. Borie ordered the various communes of the Gard to name a few citizens from whom would be chosen a single committee for the entire canton (6 Prairial).[21] Les Sables (Vendée) saw its jurisdiction extended first to the district of Challans (23 Nivôse) and then to the district of La Roche-sur-Yon (2 Floréal); while in the district of La Châtaigneraye the administration ordered a single committee in each canton (22 Germinal).[22]

(Ville), Nantes, Angers, Saumur, and Orléans, to mention only a few, had single committees for the entire commune.

[20] To mention a few of the latter: Vitry-le-François, Dieppe, Lisieux, Fontenay. Arch. Marne, Committee of Vitry-le-François, Register of deliberations, 4 Thermidor; Arch. Seine-Inf. L 5215, 28 Brumaire; Arch. Calvados, Lisieux, Committee of Section Fraternité, 9 Ventôse; Arch. Vendée L 1186, 13 Pluviôse.

[21] Rouvière, IV, 143–144.

[22] Chassin, Vendée patriote, IV, 108, 470; Arch. Vendée L 1171, 22 Germinal.

The motives for this extension are not far to seek. In the interior of the department of the Vendée, the Bocage, committees were non-existent, for it was this territory which was held by the rebels. Of the twenty-three committees whose records are still extant, all save four were in communes of the Plain and the Marsh, that is, the southern section of the department. Of the remaining four, one was on the Île d'Yeu, one at La Châtaigneraye on the eastern boundary of the department, one at Les Sables on the coast, and the fourth at Saint-Hilaire-la-Forêt, near Les Sables.

As regards the jurisdiction of the committees, therefore, the law of 14 Frimaire did not impose upon France that rigid uniformity at which the Convention had aimed. Only department committees had been broken up. There continued to exist central committees in the cities divided into sections, which was usual, and committees whose jurisdiction extended over more than one commune.

In the exercise of their surveillance, on the contrary, the committees did confine themselves to the geographical territory assigned to them. After receiving the law of 14 Frimaire the committee of Sancoins revoked its orders for a purge of the municipality of Sagonne.[23] Douai was careful to request the national agent of the district to arrest a relative of Calonne residing in another commune, believing this function was within the agent's competence (17 Pluviôse).[24]

There were, of course, some cases where committees continued to go beyond the confines of their commune to make arrests, but these were rare and usually were so loudly protested that the first experience was the last. An arrest by the committee of Saint-Malo in the territory of that of Paramé brought complaints that such acts "attack the prerogatives and dignity of the committee of surveillance of Paramé."[25] The popular society of Lunéville made similar protests against an

[23] "Le comité de Sancoins," *A. Révol.*, V, 182.
[24] Dechristé, pp. 74-75.
[25] H. Harvut, *Paramé sous la Terreur — Histoire du comité de surveillance de Paramé* (Saint-Malo, 1911), p. 10.

arrest by the Nancy committee, and at Aix it was the same in regard to the committee of Berre.[26] The committees, in short, did obey the much-quoted Section III, Article 15, and confined their activities to "the territory which is assigned to them."

COMPTES DÉCADAIRES

From an administrative point of view, one of the most important features of the law on revolutionary government was the *compte décadaire*, a regular report of the committee's activities to be submitted to the national agent of the district and the Committee of General Security. When they had established the committees, the representatives on mission had generally asked for frequent reports, but they were rarely sent. Now the district, charged with supervising the execution of revolutionary laws, and the Committee of General Security were to be informed by the committees at regular intervals.

Certain committees sent reports to the Committee of Public Safety, and after instructions to individual committees had had no effect, the Committee of Public Safety on 24 Prairial issued a printed circular, instructing the committees to correspond no longer with the Committee of Public Safety or the Committee of General Security but only with their districts. Though Article 17 of the second section "orders that the presidents of the committees shall maintain this correspondence both with the Committee of General Security and the district charged with supervising their acts," the committee wrote, "that is to be understood only in regard to the committees of Paris. All others, except in major and extraordinary circumstances, should address their correspondence to the districts, and if the latter consider that the matters communicated to them are of a nature to merit the attention of the Committee, it is their (the districts') duty to forward them to it. . . ."[27]

The reports commenced usually sometime in Nivôse, though

---

[26] H. Baumont, *Histoire de Lunéville* (Lunéville, 1904), p. 373; Arch. Bouches-du-Rhône L 1712, 20 Pluviôse.

[27] Aulard, *Comité de Salut Public*, XIV, 275.

in the outlying communes it required a bit of dunning from the national agent of the district to get the committees to comply with the law. In the district of Marseille printed circulars were resorted to, so great was the difficulty in obtaining reports from the small communes, and the same expedient was resorted to elsewhere.[28]

The reports themselves varied widely in character. Complete accounts of every decision made by the committee were usual in the cities, virtual registers which permit one to follow the activities of a committee when its official register is missing. At Bordeaux, for example, the registers of the committee set up by Julien *fils* no longer exist, but there are reports for certain *décades*, preserved in the files of the national agent, which throw some light on the committees' acts.[29]

Those from country communes are quite the reverse, but though furnishing little concrete information, they do indicate the character of country committees. Here is a typical report, from Tancarville, a small commune at the mouth of the Seine, some fifteen miles from Havre:

> Citoyens
> il ne sest rien passé dans notre commune pendans cette décade qui puisse nuire a la Republique tous le peuple qui la composse sont tous dans la bonne disposition à se conformé au loi. La plus grande partie sont bon republicain. Sont fais très exactement la publication des lois sito quel sont parvenus La lecture sent fait toute les décade a un heure à pres midy et la plus grande partie des citoÿen a siste pour les Entandre.[30]

INTERNAL ORGANIZATION OF THE COMMITTEES

The increase in their duties during the fall and winter had forced the committees of the larger communes to systematize their activity in order that nothing be neglected. Even before the law of 14 Frimaire there had been a tendency toward this division of labor. The committee of the section

[28] Arch. Bouches-du-Rhône L 1011.
[29] Arch. Gironde L 2175.
[30] Arch. Seine-Inf. L 5541.

of the Mountain at Lyon on 20 October had set up four bureaux
— a central bureau, one for denunciations, another on charity
and bakeshops, and a fourth for furnishing arms, lodging, and
barracks for the army.[31] At Bordeaux the committee set up
on 2 Frimaire organized bureaux of seals and arrests, of denunciations, of petitions, and of correspondence, and at the
same time retained a treasurer at 1800 *livres*, four clerks at
1500, a *concierge* at 1200, and six agents at 1200, the latter to
serve the warrants of the committee.[32] An establishment of
this size was, however, limited to the largest cities.

Nevertheless, committees in smaller communes also adopted
the practice of dividing their duties. The committee of Grasse
had a bureau of certificates of civism, another on archives and
correspondence, another on suspects, and a "general reporter"
who prepared the agenda for the succeeding meeting.[33] At
Beaune the committee retained an archivist, two *concierges*,
and an interpreter for intercepted letters written in German.[34]

Many committees drew up agenda of daily business, assigning to each member his special function. Save for an instruction drawn up by the representative Chaudron-Rousseau after
Thermidor, the most exhaustive regulation was that of the central committee of Grenoble (3 Pluviôse). The members had
already on 28 Brumaire formulated one set of rules for conduct-
ing meetings, which provided among other things that vague denunciations would not be accepted, that certain members would
receive denunciations, that there should be no insulting of members under penalty of a 5 *livres* fine, that officers were to be renewed every two weeks, and so on for fourteen articles.[35] The
new regulation, however, contained twenty-five provisions. The
introductory articles indicated the order of meetings: first the
minutes of the preceding meeting, then the reading of correspondence, the approval of certificates of civism, and last, any

[31] Arch. Rhône CL 203, 20 October.
[32] Arch. Gironde L 2164, 11 Frimaire.
[33] Combet, *Révol. Fr.*, LVII, 341.
[34] Barbuat, *M. Soc. Beaune*, 1911, 161.
[35] Arch. Isère L 870.

reports by members. Then followed parliamentary rules providing that the president could give the floor to only one member at a time, and that one member was to have the floor only three times on the same subject. There followed articles 15 to 21, which assigned to each member his duty:

Article 15 — The secretary shall draw up the minutes of each meeting and, when they are approved, he shall make an analysis on separate sheets to be sent every month [*sic*] to the district in conformity with the law.

Article 16 — Correspondence and reports shall be assigned to Citizens Poudret and Pyot *fils* who must perform this duty accurately.

Article 17 — Citizen Carleat is specially entrusted with two registers, that of warrants for arrest and that of certificates of civism, for which he is responsible to the committee.

Article 18 — Citizens Gourdon and Giroud are the guardians of the law; they shall make a special study of it in order to enlighten the committee, a duty which they shall perform with zeal and accuracy.

Article 19 — Citizens Joubert and Crollin are archivists. They are responsible for all papers deposited with them.

Article 20 — Citizen Blanchon, in addition to his duties as treasurer, is the steward of the committee; he is required to care for the fire in the hearth, the stove, the lighting and other matters of economy.

Article 21 — Citizen Bauthière shall be called the friend of order; he is especially charged with requesting restraint in gesture and speech of those who disturb the meeting; he shall take note of the members who ask for the floor and indicate to the president the one to whom it should be granted.

The last articles deal with the right of a member to denounce a colleague for negligence or prevarication, and the competence of the committee to judge its own members.[36]

While these dispositions are typical, certain committees went farther in the regulation of their members' lives. Bordeaux on 27 Frimaire agreed that anyone who failed to report for work at 8 A.M. was to be fined 100 *sous*, and such recommendations

---

[36] Arch. Isère L 871, 3 Pluviôse.

to punctuality and assiduity are not unusual.[37] Châlons-sur-Marne declared that any member who appeared drunk at meetings should be warned, then rebuked in the minutes for the second offense, and for the third, denounced to the Committee of General Security.[38] The Châlons committee apparently had had trouble similar to that of Bayeux, where on the first day of the second month,

. . . est arrivé le citoyen Mallet, membre du comité qui nous a paru un peu echauvé [echauffé] de vin, qui au lieu de concourir avec nous aux operations importantes qui nous sont confiées, il les a interrompües en se servant d'expressions despotiques et même injurieuse envers ses collegues il nous a menacé et n'a fait aucun cas de nos representations, a particulierement attaqué Le Cit. President qui d'abord luy a fait des sages remonstrances et a cherché à le rapeller a l'ordre mais qui dans la suitte se sentant outragé a oublié malgré luy le caractère de moderation qu'il doit conserver et la dignité paisible qui luy covenait dans ses augustes fonctions, il luy est echappé quelques traits de vivacité envers le Citoyen Mallet. Nous membres du comite de surveilliance affligé de cette scène indecente avons interposé notre authorité pour rétablir le calme et l'ordre dans notre scéance, Le Cit. President s'est rappellé ce qu'il étoit & ce qu'il devoit être il a fait excuse au comité, mais le Citoyen Mallet s'est emporté à des nouvelles injures que le comite croiroit se dehonorer en les inserant sur le papier et a fait un tumulte scandaleux, il s'est rétiré en faisant des gestes menaçantes ce qui a forcé le Comité à lever sa seance mais réfléchisant aux operations interessantes auxquelles il étoit livré ils sont repris seance ce que voyant ledit Citoyen Mallet a pris un des chevaux de luxe et est parti ainsy qu'on nous l'a dit, comme un furieux égaré et tout hors de luy-meme.[39]

This survey of the application of the law of 14 Frimaire indicates how speedily and how completely the committees conformed to its injunctions — prodded, it is true, by the government at Paris and by the representatives on mission. As a result, the committees were now a part of a centralized administration, subject to the national agent and reporting to him. Much of their arbitrary power was removed, as were those pre-

---

[37] Arch. Gironde L 2164.
[38] Arch. Marne, Register of deliberations, 11 Thermidor.
[39] Arch. Calvados, Register of deliberations.

rogatives which previously had opened the way to temptation. Now they knew the confines of their jurisdiction, the limits of their powers, and in the majority of cases they observed them. Yet they were by no means crippled, nor "purely communal and restricted to their police functions," as Lefebvre declares.[40] As we shall point out in subsequent chapters, they continued to coöperate with the army, to assist in provisioning their communes, in short to lend their aid on many occasions to the harried administration — all this in accordance with the law of 14 Frimaire.

[40] Lefebvre, Guyot et Sagnac, *La Révolution française*, p. 231.

CHAPTER X

THE COMMITTEES IN THEIR RELATIONS WITH OTHER OFFICIAL BODIES

WITH the passage of the law of 14 Frimaire the committees had reached full stature — had become members of the centralized organization which governed France. Consequently their relations with other sections of this administrative hierarchy are not without interest.

RELATIONS WITH PARIS

With the Convention itself their relations were only sporadic. Some few committees followed the example of that of Villers-Cotterêts and sent members to Paris to bear the profits of their searches for gold and silver or the results of their appeals for patriotic gifts. Generally, however, the committees conveyed their sentiments to the Convention by way of addresses, congratulating the deputies on one thing or another — the capture of Toulon, the victories of the armies against the coalized tyrants of Europe, and so on. By Thermidor the custom had become general, and the Commission on Despatches had printed a form letter acknowledging the receipt of "The address which you sent to the National Convention, dated ————— in regard to the recent conspiracy of Robespierre and his accomplices." [1]

Relations with the Committee of Public Safety were somewhat more active. Occasionally the Committee would issue a general circular, often instructing the committees in their new duties, sometimes simply encouraging them in their labors — as it did on 3 Thermidor, announcing proudly: "The Republic is established, citizens; it is the work of virtue." [2] Some com-

[1] Arch. Gironde L 2229.   [2] Arnaud, p. 505.

mittees appealed to the Committee of Public Safety when in
difficulties about the interpretation of laws, and a certain number of denunciations found their way to Robespierre's Bureau
of General Police. Yet it was usually the Committee of General Security to which the committees carried their complaints
and which they used as a threat against wayward members
and negligent officials.

Both of the committees of government intervened from time
to time in particularly troublous situations. At Orléans two
committees existed side by side, one chosen by the municipality
among its own members, the other elected by the sections; and
the Committee of Public Safety sent Eve Demaillot there to
clean up the situation. In the vast majority of cases, however,
the committees turned local problems over to the representative on mission in the region, for it was the representative,
aided by the national agent of the district after 14 Frimaire,
who was to supervise and control the acts of the local administration, replacing effectively the Minister of the Interior in
the fall of 1793.

Representatives

Thus far we have seen these deputies establishing committees, creating revolutionary armies, levying taxes, inaugurat-
ing the drive against the federalists, against the suspects, and
against religion. We have seen that the committees appealed
to them for advice, referred to them the countless petitions
presented by those detained, and plagued them with requests
for salary. Yet the committees were only a part of their burdens. They had to reorganize entire administrations in many
departments, put into effect the mass levy, aid in equipping
and feeding the army, institute the maximum, and perform a
hundred other duties. In short, the representatives were ultimately responsible for the conduct of the Terror in the departments, and if it was too terrible, the blame must be placed
on them. Carrier at Nantes, Fouché, Albitte, and Laporte at
Lyon, Ysabeau and Tallien at Bordeaux, knew well what the

committees of those cities were doing, yet they never did more than protest feebly, or, as Fouché did at Lyon, try indirectly to halt actions which were to the credit of neither themselves nor the committees. Yet later at Nantes Bourbotte and Bô on 24 Prairial suppressed the drowning committee and ordered the arrest of all thirteen of the committeemen;[3] and at Bordeaux, Julien *fils* on 15 Prairial set up a committee which, though it arrested furiously, was at least honest.

Simply from these few examples it can be seen how impossible it is to characterize the actions of the representatives as either aggravating or mitigating the severity of the committees. With no difficulty one can find examples of both. Bar dismissed the committee of Nancy because it was too lukewarm (Pluviôse); Siblot replaced the committee of Montivilliers (Seine-Inférieure), since he had found it "astonishing that there were so few arrests" (Prairial); at Fontenay, Laignelot ordered all who had been released to be rearrested, and warrants were issued for thirty-six (Germinal).[4]

On the other hand, Mallarmé released sixty-five detained at Verdun (Floréal); at Caen Bouret and Fremanger released sixty-six and dissolved the committee (Ventôse); Ysabeau and Tallien set up a commission of four to review the cases of a portion of the suspects and the committee released so many that the citizens complained (Pluviôse); at Vesoul (Haute-Saône), Augustin Robespierre released thirty-five in two days (Pluviôse).[5]

Many of these releases took place in Pluviôse and Ventôse, when the campaign of the Indulgents was at its height in Paris. Yet local events and the humor of the representative who had last passed had a greater effect than the speeches in the Convention. At Toul the new committee set up on 3 Ventôse ar-

---

[3] Lallié, "Le Comité révolutionnaire de Nantes," *R. Bretagne, Anjou,* XXVI, 129–130.

[4] Godchot, *Révol. Fr.,* LXXX, 259–260; Arch. Seine-Inf. L 5390, 22 Prairial; Arch. Vendée L 1186, 30 Germinal.

[5] Pionnier, p. 413; Arch. Calvados, Register of deliberations, 9–24 Ventôse; Arch. Gironde L 438, L 2165, 10 Ventôse et passim; Maréchal, pp. 284–286.

rested thirty-seven persons during the month; from April
1793 to Pluviôse only twenty-two had been arrested. On 3 Ventôse a new committee was set up at Nîmes. During the month
more than a hundred were arrested in the Gard; the previous
month had seen about thirty-five arrests.[6]

Briefly, in the majority of cases the initiative generally
rested with the representatives. It was they who counseled
a more moderate or a more vigorous course, and it was they
who remedied the shortcomings of the committees, pushing
them to the left or to the right as they themselves conceived it.

Not that the committees were always docile; there were
some who did not hesitate to protest against the release of
persons they believed truly guilty. Supported by the popular
society, the committee of Verdun protested to Mallarmé so
loudly against the release of a former municipal officer that
he was forced to countermand his own decree; the committee
of Macon (Saône-et-Loire) protested to the Committee of Public Safety against the release of Roberjot, brother of the deputy,
on orders of Bernard of Saintes.[7] The committee of Beaune got
along no better with Bernard, and upon his arrival there he
studiously avoided the committee's meeting place and issued a
series of decrees annulling recent deliberations of the committee.[8]

How serious or how frequent were differences of this kind
it is impossible to say; many disputes were probably arranged
by the deputies and the committees face to face. The fact that
the registers and documents extant give little indication of
animosity is no proof of its absence, for private opinions and
curtain lectures never get on paper.

Nevertheless, the representatives on mission exhibited in
many cases the confidence they felt in the committees. A great
number followed the practice of Bouret, who asked the committees of Caen and Lisieux for the names of administrators

[6] Rouvière, IV, 140; VI, 419–600.
[7] Pionnier, pp. 395–397; Ording, *Skrifter* . . . *Videnskaps-Akademi i Oslo etc.*,
p. 63.
[8] Barbuat, *M. Soc. Beaune*, 1911, pp. 165–166.

who should be replaced; Louchet requested the same from Le Havre, and Ysabeau at Bordeaux reviewed the political character of the public officials with three members sent from the committee.[9] The political power thus placed in the hands of the committees can easily be imagined, and the immensity of their influence seems even more overwhelming when one realizes that it was an almost universal practice. It is, of course, additional evidence of the tight control exercised by the committees and the popular societies, which in most places were effectively one and the same, so far as their policies were concerned.

THE COMMITTEES AND THE LOCAL ADMINISTRATION

The committee did not always await the orders of the representative to indicate which of the local public officials had lost the confidence of the *sans-culottes* of the commune. The committees themselves took the initiative and denounced to the deputies or to the administration those men not equal to the circumstances.

The committee of Angers wrote on 4 Ventôse to Francastel and his colleagues at Nantes: "You will find some changes in the project we have already submitted to Francastel for the reorganization of the municipality . . . from the department we have taken some members whom we believed more useful in other places; in the district we have excluded Aubry whom we have recognized as incapable of performing his task. . . . We are convinced, citizens, that if you ratify our work, all will go well." [10]

At the suggestion of the committee of Moulins, Fouché and Collot d'Herbois removed the *procureur-syndic* of that city.[11] At Châteauroux the committee and the district were on rather bad terms and during Pluviôse the former sent two denuncia-

---

[9] Arch. Calvados, Registers of deliberations, Caen, 8 Pluviôse; Lisieux, 11 Pluviôse; Arch. Seine-Inf. L 5327, 25 September; Arch. Gironde L 442, 23 Germinal.
[10] Bourcier, *R. Anjou*, VI, 184.
[11] Biernawski, *L'Allier de 1789 à III*, p. 289.

tions to the department and a third to the representative, in regard to illegal acts of the district.[12]

A few committees went farther — that of Bayonne, for example, which not only removed the officials without consulting the deputies on mission — an act contrary to the law — but also replaced them with individuals of their own choosing.[13] This means of caring for one's political and personal friends was not unusual, and Jeanbon Saint-André reported to the Committee of Public Safety on 21 Ventôse that the committee and popular society of Lorient had denounced officials on specious pretexts simply to provide places for their favorites.[14]

This power of denouncing public officials, coupled with the authority to visa certificates of civism, without which no administrator not elected by the people could retain his post, gave the committees the legal means of preventing an unfriendly official from continuing long in his post. It is not difficult, therefore, to appreciate the extent to which this authority increased and completed the control over appointments which was exercised by the committees and the popular societies.

DISTRICTS

To an even greater degree than with the representatives, the relations of the committees with the local administration were not universally cordial. The numberless dismissals indicate that the administration did not always enjoy the approval of the committees. Contact between them being closer and more constant, the friction was consequently greater — but this is not peculiar to the revolutionary committees, the French Revolution, or the Republic of France.

The committee of Bordeaux waged a running fight with the district during the month of Frimaire when the committee's jurisdiction extended over the entire department. The district of Bordeaux on 13 Frimaire appointed forty-eight agents

---

[12] Arch. Indre L 1538, 6, 17, 18 Pluviôse.
[13] Cuzacq, *B. Soc. Bayonne*, 1929, p. 12.
[14] Aulard, *Comité de Salut Public*, XI, 649.

charged with visiting the communes of the district to discover whether the revolutionary laws were being enforced, investigate the food supply, institute the maximum, draw up a list of those subject to the draft, confiscate the property of émigrés and those condemned, and arrest suspects. The committee was perturbed and on 18 Frimaire protested to Ysabeau and Tallien against this invasion of their rights, although at the same meeting it issued three warrants on the basis of the evidence of one of the district agents. The representatives gave them no satisfaction, so on 19 Frimaire the committee determined to receive the denunciations of these agents "as citizens, not as agents" — would not, in short, issue warrants on the orders of these forty-eight interlopers, and on the 26th struck an indirect blow at them by declaring all persons suspect who should make household inspections without previously notifying the committee. The commissioners apparently continued on their way, and on 23 Pluviôse the committee's jurisdiction was restricted to Bordeaux.[15]

At Fontenay the committee of the section of the Hospital and the district had a quarrel centering around the former's right to order the transfer of prisoners from one city to another. When the rebels had threatened the city, all prisoners were transferred to Niort.[16] When the scare had passed, the committee asked that the district arrange for the return of the suspects to Fontenay, since living was expensive at Niort and the problem of obtaining food was difficult, the suspects having no friends or relatives in that city to assist them (21 Nivôse). The district replied rather testily that it could not be done, that according to Article 12, Section II, of the law of 14 Frimaire, only the representatives could decide. The committee answered that Article 12 forbade release, not transfer of prisoners, and that it was going to write Lequinio (who incidentally had ordered the district to shoot all prisoners if the town was in danger of capture). Lequinio, without entering into the

---

[15] Arch. Gironde L 2164.
[16] Gaillard, *Soc. Emul. Vendée*, 1915–22, pp. 103–104.

legal aspect of the matter, blasted at the committee, asking it if it knew its duties and if the rebels must be at the very gates before measures of security were taken. The committee replied that it did, indeed, know its duties and would perform them with zeal and energy (28 Nivôse). The committee at least knew its way about, for nine days later it got Ingrand, another deputy, to approve the transfer of several of the most needy prisoners back to Fontenay (7 Pluviôse).[17] Most of the quarrels were of that interminable character, born of the jealousy most administrative bodies feel in regard to their functions.

Departments

With the departments, the committees had little contact. Before the passage of the law of 14 Frimaire they were, so to speak, free lances, subject only to the deputies on mission and the Committee of General Security. In certain places the departments tried more or less to subject the committees to their control, as at Mont-de-Marsan (Landes), or were given specific control by the deputy as in the Haute-Saône.[18] After Frimaire, the department was almost negligible, confined as it was to routine administration; and the district, now the all-important member of the revolutionary organization, had among its duties the surveillance of all administrative bodies, including the committees of surveillance.

National Agents

As official supervisor of the committees, it was the function of the national agent to check any abuses, any usurpations which might result from the activities of these organizations. Generally the agents were not slow in calling the committees to order, and from Nivôse on, the members seem to have confined themselves within the limits of their authority. From time to time, however, it was necessary for the agent to act,

[17] Arch. Vendée L 1176.
[18] Richard, *A. H. Révol.*, VII, 27–28; Maréchal, p. 276.

generally basing his authority on some article of the law of 14 Frimaire. When on 2 Messidor the committee of Fontenay issued a decree declaring that "spreaders of false news, even of victories," were suspect, it was informed by the national agent that it had violated Article 11 of Section II, which forbade any public authority or official to make proclamations or pass decrees extending, limiting, or contrary to the literal meaning of the law. The committee protested that it had done no such thing, but it arrested no one for spreading false news.[19] Toul's national agent quoted Article 8 of the same section, which gave to the committees and the municipalities the execution of revolutionary laws and of measures of general security, and suggested that the committee confine itself to those functions.[20]

Nevertheless, the committees were generally scrupulous about staying within the bounds of their jurisdiction. That statement may appear to be injudicious if not downright rash. The committees have been damned as the great unlawless, the petty despots of the Revolution whose acts were dictated by their own caprices. To this interpretation the history of the committee of Nantes has added the semblance of truth, and its high-handed illegality can be supplemented by many more examples. Yet the majority of committees were "within the law." If they tore people from their beds at three o'clock in the morning, there was a law of 5 September which permitted *visites domiciliaires* at night; if they squeezed money out of the wealthy, a law of 19 Brumaire permitted them to request "patriotic contributions" from the rich; if they arrested a citizen for expressing his belief that the Convention was going too far, the law of 17 September permitted the arrest of all those guilty of expressing opinions against the Revolution.

It must be understood that this is not intended as an apologia for the actions of the committees. To maintain that they conducted themselves in every circumstance according to a high sense of eternal justice, that all those arrested were enemies

[19] Arch. Vendée L 1186, 2, 13 Messidor.
[20] Denis, p. 108.

of mankind and deserved their punishment a hundred times over, would be absurd and preposterous. However, it should be borne in mind that the Convention and the Representatives gave to the committees laws which by their very nature led to abuses, laws which were vague in terminology and arbitrary in their action. The committees executed them and it was in executing these laws that abuses arose. The committees had no need of inventing means of harassing the enemies of the Revolution; they had only to confine themselves to the supply of decrees poured in upon them by a generous Convention. From a moral point of view, that is no excuse; but legally it is sovereign, and because of it the majority of the members were able to keep their heads on their shoulders after Thermidor.

The Execution of Revolutionary Laws

The committees have also been accused of interfering in affairs which rightly belonged to other administrations, in arrogating to themselves functions which were purely administrative. Yet there was no necessity for the committees' boring into the administration, insinuating themselves into affairs which were not the competence of police. The law of 14 Frimaire quite bluntly states that the application, the execution, of revolutionary law was to be shared by the committees and the municipality. The mass levy was a revolutionary law, the maximum was a revolutionary law, as was every law passed after 10 October 1793, when the government of France was declared revolutionary until peace was declared. If the committees attempted to enforce the maximum they were doing no more than their duty as defined by the organic law of France.

As a result of these new powers the committees were called upon to aid in the enforcement of the maximum on food and salaries and of economic regulations in general, of the laws on draft evasion and desertion and other matters affecting the conduct of the army. Their performance of these duties we shall enter into more fully in subsequent chapters.

These latter functions were common to the majority of the committees, but in certain communes the national agent of the municipality increased their duties according to the ability of the committees or the problems of the locality. The agent of St. Yreix (Haute-Vienne) for example asked the committee to enforce the law on the draining of swamps, the law ordering the burning of feudal titles, the law on the demolition of fortified châteaux, and the law ordering the confiscation of the property of fathers and mothers of émigrés (3 Pluviôse). (The committee's rejoinder, not unusual, was to ask him for copies of the laws in question.) On 19 Ventôse he asked that the committee watch over the forests of the vicinity and request denunciations against those guilty of any wanton destruction.[21] In the Isère the national agent of La Tour-du-Pin sent the committees of his district a questionnaire at the end of Pluviôse, asking the following questions, some of which were intended for the questionnaire the national agent himself had received from the Committee of Public Safety:

1. If the committee was established according to the laws of 21 March and 14 Frimaire.
2. If it is executing the laws of 12 August and 17 September against suspects.
3. If it is executing the law of 11 September providing that merchants shall keep their shops well supplied.
4. The law of 26 July against hoarders.
5. The law against speculating in assignats.
6. If all signs of royalty and feudalism have been removed.
7. If there are still houses bearing coats-of-arms in the commune.
8. If the law of 6 September on foreigners is being enforced.
9. If there is any commerce of the British Government in the commune.
10. If there are any citizens of the first draft in the commune.
11. If the cobbler is working according to the law of 18 Frimaire and if the tanner lack materials.
12. Does the committee supervise the requisition and supplying of arms and the furnishing of oats (for the army of the Alps).
13. If the committee watches for irregularities in the stations of the military convoys.

[21] Arch. Haute-Vienne, Register of deliberations.

14. If all soldiers without leave have been arrested.
15. Do any citizens correspond with non-juring priests or émigrés?
16. Are there any royalists or federalists in the commune?
17. Are there any false patriots who seek to deceive the people and obtain positions in the administration? [22]

Questionnaires of such type are not unusual and indicate more clearly than any other means the laws which the committees were expected to enforce.

The municipal government also referred to its committees matters which ordinarily were a part of the former's duties. At Dijon the section committees were asked to take a census of their jurisdiction and submit the resulting list of inhabitants to the commune.[23] At Grenoble the commune and the national agent assigned to the section committees tasks which were merely administrative. On 20 August the section committees had already been asked by the commune to receive the declarations of the income of married men with more than 10,000 *livres* income. On 10 Nivôse (the law of 14 Frimaire was already in effect) the commune asked the committees to name members to keep order at the markets and see that the maximum was observed; on 12 Nivôse the national agent requested a list of the deaf and dumb in the section; on 16 Floréal the substitute of the national agent ordered the committees to collect one pound of old linen from each citizen as ordered by the Committee of Public Safety on 18 Germinal; on 17 Germinal the municipality asked for a list of those who could make bayonets; on 25 Germinal the municipality wanted a list of persons having old barrels; later the committee of Section 7 was criticized for being delinquent in furnishing a list of the agents of the Executive Power or other authorities residing in its section, a list of youths between eight and eighteen to form the popular society's Company of Hope, a list of draft evaders, and a list of nobles and foreigners resident in the section. The committee replied that there were no agents of any authorities residing

[22] Arch. Isère L 897.
[23] Arch. Côte d'Or L IV a 47/a, 20 of 1st month.

in the section; that the list of the youths had been sent to the commandant; that there were no suspects or foreigners in the section; and added that there were only four pigs in the section.[24]

At Lyon the practice of using section committees also developed extensively. In addition to summoning workingmen to assist in the army workshops the committees were asked to list all masons and laborers for the work necessary in repairing the damaged city; to deposit all shoes either gifts or confiscated at the sacristy of Saint-Pierre; to remove from among the property confiscated all blankets, sheets, and mattresses to furnish the barracks of the revolutionary army just arrived from Paris.[25] On the same day the head of the administration of national property, in view of the fact that many of the debtors of the Republic (that is, tenants of property which the Republic had confiscated) were not paying their rent, asked the committee of the section of Equality to grant no permits to move unless a receipt were shown.[26]

The law of 14 Frimaire, therefore, by its ambiguity in assigning to the committees as well as the municipalities the duty of executing revolutionary laws, permitted the national agent of the district and the communal government to pass on to these erstwhile police organizations any routine tasks which they could handle easily. By making no clear distinction the convenience of the agent and the municipality was served and the Republic gained, probably at no cost, willing assistants to carry on the administrative burdens of the state.

"Purveyors to the Guillotine"

The bloody legend of the French Revolution included the members of the revolutionary committees as fiendish purveyors to the guillotine, cackling quietly to themselves as the blade descended upon the necks of their enemies. To enliven

---

[24] Arch. Isère L 868, 869.
[25] Arch. Rhône CL 261, Frimaire; CL 51, 5 Nivôse, 17 Nivôse.
[26] Arch. Rhône CL 151, 3 Pluviôse.

their argument their critics quoted such bits of grisly humor as this letter from the committee of Angers to the deputy Richard: "The committee asks you to send it the *sacram sanctam guillotinam* and the republican ministers who celebrate its offices. Not an hour of the day passes that doesn't see the arrival of initiates whom we wish to induct into its mysteries." [27] Fougères (Ille-et-Vilaine) asked for "a batch of these beggars to be disposed of inside our walls." [28] At Nantes, at Angers, and in Brittany generally, brigands and their priestly mentors were treated quite unceremoniously, and the various Military Commissions which traveled through the departments of Brittany and the West generally found the committees more than eager to "rid the soil of liberty" of the rebels, the more so since "all these monsters [were] eating up the food which must be spared for the children and the defenders of the Republic."

At Bordeaux the story is repeated. The successive committees made arrests at the request of the Military Commission in operation there, but after the law of 14 Frimaire they became sticklers and insisted upon four signatures on the orders issued by the commission instead of only two as had been the practice.[29] Reports on the counter-revolutionary activity of rebels were submitted by the committee to the department, then directly to the Commission itself after the passage of the law of 22 Prairial, since the court, according to that law, must have a "swifter pace." [30]

In the Bouches-du-Rhône the committees were engaged in the same task, examining the records of the sections, arresting *sectionnaires* and shipping them along to the Military Commission at Marseille and later to the Popular Commission sitting at Orange.[31] Lyon's committees were not too busy to

[27] "Correspondance," *Anjou Hist.*, XXVI, 39–40.

[28] T. Lemas, *Les Commissions militaires révolutionnaires dans l'Ille-et-Vilaine* (Paris, 1893), p. 85.

[29] Arch. Gironde L 2164, 6 Nivôse et passim; L 2165 passim.

[30] Arch. Gironde; *ibid.* and L 2175, 2 Messidor.

[31] Arch. Bouches-du-Rhône L 1712, 16, 17 Pluviôse, 7 Germinal et passim; L 1011, 1 Germinal, 22 Messidor; L 1060, 24 Pluviôse; Lourde, III, 362–365.

coöperate with the Military Commission set up there. Lebon's "infamous" tribunal at Arras not only found assistance from the committees but drew from their membership in constituting its jury. Some of the jurors, however, attempted to impede the rapid progress of the court and were jailed by Lebon for their pains. When the tribunal was transferred to Douai in Floréal, it relied upon the committee there for information on the accused.[32]

These were, of course, the troubled districts, where spirits ran high and — at least in the West — it was a case of eat or be eaten. Yet even in these districts, where the rebellion of the Vendée or the anti-Jacobin resistance had created obvious victims, there existed a few committees who refused to lend themselves to supplying the guillotine. The committee of Laval, acting on the advice of its colleagues at Rennes who declared that the committees' functions were limited to the surveillance of the administration and suspects, ignored the order of the Military Commission to prepare the cases against the detained (3 Floréal). They did, however, turn over to the national agent of the district whatever evidence they had in cases of conspiracy, desertion and other serious offenses, and it was he who forwarded them to the courts of the Military Commission.[33] In the Vendée is seen once more the usual hesitant position, for although the committees did indeed send brigands before the Military Commission sitting at Fontenay, it was not with the enthusiasm nor in such numbers as in the departments to the north.[34] At Caen, although two members were appointed to examine the deliberations of the sections and the departments and "make extracts from them if they believe it to the interest of the public welfare," no one was guillotined within the walls, and only two Caennais involved in the federalist revolt were put to death.[35]

[32] Arch. Nord L 10185; Paris, 187, 210, 218, 221–222 et passim.
[33] A. Galland, "Le Comité révolutionnaire du district de Laval," *B. Comm. Mayenne*, 2e série, XVII, 399–400.
[34] Arch. Vendée L 1186, L 1171, L 1248 passim.
[35] Arch. Calvados, Register of deliberations, 23 Nivôse; Guillonet, *A. Révol.*, I, 573.

In the quiet departments of France the committees had little business with the guillotine. Occasionally a few counter-revolutionaries would be sent before the criminal tribunal or to Paris to appear before Fouquier. Rarely did the committees follow the example of the municipal committee of Dijon, which sent several of its members to Paris in order to present a list of "candidates" to Fouquier.

Occasionally one of the great committees ordered the transfer to Paris of persons whose punishment was to forward the march of the Revolution. The Nantes committee was sent to Paris for trial; in Messidor the Committee of Public Safety ordered the transfer to Paris for trial of the recently dismissed municipality of Orléans. In all these cases, however, the committees were simply obeying the orders of their superiors, so that, save for those in the departments in which there was, or had been, armed opposition to the authority of the Convention, the committees had little part in bringing the guillotine to the departments, or in furnishing the machine on the Place de la Révolution at Paris with likely subjects.

Relations with Other Committees

Most important from the point of view of a comprehensive system of surveillance were the relations which existed between the committees themselves. Had the committees refused to honor the warrants issued by their colleagues in other towns, had they insisted upon sitting themselves in judgment in regard to every individual arrested within their territory, suspects could have escaped detention with ease.[36] There was no law requiring the committee of Dijon, for example, to arrest, simply on the orders of the committee of Besançon, a former citizen of Besançon who had fled to Dijon and against whom the committee of Dijon had no complaint. Yet in the thousands

[36] Even with the coöperation which did exist among the committees, many counter-revolutionaries found a refuge in the countryside in communes where no committee existed or where, if it existed, the larger landowners exercised a strangling control.

of similar cases which fill the files of the committees, instances of categorical refusal to serve the warrant in question are extremely rare.[37]

From the quantity of reports of failure to apprehend fugitives, it would seem that the percentage of captures was low. The impression is, of course, heightened by the fact that requests for arrest were dispatched to a number of obvious places, and the failure at one town is no indication of the results at another. If the suspect was apprehended, the complaining committee was notified, a warrant was forwarded to the arresting committee, and the suspect was conducted back to his commune "from brigade to brigade," unless he wished to pay the expenses of a coach.

In addition to these amicable relations of equals with equals, some committees, despite the law of 14 Frimaire, strove to continue their influence over their colleagues in the smaller communes of their department or district. Instructions or advice were occasionally circulated in the departments. It was, however, not usual, and aside from grumbling at the indulgence of their less aggressive colleagues, they generally limited themselves to a meaningless reproach.

The Popular Societies

Almost everywhere the committees maintained close contact with the popular societies, groups of patriots who shared to a large extent the opinions of the Paris Jacobins and who by Brumaire had become semi-official members of the state.[38]

---

[37] This statement, accurate as it is, should be tempered by the observation that it was possible for an interested committee to assert its inability to apprehend the suspect if it judged the charges unwarranted.

[38] The Committee of Public Safety on 23 Brumaire asked the popular societies to compile and send lists of citizens fitted for office. Mautouchet, *Le Gouvernement révolutionnaire*, p. 119. This semi-official character is also evidenced by the circular attached to the letter sent by the Jacobins of Paris to the municipal committee at Dijon which carried on a regular correspondence with the Paris society. In the circular, the club asked the committee to be so kind in the future as to send all their letters addressed to the club "under cover of the Convention, or of the ministers of war and of the marine to spare us. the great expense of postage." Arch. Côte d'Or L IV a 47i/1, 22 Frimaire.

The intimacy of their connection with the committees exhibited itself many times and in many ways. Frequently it was the popular society which named the committee and provided replacements after the resignation of officials in consequence of the law of 14 Frimaire. In that "interesting operation" the arrest of suspects the societies lent a willing hand, officially denouncing individuals with some such "Whereas" as this one of the club of Melun: "Whereas public opinion, both in this commune and in the popular society, has emphatically declared" that Citizen So-and-So is suspect and so on.[39]

Quite often the clubs had committees of surveillance themselves whose duty it was to receive denunciations and declarations and further the work of the official committee in every way possible. The popular society of Nîmes went even beyond this. Pelissier, one of its members, confessed later that "several patriots having realized that the committee of surveillance did not perform its duties as punctiliously as was to be expected," a special committee of twelve was named by the club. Having won the coöperation of the public accuser, the committee brought about the arrest of 152 persons within several hours.[40] The society of Pau was equally skeptical about the official committee and set up a group of its own to exercise surveillance over the committee of surveillance.[41]

Once in a long while a commune's committee and club would have a falling out. At Draguignan the moderates gained control of the club for a short period and voted a proposal to release all those under arrest in the house of detention. Another motion that the committee be dismissed was made at the same time, but the meeting was halted by the sudden arrival of the national guard. The decisions of the previous meeting were revoked the following day despite the moderates' efforts, and the committee was safe.[42] At Angers the reaction

[39] Campagnac, *A. Révol.*, II, 472–473.
[40] Rouvière, IV, 153 note 1.
[41] Richard, *Basses-Pyrénées*, p. 66.
[42] Patin, *B. Soc. Draguignan*, XVII, 81–84.

against the committee, which led to its suppression in Ventôse, started in the popular society with charges of "blood-drinking" levied against the committee. The Société populaire de l'Est was suppressed as a result.[43] At Hondschoote the committee expressed its disapproval of the local club more calmly. The members never attended its meetings.[44]

More often, however, the club and the committee presented a united front to the opposition. The committee of the Liberty section of Narbonne on 23 Pluviôse had dragged before it General Marbon who had declared that the club was three parts aristocrat. Taxed with his remarks, he went back on a few, but maintained steadfastly that the society discussed nothing but minutiae. When the committee triumphantly showed that the club sent agents to the markets each day to supervise sales, the general huffed off with the unanswerable declaration that nevertheless the maximum was not being observed.[45] The Loriol committee also tried to protect the fair name of the club by drawing up a set of regulations for the conduct of affairs because of the fact that the president of the society had come to one meeting so drunk he was unable to count the votes.[46]

It is hardly necessary to insist upon the position of the committees as important members of the revolutionary organization. Their relations extended both horizontally and vertically throughout the entire Republic. They themselves were organized into an interlocking network which made the escape from revolutionary justice difficult. Often they were called upon to supplement the regular governing bodies in the execution of laws which were more functions of administration than of police. The vigilant and suspicious surveillance which they

---

[43] F. Uzureau, "Le procès des terroristes angevins," *Anjou Hist.*, IV, 514.
[44] Lefebvre, *Les Paysans*, p. 838.
[45] Arch. Aude L 2221.
[46] A. Faucher, "Le Comité de surveillance révolutionnaire de Loriol," *Comité des travaux historiques et scientifiques, Section d'histoire moderne et contemporaine, Notices, Inventaires, et Documents*, VII, 130 note 3.

exercised over the public servants of the nation, coupled with their undoubted powers of repression and coercion, resulted in a bureaucracy wholly satisfactory to the Jacobin party. The law of 14 Frimaire had made them an integral part of the government.

CHAPTER XI

THE FOOD CRISIS

THE MAXIMUM

SUSPECTS and revolutionary committees have been so long linked together in the minds of historians that it has become almost impossible to conceive of the committees in any other relationship. We have seen that a large part of the committees' days was spent in routine work, visaing certificates of civism and passports, inspecting the mail, and in many instances assuming the responsibility for superintending houses of detention, functions which are of course related to their task of watching over suspects. The levying and administering of revolutionary taxes, the collection of "patriotic contributions," the search for hoarded treasure, are functions which commence to merge into pure administration. With their interest in enforcing the economic legislation of the Terror the committees are almost entirely divorced from the surveillance of suspects.

It is true that the law of 29 September 1793 (the maximum) declared that all persons who bought or sold above the fixed price were to be treated as suspects, and the committees duly arrested such persons. Yet an examination of the documents indicates that they were as much interested in provisioning their communes as in punishing offenders, perhaps even more. Such an attitude could have been anticipated, since a strictly enforced maximum would have a tendency to keep goods out of the usual markets and drive trade underground.

An incident in the small commune of Blevaincourt (Vosges) will illustrate this victory of interest over principles. The innkeeper was denounced for selling wine above the maximum; and when the committee sent to buy some, it found that the charge was true. The committee, however, did nothing but warn him, for he was the only innkeeper in town. Nevertheless, he had been anxious to close his inn and he took down his sign and wound up his affairs. The committee ended the incident with a lament on the difficulty of life under the maximum. "It is indeed unfortunate to be poor and a good patriot, for only those who have the price carry off the merchandise." [1]

The committees were not alone in this indulgence, for public opinion, save in the larger cities, was firmly set against turning over real goods for worthless assignats. Consequently there was much grumbling about the failure to enforce the law, but the committees' efforts, even where they were willing to exert themselves, were usually hampered by the refusal of the grumblers to make categorical denunciations.

The task set for the committees, therefore, was a discouraging one, and many of them were anxious to escape it. Sometimes even after receiving denunciations they took no action or referred the matter to another administration, but the ever-present national agent was always at hand to remind them of their unpopular duties. Consequently, to give evidence of their zeal they usually took half-hearted steps to apprehend violators.

In some localities certain members were named to police the markets to discover whether the pegged prices were being observed.[2] At Grenoble the over-burdened section committees were ordered to send several members to the markets of their sections.[3] At Lyon the member commissioned to supervise the markets was authorized to seize and sell the merchandise of any person caught violating the law.[4] Yet in the vast majority of communes the committees' only concern with the maximum resulted from denunciations, dumped in their lap as it were, and about which they had to do something. Simply put, the committees' concern with the maximum was superficially widespread, but hardly intensive.

The even more unpopular maximum on wages the committees

[1] Schwab, *Révol. Vosges*, 23e année, pp. 43–44.
[2] Arch. Calvados, Bayeux, Register of deliberations, 6 Floréal; Arch. Isère L 897, Pluviôse.
[3] Arch. Isère L 854, 13 Nivôse.
[4] Arch. Rhône CL 261, 26 Brumaire, 4 Frimaire; CL 153.

neglected almost entirely, perhaps because the majority of the members were workingmen themselves. The committee of Allauch (Bouches-du-Rhône) reported to the district that the workmen of the commune were not observing the law, which was probably not news to the district,[5] and several who demanded exorbitant wages were denounced to the justice of the peace by the committee of Châteauroux.[6] Aside from these feeble acts, and a few more like them, the records of some two hundred committees fail to reveal any interest in enforcing the maximum on salaries.

HOARDING

The committees, like the regular administration, had been unable or unwilling to enforce the maximum. Their complacency stopped there, however, for in the drive to break up hoarding, and in general to assure their fellow citizens a sufficient supply of the necessities of life, there seemed to be no end to which they would not go.

The sovereign remedy for hoarding was a house-to-house canvass of the community, verifying the declarations already made and removing any surplus merchandise. At Dijon the section committees were asked to make these *visites domiciliaires* at least once a month; elsewhere they were less regular, depending upon the fancy of the municipality or the committee. Even though the registers carry few notices of seizures, it still remains difficult to evaluate the efficacy of these searches. The fear of the committees and the penalties for hoarding must have served their purpose in many cases and prevented any undue accumulation of supplies. The mere fact that the committees were making searches was sanction enough. In other cases the hoarders, and there certainly were such persons, had undoubtedly exercised an ingenuity more artful than that of the committeemen, and their store went undiscovered.

In the matter of requisitions levied against the country com-

[5] Arch. Bouches-du-Rhône L 1011, 20 Prairial.
[6] Arch. Indre L 1538, 21 Floréal.

munes the city committees had little business, their jurisdiction being limited to their own commune. Before the law of 14 Frimaire, however, the committee of twenty-one of Grenoble, then a department committee, asked the municipality for a copy of the requisitions made to supply the city, evidently with the intention of discovering delinquents.[7] At Melun the committee arrested several peasants who had refused to satisfy requisitions ordered for the provisioning of Paris.[8] In Finistère members of the committees served on the "roving commissions" set up by the deputy Bréard to scour the countryside for 25,000 quintals of wheat, with little success, apparently, for on 5 Frimaire only 80 quintals were in the city granaries, and it was necessary to borrow 1500 from the Marine.[9] The general practice, however, was to employ the *gendarmerie* and revolutionary armies to enforce the requisitions, or, as in the Vosges, the national guard.[10]

In the smaller communes the committees seem to have participated in the hoarding conspiracy, for their registers are almost devoid of activity. At Aix-les-Bains, however, the committee acted a number of times to satisfy requisitions. Calling the recalcitrant citizen before it usually sufficed, and the requisition was met, though on one occasion it borrowed a *gendarme* to force the people of La Biolle to bring their hay in to Chambéry, since the "people are not diligent in executing the requisitions made of them." [11] Yet the committee itself was not above reproach, for one of the members was denounced for saying to a citizen who came to him with a requisition from the district, "You would get your wheat a lot easier, if you brought some hard money instead of your papers." He delivered, apparently, for no action was taken.[12] The commit-

[7] Arch. Isère L 870, 23 Brumaire.

[8] Campagnac, *A. Révol.*, II, 552.

[9] P. Levot, *Histoire de la ville et du port de Brest pendant la Terreur* (Paris, 1871), p. 167.

[10] F. Bouvier, *Les Vosges pendant la Révolution* (Paris, 1885), pp. 259–60.

[11] Vermale et Rochet, *M. Soc. Savoisienne*, XLV, 4e fascicule, 43–44, 46, 49–51.

[12] *Ibid.*, p. 38.

tees' usefulness in the fulfillment of requisitions was, all the same, quite limited; only in the Year III, when the competence of the committees extended over the entire district and when the threat of famine was even more serious, were the committees able to act more freely in matters of requisitions.

PROVISIONING THE COMMUNES

Visites domiciliaires with all their theoretical efficiency were, in the opinion of many committees, no solution at all. Some of them, not without a certain selfish interest, undertook more effective steps to solve a problem which seemed to have no solution.[13] The measures adopted were almost as numerous as the committees which executed them. An obvious solution was simply to place the responsibility on the shoulders of the merchants, as at Nîmes where the local committee of public safety announced that all merchants who closed their shops or failed to keep them well supplied were suspects.[14] Ysabeau and Tallien at Bordeaux ordered the committee to arrest all merchants suspected of declaring bankruptcy as a means of escaping their responsibilities, and if they were guilty, to send them before the Military Commission.

In agricultural districts the same policy of force was used to hasten the threshing and storing of grain to prevent its destruction by inclement weather or enemies of the people.[15] The committee of Amplepuis was forced to take steps when it met with the sullen opposition of the farmers. It published an order a second time on 18 Nivôse, a third time on 25 Nivôse, and

---

[13] In certain centers, special food commissions relieved the committees of these responsibilities. Such organizations existed, among other places, in the Oise, at Bordeaux, in the Pyrénées Orientales, and at Beaulieu (Corrèze). At the latter city, the committee was skeptical of the commission's abilities and by its complaints obtained the creation of a new commission which included two members of the committee. E. Cantouny, "Le Comité de surveillance de Beaulieu," *Bulletin de la société de lettres, sciences et arts de la Corrèze (Tulle)*, XLIV, 9–10.

[14] Rouvière, IV, 21.

[15] For example at La Tour-du-Pin, Arch. Isère L 888, 11 Nivôse; at Raucon, Arch. Haute-Vienne L 862, 17 Nivôse; at Custine, Arch. Meurthe-et-Moselle L 3183.

being skeptical, sent four of its members to verify the declarations that the law had been complied with. On 29 Ventôse it was forced to hire laborers to thresh the wheat of the delinquents.[16]

Other committees tried to break up the farmers' practice of sowing only enough grain for their own use. The Grasse (Alpes-Maritimes) committee notified the municipality of two fields which were uncultivated, and two proprietors were forced to sow despite their objections.[17] The committee of Amaye-sur-Seulles (Calvados) had fears of a similar situation in its commune and invited all citizens to appear at the city hall within forty-eight hours to receive their share of the grain for sowing.[18] Carouge (Mont-Blanc) went farther and forbade the exportation from France of all foodstuffs, even though the product of soil in France owned by foreigners.[19] Such measures were effective enough but had the inconvenience of being illegal. At Dourdan (Seine-et-Oise) where many Parisians were buying their supplies the committee issued an order forbidding all persons to send foodstuffs out of the commune on pain of being declared suspect. On the report made in regard to this decree Robespierre wrote: "Write to the committee and enlighten it in regard to the inconveniences of this measure and tell it to revoke its orders." Paris shall not starve, even though Dourdan does.[20]

The committee of Orléans concerned itself with the shipments of food which came and went through the city. On 1 Germinal a letter from the committee of Beaune led it to investigate the shipment of a large quantity of sugar to the latter city. On 2 Germinal it arrested the two persons responsible and discovered that they had purchased the sugar at 30 *sous* a pound (the maximum price at Orléans) and sold it at

[16] Arch. Rhône CV 10, fo. 29.

[17] Combet, *Révol. Fr.*, LVII, 339.

[18] Arch. Calvados, Register of deliberations, 28 Ventôse.

[19] F. Dullin, "Conflit entre les membres de la garde nationale et le comité révolutionnaire," *B. Acad. Delphinale*, 4e série, IV (1900), 198.

[20] Ernest Hamel, *Histoire de Robespierre* (Paris, 1865–67), III, 604.

3 *livres* 5 *sous* (65 *sous*) plus 2 per cent commission![21] The same committee on 14 Germinal wrote to the committee of Artenay for the names of the persons at Orléans who had shipped some prohibited merchandise discovered by the committee of Artenay. A few days later it ordered all the agents of the food commission of Montluçon to present their bills of lading to the committee so that it could discover whether any unauthorized purchases had been made.[22]

Food-rationing was resorted to in other cities. At Troyes it was the section committees' function to distribute the cards issued against the *greniers d'abondance*.[23] At Landerneau (Finistère) a scandal resulted from the committee's distribution of cards for the scarcer commodities. Some certificates were forged, others were signed and passed out in blank, to be filled in later in such a way that preference was given to the bearer in the distribution of food.[24]

The committee of Compiègne on 24 Ventôse issued strict regulations on the sale of meat and suggested that the wealthy be economical in their purchases or be declared suspect.[25] The members at Beaune went so far as to request the district to forbid the peasants to hold their customary festivals at the time harvesters were hired, since they used up their eggs, cream and butter in making cakes instead of bringing it into market at Beaune.[26]

A few committees directed their attention to the "means of production." The committee of the Gourguillon section at Lyon, for example, confiscated the oven and accessories of a baker who refused to make bread for the public, and turned them over to one of his rivals.[27] In the neighboring town of Amplepuis the committee ordered that all save two mills be

[21] Arch. Loiret L 1179.
[22] *Ibid.*, 19 Germinal.
[23] Babeau, II, 97.
[24] Duchatellier, *Brest*, pp. 39, 41, 44.
[25] Baumont, *B. Soc. Oise*, VI, 84.
[26] Barbuat, *M. Soc. Beaune*, 1911, pp. 189, 309–310.
[27] Arch. Rhône CL 203, 27 Frimaire.

dismantled, for "one says" that white bread is still being made, and the committee can only supervise the grinding of the "flour of equality" at two mills.[28]

The mills at Les Sables (Vendée) were the center of a dispute which raged for months. Regulus Plantier, inspector of the army food supplies, had been monopolizing all the mills of the city for grinding flour for the army. On 6 October he was arrested and questioned by the committee in the presence of the representative Fayau, but no decision was reached.[29] The matter was up again on 22 Brumaire, for Plantier was now using all the mills at Les Moutiers and Saint-Gilles, as well as those at Les Sables. After the customary "mature deliberation" the committee decreed that Regulus Plantier should answer with his head for the public tranquility (there were angry mobs outside the bakers at Les Sables); he was forbidden to use the mills reserved for the use of the city; he was ordered to see that the army was provisioned without recourse to purchases from the bakers of Les Sables, thus depriving the people of their food. Should he fail in this respect, he was to be turned over to the courts; meanwhile he was declared suspect and was to be denounced to the Committee of General Security.[30]

Plantier was not a whit disturbed, and ten days later he collected a large supply of bread from the bakeshops of the city. In a rage the committee wrote to the municipality "forbidding it to allow the bakers of the city to give flour and bread, intended to feed the people, to the person in charge of the army rations" (2 Frimaire). Not content with this, it ordered on the following day that four millers were to grind for all bakers without distinction or be prosecuted *révolution-nairement*, since they would be guilty of an attempt on the welfare of the public. To make certain that its orders were executed it placed the millers under arrest at their mills for

[28] Arch. Rhône CV 10, 11 Ventôse.
[29] Chassin, *Vendée patriote*, IV, 19.
[30] Arch. Vendée L 1215.

two weeks, with two guards to see that all bakers could enter freely and that all of Plantier's men were excluded. At the end of this period the millers were to be tried and fined for disobeying the previous instructions of the committee.[31]

The affair seemed settled until 12 Nivôse, when the committee discovered that Plantier was off to Paris, and rather than have itself maligned it sent all the documents of the affair to the two great committees. A pamphlet attacking one of the members, who was a *curé* and president of the district, was Plantier's reply, and he seemed to have the last word, for on 3 Floréal the committee was reorganized by Hentz and Francastel, and the offending member, charged with dishonesty in connection with national lands, was removed from his post.[32]

Not many committees had the courage of that of Les Sables. Indeed, the neighboring committee at Fontenay exerted itself to draw up a report on the food supply of the city and then wrote the municipality counseling "grand measures." So the municipality wrote to the district, and no more was heard of the matter.[33] The committee of Loriol was almost as muddle-headed. It asked the popular society to devote a meeting to the discussion of the problem of the food shortage. The municipality tried to get the workers into the fields by forbidding the playing of billiards and bowls, thus rescuing the workers from idleness. It likewise put a ban on the sale of wine at inns save to travelers. Nevertheless the committee had to report failure to the Committee of General Security, remarking in a bewildered way: "Instruction, advice, open discussion of the subject at the popular society, a proclamation by the municipality, nothing has been forgotten." [34]

Despite these few dullards and some more like them, a respectable number of committees had the initiative and the

---

[31] Arch. Vendée L 1215, 2, 3 Frimaire.
[32] Chassin, *Vendée patriote*, IV, 173, 469.
[33] Arch. Vendée L 1186, 28 Pluviôse.
[34] Faucher, "Le Comité . . . de Loriol," pp. 141–142.

ingenuity to take steps to mitigate the severity of the threatened famine. In these efforts to shore up the creaky economic system of France they went beyond their character of mere police and became administrators; from repression they passed to coercion; they stirred themselves from their passivity and took positive steps to bring about the provisioning of their commune. Some, who themselves had not sufficient energy to remedy the evils, protested constantly to the municipality or to the national agent, putting a very real pressure on them to enact measures which would alleviate the plight of their fellow citizens.

To what extent the committees were the responsible agents in assuring the food supply of France it is impossible to determine. They did make a serious effort, and although the unkind may declare that the acts of the committees were the acts of interested persons, for the members were faced with starvation as well, they had the will to force matters through to a conclusion, which entitles them to a bit of indulgence when the final judgment is made.

CHAPTER XII

WAR

Draft Evaders

Roused by Barère to one of its defiant moods by the repeated failures of the Republican armies during the spring and summer of 1793, the Convention on 23 August decreed the *levée en masse*. Barère, the champion of the new law, painted a stirring picture of France as a great camp where every citizen without discrimination would be engaged in the tasks of war. The deputies were captivated, but to the young men between eighteen and twenty-five who were called upon to defend the nation with their lives, the prospect was not so inspiring. As a result, in certain localities the opposition to the new levy, though not so serious as that of five months before, led once more to armed resistance.[1] Generally opposition was an individual enterprise, a flight into the woods, or hiding away in barns by day and foraging for food by night.

The Convention answered, as was its custom, with severe laws. On 2 Frimaire it declared that those members of the first levy who had abandoned their homes to escape service were declared émigrés, unless they surrendered themselves within ten days after the publication of the law.[2] As usual, it was the committees who were called upon to enforce the

---

[1] Mathiez, *Révolution française*, III, 44.

[2] *Arch. parl.*, LXXIX, 650. Their parents, as parents of émigrés, were therefore suspects, but despite this technicality — or perhaps because it was a technicality — the committees rarely deprived them of their liberty. The Laval and Châtelard (Savoie) committees made a few such arrests of parents, and at Beaune and Roquebrussanne (Var) the possibility of such an arrest was used as a threat. Elsewhere the law seems to have been ignored. Galland, "Le Comité révolutionnaire du district de Laval," *B. Com. Mayenne*, 2e série, XVII, 398; Vermale, *M. Soc. Savoisienne*, XLV, 4e fascicule, 250; Barbuat, *M. Soc. Beaune*, 1911, p. 223; E. Poupé, "Le Comité de surveillance de la Roquebrussanne," *B. Com. Hist.*, 1907, p. 298.

law, and with few exceptions, they were on the alert for any draft dodgers who might be hiding in their communes. In their pursuit of evaders, the committees, of course, followed no uniform method. Some displayed the same apathy as that of Fontenay and merely drew up a public notice, ordering those drafted to join their battalions.[3]

The committee at Châlons-sur-Marne was a bit more energetic and wrote to the local saltpeter works for a list of their employees of the statutory age to discover whether they had permission to absent themselves from the army, and the Orléans committee wrote for the same purpose to the local foundry.[4] The Beaune committee compiled a list of those subject to call by examining parish registers, and in Germinal it wrote to all the communes of its district trying to frighten them into making their conscripts depart.[5] No doubt it was sheer bluff, as was Toul's circular to the national agents of its district: "If we later discover," the committee wrote, "that even after we have warned you, someone in your commune has evaded the levy, we shall not fail to denounce you and have you punished."[6]

The Châtelard committee also entertained doubts about the good intentions of the local officials and on 12 Messidor organized a raid to clear the countryside of draft evaders, or failing them, of their parents. The details of the expedition were carefully worked out, down to the bottle of wine the various communes were to supply to each member of the searching party. The raid netted 145 fathers and mothers who were politely given time to supply themselves with four days' provisions, but only four young men were taken into custody.

---

[3] Arch. Vendée L 1186, 6 Germinal. Once more an example of Fontenay's fear of compromising itself. Later (14 Messidor) it refused the request of the local commandant to assemble all men between eighteen and twenty-five years on the town square, giving as the reason that it was the municipality's business. *Ibid.*

[4] Arch. Marne, Register of deliberations, 2 Floréal; Arch. Loiret L 1179, 12 Germinal.

[5] Barbuat, *M. Soc. Beaune*, 1911, pp. 295, 301.

[6] Denis, p. 105.

Legally the property of all these prisoners should have been
seized, but just as in the case of other confiscatory legislation
of the Terror, the law was not enforced.[7]

THE COMMITTEES AS MILITARY POLICE

The mass of army business referred to the committees can
undoubtedly be explained by the lack of a completely organized military administration. By the winter of the Year II
there were — at least on paper — almost a million men under
arms, and as Robespierre had observed in August, "What are
you going to do with all that mob?"[8] The mere problem of
clothing, arming, and feeding it was overwhelming, but added
to these difficulties was the question of desertion, leaves and
hospitalization.

Having coöperated in getting the young men into the army,
the committees had also to see that the recruits stayed there.
Consequently, chasing deserters became another one of their
duties; nor was it confined to the frontiers, for the committee
of the Center section of Dijon and the committee of Châteauroux arrested deserters.[9] Châteauroux, indeed, allowed its enthusiasm to run away with it in enforcing the law of 22
Frimaire, which ordered the arrest of all persons who did not
return immediately to their battalions. The exemptions naturally to be granted to those on leave, and those invalided out
of service, had been so obvious that they had been omitted
from the law, with the result that within three successive days
the committee arrested thirty-one "deserters." At the end of
the third day it commenced to have doubts, and sent two members to consult the deputy on mission in the department.[10]

---

[7] Vermale, *M. Soc. Savoisienne*, XLV, 4e fascicule, 224, 250, 258–260. On
17 Frimaire the Convention decreed that the property of all minor émigrés and
their parents should be confiscated as well as that of the parents of émigrés
of legal age, unless the former could prove they had made every effort to prevent the emigration. In law the draft evaders were émigrés, as we have already
mentioned.

[8] Mathiez, *La Révolution française*, III, 54.

[9] Arch. Côte d'Or L IV a 47/a, 19 Prairial; Arch. Indre L 1538, 21 Floréal.

[10] Arch. Indre L 1538, 2–4 Floréal; L 368.

Throughout France the committees were also entrusted with the problem of determining whether the health of a soldier on sick leave permitted him to return to action. They relied of course upon the testimony of a doctor, although the committee of Aix-les-Bains sent three men already supplied with doctor's certificates to the military hospital for confirmation. There, two of the three were ordered back to the frontiers.[11]

During the winter the committees usually came upon soldiers on leave merely by accident, since there was no system of registration by which they could know what soldiers were officially present in their commune. By spring, however, the Bureau of Leaves at Paris communicated to the committees directly the names of those on sick leave, the extent of their furlough, and other information necessary for the business of controlling the movements of the soldiers.[12]

WAR SUPPLIES

The shortcomings of the military administration also forced the committees to interfere in the urgent problem of army supply. Fraud on the part of the army contractors was occasionally brought to the attention of the committees and aroused in the members the proper amount of alarm and indignation. The Châteauroux committee was informed by the district that defective uniforms had been furnished it, and the committee was asked to investigate. The experts summoned by the committee testified that the district had indeed been defrauded, so the public accuser was instructed to prosecute the contractors, and the district was denounced to the Committee of Public Safety.[13] The Châteauroux committee was also called upon

---

[11] In centers where permanent military hospitals were established, committees were appointed especially to supervise these institutions. Several members of the local committee of surveillance were included and shared with two members of the municipality and the commandant the responsibility for the good order, economy and general efficiency of the hospital (Law of 3 Ventôse). All over France committeemen participated in this surveillance.

[12] Arch. Nord L 10186 (2 and 3); Arch. Meurthe-et-Moselle L 3289, Thermidor, passim.

[13] Arch. Indre L 1538, 19, 29 Nivôse, 2 Pluviôse.

to denounce the district of Argenton, since the latter's detach-
ment of soldiers complained loudly about their shoes when
they passed through Châteauroux. Since the two cities are
some eighteen miles apart, it is not unlikely that the fault was
with their feet and not the shoes.[14]

Scandals were not as frequently unearthed in other centers,
but at Orléans, Melun, Loriol, Narbonne, Nancy, and Caen
the committees from time to time appointed members to examine material supplied by the contractors, either on their own
initiative or at the request of the administration. Several of
the committees discovered that soldiers were sending home
either property they had received as part of their equipment,
or sometimes simply booty. Nancy found several cases of this
kind, and the Beaune committee recognized the abuse to be
so widespread that two members were assigned to meet the
diligence simply to ferret out what they could. At various times
they discovered shoes, socks, shirts, corkscrews, a box of
sugar and a box of gunpowder. This praiseworthy filial spirit
may explain in part the "ragged" soldiers of the Republic.[15]

In the actual production and supply of war materials the
committees also participated. The Committee of Public Safety
on 26 Floréal instructed all committees to supply the local
saltpeter factory with the necessary casks, and there was
hardly a committee which did not conform to these orders,
either requisitioning the casks or purchasing them outright.[16]

In a few communes the committees' official interest in saltpeter commenced earlier than Floréal. According to the decree

---

[14] Arch. Indre L 1538, 6 Pluviôse.
[15] Godchot, *Révol. Fr.*, LXXX, 258; Barbuat, *M. Soc. Beaune*, 1911, p. 295
et seq.
[16] Arch. Meurthe-et-Moselle L 3156; Arch. Gironde L 2232. Since France
had no natural deposits of saltpeter, used in the manufacture of gunpowder, it
was necessary to exhaust every possible source, no matter how small. Workmen removed the soil in cellars, in barnyards, and other places where decaying
animal matter had left deposits, and transferred it to the refineries, where the
saltpeter was dissolved with water, and then extracted by wood-ashes or
potassium carbonate. It was for this reason that the committee of Pithiviers
denounced many residents of Thignonville for refusing to hand over their
wood-ashes. Arch. Loiret L 1186, 11 Brumaire III.

of the Committee of Public Safety (29 Frimaire) the refineries were to be set up by the municipalities of the Republic. The committee of Loriol, however, assisted the popular society in establishing the plant in that commune. At Grenoble and Lyon, both of them communes where the many section committees were repeatedly called upon to assume part of the municipality's burdens, the administration requested inventories of copper boilers and other useful tools at bakers and brewers, and a list of persons capable of assisting at the refinery.[17]

Supervision of cobblers in requisition to make shoes was included among the duties of many committees, for it was not unusual that the workmen fell behind for some reason which they presented as being plausible. The committee of Saint-Ouen (Vosges) and that of Equality section at Lyon took the simplest course and threatened to imprison those behind in their allotment.[18] A more sensible procedure was followed by the committee at Saint-Junien (Haute-Vienne). Cobblers and those who made cartridge boxes were to decide among themselves which part of the hide was best for their work, so that there could be no excuse of not having proper material. The tanners were therefore put in requisition to supply these portions of the hides to the workmen. Meanwhile the superintendent of the military warehouse was ordered to forward to the committee a list of the shoes and cartridge boxes supplied him by each of the workmen, and to report at intervals to keep the list up to date. Until a workman had fulfilled his requisition, he was forbidden to work for a private customer.[19]

Other odd jobs often came the way of the committees. The overworked Lyon committees were to list all hatters and all leather-workers of their sections and to tell all women who wanted to sew tents for the army to report at the Cordeliers.[20]

---

[17] Faucher, "Le comité . . . de Loriol," pp. 143–144; Arch. Grenoble LL 19, 16 Nivôse; Arch. Rhône CL 250 (1).

[18] Schwab, *Révol. Vosges*, 24e année, p. 21; Arch. Rhône CL 153, 15 Nivôse.

[19] Arch. Haute-Vienne L 872, 27 Messidor.

[20] Arch. Rhône CL 261, 24 Pluviôse; CL 261, 2 Pluviôse.

At Lisieux the committee of the Fraternity section asked the other committees of the commune to inventory all weapons on sale and to forbid the armorers to sell any without the permission of the committee, since arms were in requisition.[21] Dijon's Center committee was asked to arrest Citizen Jaset, who had refused to work on requisition for the local arms factory, who had declared, in fact, that "il se torchoit le derrière du requisition. . . ."[22] In the district of Narbonne the committees were told to make household inspections, to gather all superfluous pots, cans, bowls, coats, and overcoats.[23]

Certain committees also turned their attention to the transportation facilities of the army. They were especially concerned with conditions at the halting-places set up along the main routes where the carters were to feed their animals and obtain material for any necessary repairs. The director of *étapes* and convoys was arrested by the Caen committee on 8 Nivôse for irregularities, and at Loriol the committee denounced to the district the contractor of the *étape* for supplying bad fodder and generally neglecting the horses and mules which came through. The contractor perhaps had a friend in the district administration, for nothing more was heard of the affair.[24]

The committees made other efforts to increase the efficiency of the supply system. Châteauroux sent a member to investigate the complaint that carters were only bringing half a load of coal to the forges, which "compromised the Republic and its opportunity for military success."[25] At La Cadière (Var) the committee was urged by the representative to keep an eye on those repairing the roads over which the supplies moved forward to the Army of Italy.[26] Narbonne's committee sent three members to the fodder depot to see that boats were

[21] Arch. Calvados, Register of deliberations, 5th of 2nd month.
[22] Arch. Côte d'Or L IV a 47/a, 1 Messidor.
[23] Arch. Aude L 2222, 29 Brumaire.
[24] Arch. Calvados, Register of deliberations, 8 Nivôse; Faucher, "Le comité . . . de Loriol," pp. 135–136.
[25] Arch. Indre L 1538, 7 Prairial.
[26] "Le comité de Surveillance de La Cadière," *B. Soc. Draguignan*, XXVIII, lvii.

loaded and unloaded quickly and that the carts departed promptly for Perpignan.[27] The neighboring city of Carcassonne later suggested that foreign deserters be put to work in the saltpeter plant and in the army stables, assisting in hostling and in trussing up fodder.[28] The committee of Les Sables also felt that prisoners should earn their keep. On 2 Frimaire it ordered each ironfounder of the commune to make a chain so that the brigands could be set to work cleaning the streets and squares, and performing any other labor useful to the Republic.[29]

Not content merely with intruding in the service of supply, a few committees carried their activity as far as the technical side of military operations. The committee of Toul was perhaps most energetic of all. On 12 Brumaire it commenced raising and arming the levy of Toul, sending agents to beg clothes from the citizens and laying plans for the morrow. It adjourned at 2 A.M. on 13 Brumaire, but at 7 A.M. it was at work again. The members ordered all merchants to bring to the committee whatever equipment they had and then sent a *gendarme* and a drummer to proclaim through the streets of the city that all young men between eighteen and twenty-five years were to present themselves to the committee. That evening they met at 7 o'clock and instructed the recruits to appear the following day. The next morning the 300 recruits were again assembled and given their arms and equipment, including a pair of shoes each, and a 50 *livre* bonus. After a review they were packed off to Lunéville to the sound of martial music and much cheering.

The committee's work was not done, however. It had borrowed 12,000 *livres* to pay a part of the bonus, and to distribute among the wives and parents of the soldiers. To obtain the remainder of the bonus and to be able to continue the financial aid to the soldiers' dependents, the committee levied a revolutionary tax on the detained and "suggested" that the

[27] Arch. Aude L 2223, 11 Ventôse.
[28] *Ibid.*, L 2125, 5 Thermidor.
[29] Arch. Vendée, L 1215.

wealthy citizens contribute in proportion to their fortune. By 10 Frimaire it had collected 50,000 *livres,* all of which was used for pensions or the fabrication of equipment.[30]

The committee at Les Sables on 9 October called on the commandant of the division of Sables and an architect to deliberate "upon the fortifications to be completed to assure the city against the attacks of the brigands." The conference decided upon certain improvements at vital points in the defenses, and the soldiers were ordered to proceed with the work. On 12 Brumaire an examination of the repairs by several committeemen revealed that there had been great negligence at certain points, and the committee suggested that the staff of the artillery batteries be purged. On the 16th the purge was held, and the three superior officers were indicated to the commandant as unworthy of serving the Republic.[31]

The department committee at Limoges also took it upon itself to conduct a purge, since the staff of the Fifth battalion of the Haute-Vienne had "bad principles." The representatives Brival and Lanot gave their approval and the companies were instructed to elect new officers. According to the committee, only one company made a bad choice, and it was being undermined by aristocrats. The committee arrested the officers in question "and alarms ceased." [32]

As was the case with the crisis in food, the many problems arising from the war demanded that the committees once more abandon their simple role of surveillance of suspects. If the pursuit of draft evaders and of deserters was merely police work, the inspection of military supplies, of the convoy stations, and of military hospitals, and coöperation in the establishment of saltpeter refineries carried them into the realm of administrative action. Nor was it mere malicious meddling in the affairs of others; frequently it entailed additional labor,

---

[30] Denis, pp. 28–38.
[31] Chassin, *Vendée patriote,* IV, 108; Arch. Vendée L 1215.
[32] Arch. Haute-Vienne L 836, 18 September.

additional hours freely given to the Republic, all directed toward that desideratum of every government, "getting things done."

Here again it is impossible to assign them precisely their due in the achievements of the Revolution. It is incontestable, however, that they not only prodded the regular administration at the proper intervals, but that they themselves assumed responsibilities and toiled unselfishly to increase the efficiency and quicken the pace of the military administration.

CHAPTER XIII

THE LAWS OF VENTÔSE

THE INDULGENTS

THE compact concluded between Robespierre and the Dantonists in Frimaire led to a reaction against the violent Hebertism of the fall. Though Hébert and his crew went to the guillotine only in Ventôse, their influence and their policies were decisively checked; in the departments the law on revolutionary government made it difficult for the representatives or the committees to continue their radical activities; at Paris, a concerted political campaign muzzled the Hebertists.

The alliance of the two leaders was perhaps too successful, for their efforts to recall the nation from the extremes of radicalism had the usual result; in pendulum fashion, the political temper swung over to indulgence, and Robespierre was faced with a new deviation from the party line.

The speeches of Danton and the writings of Desmoulins in the *Vieux Cordelier* gave the keynote of the campaign, and the reaction of the populace soon revealed itself. On 22 Frimaire a crowd of women stormed the Convention and asked for the release of their husbands, guilty of no crime, but still held as suspects in houses of detention. The following *décadi* (30 Frimaire) the women were out in force again, clamoring for the report on suspects that had been promised them by the Convention. The press of work was the explanation offered by the Committee of General Security for its delay, and Robespierre, to quiet the petitioners, proposed a special commission, composed of members of the two committees of government, to examine the cases of those detained.[1]

Before the commission could be organized, Desmoulins's

---

[1] *Arch. parl.*, LXXXI, 384; LXXXII, 35 et seq.

famous "Number 3" appeared. His attacks against the Hebertists continued, but at the same time, Camille lashed out against the Terror and its agents. "Today in France, the only people who do not make laws are the 1,200,000 soldiers in the armies, for the agents of the Convention make laws, the departments, the districts, the municipalities, the sections, the revolutionary committees make laws, and God spare me, I believe the fraternal societies make them too." He ridiculed the system of suspects by drawing upon the history of the decadent Roman Empire:

If a citizen was popular, he was the rival of the prince. . . . Suspect.

If, on the contrary, you shunned popularity and stayed at your own fireside, this retired life made you noticed, gave you a certain reputation. . . . Suspect.

If you were rich, there was imminent danger that you would corrupt the people by your largesse. . . . Suspect.

If you were poor, well then, invincible emperor, you had best keep an eye on this man. No one is more enterprising than the man who has nothing. . . . Suspect.[2]

Robespierre attempted to reply and on 5 Nivôse made his speech on revolutionary government, ridiculing the idea that the safeguards of peace should be preserved in time of war. The attack on the Indulgents had begun, and on the following day, when Barère made his report on the committees of clemency, decreed on Robespierre's motion of 30 Frimaire, he minimized the injustices of the committees. He resorted to the usual explanation, that in crises, crisis government was necessary. He showed that the suspects were as truly enemies of the Republic as though legal proofs had established their guilt, and aping Desmoulins declared "nobles, suspect; priests, suspect; bankers, foreigners, stockbrokers, citizens disguising their circumstances, suspect; men complaining of everything a revolution accomplishes, suspect; men downcast by our successes at Maubeuge, Dunkirk and in the Vendée, suspect."

[2] *Le Vieux Cordelier* (1825 edition), pp. 49–51.

He then delivered a rather eloquent apology for the committees: "We do not wish to decree the infallibility of the committees of surveillance. They are composed of men, of men
exalted in their love for liberty, of men surrounded by the
passions of others, even though they have none of their own.
Their errors must be corrected, their abuses mended, their
crimes punished; but their necessary powers should not be
weakened. . . . The manufacture of arms is not prohibited
because assassins use rifles, nor is the printshop proscribed
because slanderers use it every day." Barère's defense was
too eloquent, for instead of approving his proposed commission
(damned by Billaud-Varenne as a "committee for aristocracy"),
the Convention repealed the decree of 30 Frimaire which had
set it up.[3]

The result of the campaign of the Indulgents is known. Danton and his followers were guillotined on the Place de la Révolution on 16 Germinal, and the powers of the Committee of
Public Safety were increased. But before this victory could
be gained, the Convention had to appease the *sans-culottes*,
the women who had invaded the Convention, the citizens who
had spoken bitterly of the repeal of Robespierre's law of 30
Frimaire.[4] To calm them, to give them pledges, the laws of
Ventôse were passed.

It was a return to the tactics of June and July 1793 when
the Montagnards, hoping to break up the potential support
of the Gironde, had offered substantial reparation to the peasants and the middle classes. At that time, to win over the
peasants, émigré lands were to be sold in small parcels, the
communal lands distributed, and the remainder of the feudal
dues abolished; for the middle classes, the salaries of public
officials were raised, and married men with less than 10,000
livres income and bachelors with less than 6,000 were exempted from the forced loan.[5] Now it was the turn of the

---

[3] *Arch. parl.*, LXXXII, 365–369.
[4] P. Caron, *Paris pendant la Terreur* (Paris, 1910–14), II, 33–34, 42, 47–48,
49.
[5] Mathiez, *Révolution française*, III, 9–10.

sans-culottes to profit, and the systematic expropriation of the suspects was to be the means. Barère admitted as much when on 22 Floréal he reported on the progress made in executing the laws. "The decrees of the month of Ventôse," he announced, "were intended to make the revolution profitable for those who support it (*ont voulu faire tourner la révolution au profit de ceux qui la soutiennent*) at the price of ruining those who oppose it, and to relieve the unfortunate with the property of the Republic's enemies." [6] By such measures the loyalty of the city workingmen, of the needy patriots, was to be opposed to the indulgence of the Dantonists, which, from the Mountain's point of view, was only a cloak for the greed and selfishness of the middle classes.

"Wealth is in the hands of a large number of the Revolution's enemies," Saint-Just trumpeted on 8 Ventôse: "Poverty makes the working people dependent upon their enemies. . . . The property of patriots is inviolable, but the possessions of conspirators are there for the unfortunate. The unfortunate are the powers of the earth. They have the right to speak as masters to the governments which neglect them." [7] The inference was unmistakable — the government shall give them wealth, and their stomachs shall be full and their mouths closed.

Saint-Just had defended the system of detention in the same speech — indeed, the ostensible occasion for the report was the Convention's request of 4 Ventôse on a method of setting free the innocent, imprisoned by men in "new *bonnets rouges*" who "had forced their way into the committees. . . ." [8] "Detentions are inseparable from the progress of reason and justice" was his opinion, "for upon detentions depends the defeat or triumph of our enemies." And later, "You wanted a republic; if at the same time you refuse the measures which can establish it, it will bury the people in its ruins. Only by the total destruction of all those things which oppose it can a

---

[6] *Moniteur*, réimp., XX, 446.
[7] *Moniteur*, réimp., XIX, 568.   [8] *Moniteur*, réimp., XIX, 548.

republic be firmly established." More pointedly, he attacked the Indulgents, Desmoulins and Lacroix especially, and hurled out this prophetic warning: "The *grands coupables* wish to tear down the scaffold, for they fear to mount it themselves." [9]

At length he concluded with this twofold decree:

The Committee of General Security is invested with the power to set at liberty patriots who have been detained. Any person who petitions for his liberty shall give an account of his conduct since 1 May 1793.

Article 2. The property of patriots shall be inviolable and sacred. The goods of persons recognized as enemies of the Revolution shall be confiscated for the benefit of the Republic; they will be detained until peace is declared, and then be banished forever.

The first article indicates clearly that the Committee was not expecting to make any great delivery of prisoners. The burden of petitioning was to be left to the detained, the Committee itself assuming no responsibilities in the matter.

Danton, distrustful of a decree so ineffective, suggested that the committees of surveillance of the Republic send reports on those they had detained, and the measure was approved and sent to the Committee of Public Safety.[10]

The Execution of the Laws of Ventôse

In execution of this decree, the Committee of General Security sent out to the national agents of the districts a table in blank, which, when filled in by the local committee, would give the information needed to determine who was to be released and whose property was to be confiscated. It was constructed thus:

Name of detained; his residence before his arrest; his age; the number of his children; their age; where they are; if he is widower, bachelor, or married.

The place where he is detained; since when, at what period; by whose order; why.

His profession before and after the Revolution.

[9] *Moniteur*, réimp., XIX, 566–567.
[10] *Moniteur*, réimp., XIX, 611.

His revenue before and after the Revolution.

His relations and contacts.

The character and political opinions he has exhibited in May, July, and October, 1789; on 10 August; at the time of the flight and of the death of the tyrant; on 31 May and during the crisis of the war; if he has signed liberticide petitions or decrees.

The committees are to give the above information in regard to persons resident in their jurisdictions before their detention, whether they are detained in their jurisdiction, or whether they are detained elsewhere.

The committees of surveillance are to fill out this table in regard to persons ordinarily resident in their jurisdiction, and arrested in another section, adding by whose order and for what reasons, if they know them.

The national agents of the districts will reprint the present table in sufficient numbers, according to the number of detained in each district, and will send them to the committees of surveillance to be filled out within a period of a week. The directories of the districts will send certain of their members to speed up this salutary operation. They will see that the tables are filled out in regard to those subsequently detained.

The national agents will send the completed tables, without delay, to the Committee of General Security of the Convention and will countersign the envelopes.

The members of the Committee of General Security
Lavicomterie   Lebas   Vouland   Louis (of Bas-Rhin)
Dubarrau   Vadier   Amar   David Ruhl   Jagot
Elie Lacoste   Moïse Bayle
Paris—————Ventôse, Year II of the Republic.

By the end of Ventôse some of the committees had commenced gathering the information demanded and were forwarding the tables to their national agent.[11] In the majority of cases, however, the compilation was not begun until the month of Germinal and often was not completed until several months later. The charts of Orléans were only handed to the national agent on 4 Floréal. At Les Sables 54 had been sent in by 16 Floréal; by 19 Messidor, 126. In the district of Marseille, Prairial was the month in which most of the committees com-

[11] Nancy, Arch. Meurthe-et-Moselle, L 3183, 25 Ventôse; Montivilliers, Arch. Seine-Inf. L 5390, passim; Barbuat, *M. Soc. Beaune*, 1911, p. 288.

piled the information. The committee of Vitry-le-François had not finished in Thermidor, nor had the committee of Dax, the latter, in fact, having received the blanks only on 8 Prairial.[12]

Several explanations for these delays immediately present themselves. In the first place, some of the administrations may have had no liking for the whole expropriation scheme and have played for time, the proper tactics as it turned out. The committees also may have had objections to submitting their handiwork to the examination of the Committee of General Security. A more charitable view would be that the committees and the district were occupied in other pressing business and had insufficient time to perform both duties speedily and efficiently. But whatever the reasons, the committees did not follow the injunction of the Committee and complete the task within a week.

Tardiness, however, was a minor complaint. Vague remarks, improbable estimates of revenue and other obvious inaccuracies, led the two great Committees to issue a joint circular on 22 Germinal, instructing the committees that there was to be only one name on each chart, the chart to be in quarto, "by which you will economize material, words and time."

"What the committee wants are facts, precise information and not vague observations," said this circular. Furthermore, it continued, "it is important that the revenues of the detained be stated precisely in order that the Republic may determine its share . . . it is also necessary to indicate the number of children, their place of residence, to give the nature of their contacts so that no guilty person shall escape the justice of the nation."

The committees were warned against "intrigue and aristocracy" which probably would plague them "with petitions, traps and lies. In case your conscience is not sufficiently en-

[12] Arch. Loiret L 1179; Arch. Bouches-du-Rhône L 1011, passim; Arch. Vendée L 1215; Arch. Marne, Register of deliberations; Richard, *A. H. Révol.*, VII, 37.

lightened, you could ask information of your fellow citizens, inviting them to obtain it for you and at the same time posting the table with the facts you have already obtained." This last measure was optional, however.[13]

A few committees adopted the suggestion and posted in a conspicuous place the tables they had already filled out. The committee of Issoudun, which should have known better since it was the only "terrorist" organization in the town, posted its tables with the result that it was besieged with persons proffering information. The depositions in regard to Citizen Collet, all favorable, cover thirty-three folio pages, and there were other suspects who enjoyed only to a lesser degree the good opinion of their fellow citizens. The committee solemnly heard out the protests and then sent off the tables as originally compiled.[14] Generally, however, the committees kept their own counsel and made no effort to discover the opinions of the rest of the commune.

In a few localities the committees, to economize time and spare themselves the effort, sent the charts to the houses of detention to be filled out by the suspects themselves. The Neufchâtel committee sent off a number in this fashion, generally endorsing the notes the suspects wrote in regard to their political opinions, but retaining a certain number to be filled out by the members themselves. The Troyes committee followed the same practice, sending some to suspects, reserving others for its own attention.[15]

Undoubtedly this attention to exceptional cases will leave the impression that the committees were executing the laws in the same dilatory and independent fashion as they had been during the fall of 1793. On the contrary, the execution of the law of 8–13 Ventôse was certain, even though not as swift as the Committee of General Security had optimistically requested. It is true that a certain amount of correspondence between the

---

[13] Arch. Meurthe-et-Moselle L 3156.
[14] Arch. Indre L 1552, 18 Floréal et seq.
[15] Arch. Seine-Inf. L 5405; Babeau, II, 295.

committees and the national agent was necessary. But these letters were sent by the national agent most frequently to obtain the signatures of the members on the charts (which was not necessary, since only the national agent was to endorse them) or to have the committees recopy the tables, with the name of only one suspect on each, again a provision not mentioned in the original instruction.

Three months previously it had frequently been necessary for the national agent to send out dunning letters before the reports by *décade* were regularly communicated to him. By Germinal similar letters, pleading for the completion of the tables, were almost unknown, and the reports on those detained poured into the districts with a regularity commendable in organizations once so haphazard in their conduct of business. By 22 Floréal Barère reported that 40,000 of the reports had been received by the Committee of General Security. If Mathiez's estimate of the number of suspects detained in France is at all accurate (90,000) the committees had been making a reasonable amount of progress.[16]

It is no secret that the laws of Ventôse were never enforced in France, that the fall of Robespierre and the return to Girondist principles signified the end of any such wholesale confiscation. Nevertheless the tables were not wasted. After the Terror ended and the prisons were thrown open, they were employed in many cases to separate the "oppressed patriots" from the "truly guilty." The Committee of General Security itself ordered hundreds of releases on the strength of the tables, sometimes supplemented by the *comptes décadaires.*[17] For the same purpose the representatives on mission occasionally made use of copies of the charts when they could put their hands on them.[18]

---

[16] *Moniteur*, réimp., XX, 446; Mathiez, *A. H. Révol.*, VI, 75.

[17] Belloni, p. 474. On pages 473–476 Belloni gives a large number of orders for release, worded generally: "After examination of the tables of the committee of surveillance of the commune of ———, the Committee of General Security orders that the following citizens be set at liberty. . . ."

[18] At Toul, Denis, pp. 113, 139; in Finistère, Duchatellier, *Brest*, p. 381.

In making use of these tables the Committee and the representatives were in most cases leaning on a broken reed. Frequently the sixth column contains only the comment "Counter-revolutionary" or "The committee has no information," and it was for this reason that the committees of government demanded facts and precise information in their circular of 22 Germinal. Both should have known that there were no facts, that in most cases there were tendencies, suspicions, rumors, and nothing more.

The Expulsion of Nobles and Foreigners from the Ports

The arrest of Danton and his followers on 11 Germinal eliminated the last of the deputies who attempted to hold head against the increasing concentration of power in the hands of the Jacobin clique now settled in the Committee of Public Safety. Several weeks later, on the 26 and 27 Germinal several decrees strengthened the powers of the Committee over the entire administration and, at the same time, enacted severe measures against ex-nobles and foreigners.

Foreigners during Ventôse and Germinal had fallen into disrepute again. Both Hébert and Danton were haled before the Revolutionary Tribunal on charges of plotting with the foreigner, and in both cases a sprinkling of genuine foreigners was added to give the appearance of authenticity. Anacharsis Cloots, the orator of the human race, the Dutch banker Kock, and the Belgian secret agent and banker Proli were added to the *journée* which accompanied the despicable Père Duchesne to the guillotine. Danton saw his cause confounded with that of the Spanish banker Guzman, the two Freys (actually these two Moravian Jews were named Dobruska), and their secretary Diedrichsen. All of them, as Mathiez has shown, had unsavory reputations and had been fishing in the troubled waters of the Revolution.

It was not surprising, therefore, that those revolutionaries who were developing a strong case of nationalism should once more limit the activities of foreigners as well as the tried and true enemy, the aristocrat. Under the law of 27 Germinal no ex-noble or citizen of a belligerent nation was to be permitted to reside in Paris, in the sea-ports, or in fortified towns. Within ten days of the publication of the decree all such persons must present themselves to the local committee and receive passports indicating the destinations they had chosen. The committees were to keep registers of all such passports issued and report to the two Committees. Under the sponsorship of Couthon, a number of exceptions were later added to the law — minors, foreign wives of Frenchmen, and so on, were to be exempted.[19]

Once again there was almost universal enforcement of the law in those communes concerned. In most departments, the distribution of passports commenced during the early *décades* of Floréal, though at Quimper it was 30 Floréal by the time the municipality sent the committee a list of those to be expelled.[20]

Some committees persisted in perverting the law to suit their own convenience. The members at Quimper issued only four or five passes, since they judged it simpler to arrest all the ex-nobles as suspects, and at Saint-Brieuc (Côtes-du-Nord) the committee adopted the same solution.[21] Rouen was guilty of a similar extension of the law. It commenced enforcing the law on 1 Floréal, but results were only mediocre, and accordingly, on 23 Floréal a general round-up was ordered. The members of the committee, the gendarmes, sixty members of the popular society and five hundred national guardsmen were to assist. At 4 o'clock the following morning, with the city gates closed, the chase commenced, netting 271 persons, *ro-*

---

[19] *Moniteur*, réimp., XX, 224–225, 234–235, 243, 251–252.

[20] At Caen, 5 Floréal, Arch. Calvados, Register of deliberations; at Orléans, 7 Floréal, Arch. Loiret L 1178; Grenoble, 8 Floréal, Arch. Isère L 878; at Bordeaux, 8 Floréal, Arch. Gironde L 2165; in the district of Marseille, the *décade* of 11–20 Floréal, Arch. Bouches-du-Rhône L 1011, passim; Les Sables, before 13 Floréal, Arch. Vendée L 1215, 13 Floréal; Quimper, 1 Prairial, Trévédy, *R. H. Ouest*, XII, 753.

[21] Trévédy, *R. H. Ouest*, XII, 753–754; Galmiche, "Nouveaux documents sur le comité de surveillance de Saint-Brieuc," *A. Bretagne*, XXXVIII, 406.

turier as well as noble. Seventy-five were released, about forty referred to the committee or the municipality, while the remainder were kept under arrest, their cases being referred to the public accuser as being guilty of counter-revolutionary crime.[22]

The Bordeaux committee, on the contrary, was more than generous, despite its determination to arrest all aristocrats who could not prove their civism. A large number of the hundreds who applied were permitted to take advantage of the many exceptions written into the law, and in other cases the committee suspended action for several days with the suggestion that the petitioner find some documents which would prove that he was not a noble. The committees, in fact, had to set themselves up as a sort of College of Heralds to decide who was noble and who was not before they could expel the offending person.[23]

The moral of this chapter is obvious. The governmental reorganization undertaken by the law of 14 Frimaire had begun to bear fruit. Subordinated to the local national agents, the committees were becoming increasingly responsive to the orders sent down from Paris. The speed and the universality of the application of these two laws are rather a shock to those whose acquaintance with these amateur administrators is limited to the stormy months of the fall of 1793.

[22] Clérembray, *La Normandie*, 1899, p. 422.
[23] Arch. Gironde L 442, 8, 16 Floréal; L 2165, 9 Floréal et seq.

CHAPTER XIV

THE LAW OF 21 MESSIDOR AND THE OPENING
OF THE PRISONS

THE LAW IN EXECUTION

THE last terrorist measure which the committees were called upon to enforce, the law of 21–22 Messidor, was of the Terror and yet not of it. During the winter and spring of the Year II large numbers of peasants had been arrested as fanatics, for making false declarations of their estimated harvests, or for other violations of the economic legislation intended to simplify the problem of feeding France. The result was the aggravation of the shortage of labor, created partly by the number of peasant boys with the armies.

Vadier, a member of the Committee of General Security, therefore proposed on 21 Messidor that all laborers, harvesters, day-laborers and artisans in the rural areas and in towns of less than 1200 inhabitants, detained as suspects, should be provisionally released. The second article excepted those who had borne arms against the Republic and those guilty of high treason, which in effect meant the Vendeans and Chouans. The committee in the district capital was to make the release, acting with the advice of the committee of the suspect's commune, a provision which indicates that the Committee of General Security was commencing to profit from the observations of the representatives in regard to the weakness of the country committees.[1]

---

[1] Mathiez, in his *Girondins et Montagnards* (Paris, 1930), p. 135 note, declares with no evidence that Vadier's decree was aimed at saving the property of farmers from confiscation under the laws of Ventôse. But the release granted by the law of 21–22 Messidor was only provisional, and a decision of the Committee of Public Safety declared that the tables to be prepared under the Ventôse decrees should include as still suspect those released on bail (*sous caution*). Arch. Isère L 906, 30 Germinal. More than likely the farmers would still be considered suspects by the Committee of Public Safety.

Laborers, simply because they were laborers, had been set at liberty before. The Douai committee on 18 Prairial had released two citizens who would "continue their work as farmers. . . ." In the same month the representative Siblot asked the committee of Neufchâtel (Seine-Inf.) to send him the Ventôse tables of all those capable of working.[2] Augustin Robespierre had released twenty inhabitants of Haute-Saône "since the majority are farmers and necessary in the coming sowing" (18 Pluviôse). In the Puy-de-Dôme, Couthon permitted the committee of Issoire to suspend or modify the arrests of farmers, artisans, non-nobles and poor priests (27 Brumaire).[3] Now, however, the government was extending the practice throughout the Republic, confidently relying upon the discretion of the district committees to prevent the overthrow of the entire system of detention.

The favor with which the committees regarded the law is made quite evident by the speed with which they put it into effect. A glance at Appendix V will show that by 3 Thermidor action had been taken in twenty out of the twenty-three departments where information was sought: letters were written to the country communes and jail ledgers were examined to discover if any peasants had been sent to the district capital for detention. The urgency of the measure was constantly emphasized. The committee of Lisieux informed the country committees that "the law demands instant execution." At Montargis, the village committees were notified on 24 Messidor, on the 25th their delegates arrived at Montargis with the necessary information, and twenty-two were released immediately.[4] The committee of Romans (Drôme) insisted upon speed in its letter of 29 Messidor to the committee at Saillans:

Citizen colleagues:
We believe that you are familiar with the law of 21 Messidor . . . in the house of detention of the district of Romans, we are holding

---

[2] Arch. Nord L 10144; Arch. Seine-Inf. L 5401.
[3] Maréchal, p. 287; Mège, p. 290.
[4] Arch. Calvados, Register of deliberations, 28 Messidor; Arch. Loiret, Register of deliberations.

some of the citizens of your commune; we beg you to tell us immediately: First, if your commune has less than 1200 inhabitants;
Second, if there is anyone in a position to take advantage of the law;
Third, and last, in the event that there are some, if they are included
in the second article of the said law? [This article forbids the release
of those who have borne arms against the Republic.]

Since this law requires the greatest dispatch in its execution we
request that you do not lose an instant in giving us all the information we have asked in conformity with the requirements of the law.[5]

For Orléans even this was too slow. Since "it would take
too much time to write to the revolutionary committees of all
these places [the canton capitals] to gather information, and
since the weekly reports of the committees to the district
administration will enable the administration to give us information regarding the arrests to which the above-mentioned law
could be applied," the committee decided to consult the district.
The same day it released eight persons from prison after a
summary examination by two members, and only wrote to the
committee of their commune after they had been released.[6]

Nancy was as precipitate. On 25 Messidor, the day the law
was known to the committee, the members adjourned to the
commune of Champenoux to consult with the committee there,
and on the following day it sent agents into six other communes
to gather necessary information.[7]

The speed which the committees brought to the fulfillment
of this new duty sometimes carried them beyond the limits
which the law had set. The committee of Semur (Côte d'Or)
released a nun held for fanaticism when she swore she would
help her mother in the fields. On 5 Thermidor the committee
of Vézelise had written the Committee of General Security
asking if "this benevolent decree includes ex-nobles and priests
who were in the habit of exploiting their property and against
whom there are no charges of counter-revolutionary crimes."
Without waiting for a reply — one can imagine the attention

---

[5] Chevalier, p. 9.
[6] Arch. Loiret L 1181, 27 Messidor.
[7] Arch. Meurthe-et-Moselle L 3326.

this would get from the Committee of General Security within the succeeding few days — the committee released a noble, who, before his arrest, had led a miserable existence, "banished from all society." The committee was almost sorry for him.[8]

The Douai committee took liberties with the population restriction and released several citizens who lived in a commune of 1600 inhabitants, but "in view of the fact . . . that more than half of them [the inhabitants] were children and considering the number of defenders of the fatherland supplied by this commune" the committee felt that it was not endangering the Republic.[9]

The limitation of the "dispensation" to communes of 1200 inhabitants was indeed an unpopular provision.[10] The committee of Orléans, in reporting rather proudly its speedy execution of the law, told the Committee of General Security that "a number of farmers, residents of communes of over 1200 inhabitants, were still imprisoned. Since their labor makes them precious to the Republic" the committee suggested that the restriction be removed. A committee of the Indre was even more outspoken. It queried the Committee of Public Safety as to the meaning of 1200, the committee being uncertain whether it meant persons or voters. It declared that the law as passed still deprives the Republic of many farmers, who are actually only the "dupes of the aristocracy" and would do little harm if they were released.[11]

The committee of Hazebrouck also felt it had a legitimate complaint. The majority of the communes of its district had more than 1200 persons, but "this surplus does not result from the fact that the land-holdings are smaller here, but is due to the fact that these communes are greater in extent and have in the center of them a sort of village which is inhabited by

[8] Arch. Côte d'Or L IV a 154 (c) 1, 1 Thermidor; Arch. Meurthe-et-Moselle L 3442, 5, 10 Thermidor.

[9] Arch. Nord L 10142, 29 Messidor.

[10] Vadier's original proposal had been for communes of less than 500 inhabitants, but was raised to 1200 on an amendment from the floor. *Moniteur*, réimp., XXI, 184.

[11] Arch. Loiret L 1181, 2 Thermidor; Arch. Indre L 368, 8 Thermidor.

artisans who are useless in the fields. Also, this being the frontier, in addition to the contingents supplied to the army in proportion to their population, there are still more laborers occupied in engineering, carting, and chopping and transporting wood for the navy." Without injuring the cause of the Republic the committee believed it could release "all the workmen imprisoned for private opinions resulting from fanaticism or other partialities. . . ."

The committee, after Thermidor, saw its position justified. Florent-Guyot on 22 Thermidor released citizens of Caestre, which the committee well knew had more than 1200 inhabitants, for on the same day on which they had written the letter quoted above two delegates from Caestre had testified that their commune had 1550 inhabitants. (In the register the deposition of the men from Caestre is scratched out — whether before or after the release, it is impossible to say.) The representative had justified his release by declaring that Caestre had only 600 men, apparently working on the principle that a normal commune has half men and half women, therefore Caestre, with less than 600 men, *must* have less than 1200 inhabitants. The commune was bewildered by all this actuarial computation and went to the council-general of the commune for an explanation. There the committee was completely reassured by the council-general. The law said, according to this authority, "communes which did not exceed 1200 men." The committee's mystification was only ended by the reception of the law of 29 Thermidor, which removed entirely any restrictions based on population.[12]

Of persistent refusal to enforce the law there seems to have been little. We have already referred to three departments of the twenty-three where our search yielded no results. Gironde was under the influence of Julien, *fils*, and from Prairial to Thermidor underwent a reign of terror more severe than any

---

[12] Arch. Nord L 10197, 29 Messidor, 22 Thermidor. Some of this confusion may have resulted from the similarity in pronunciation of *homme* and *âme*, the latter being often used synonymously with *habitant*.

it had previously known. Lack of documents prevents any dogmatic statement, but it was not improbable that the law was suspended. In the Bouches-du-Rhône documents are again scarce for this period, but on 14 Brumaire III the department was specifically mentioned in the Convention as one of those where the law was not being enforced.[13]

The situation in the Haute-Vienne, however, is less understandable. The department had had a few moments of alarm in the summer of 1793, when the Vendeans were marching toward Poitiers, but calm was soon restored. Since then it had been an average, quiet department, and the committees were not noted for their severity. Nevertheless, the first notice of the law at Limoges was on 7 Fructidor, when the law was applicable to laborers in all communes. (Law of 29 Thermidor.) At Saint-Junien, 17 Fructidor was the date of the first release, while Saint-Yreix on 21 Fructidor motivated three releases "by the new law which permits committees of surveillance to release laborers and artisans."[14] It is hardly probable that no laborers of communes of less than 1200 inhabitants were arrested. In such a case, one of the committees would have undoubtedly mentioned the fact. One can only adopt an explanation so often put forward by the terrorists themselves, some "malevolent" persons were simply nullifying the law on their own authority.

There are, in addition, a few isolated examples of outright opposition. At Issoudun (Indre) the majority of the committee, throughout the Terror unyielding in its Jacobinism, seemed to have deliberately nullified the law. The committee duly acknowledged receipt of the law and wrote to the country communes as required, but four days later, when a member suggested that the committee devote its energy to the law of

[13] *Moniteur*, réimp., XXII, 426. The remark was not completely justified, for the Aix committee had released thirteen peasants, fathers of émigrés or of fugitives, on 23 Thermidor, all under the law of 21–22 Messidor. Salon had on 7 Brumaire III released several *sectionnaires* under the same law. Arch. Bouches-du-Rhône L 1712.

[14] Arch. Haute-Vienne L 843; L 872; Saint-Yreix, Register of deliberations.

21 Messidor, one of his colleagues suggested that the committee write the Committee of Public Safety for information on the method of procedure, which was decreed. It was the first time the committee had shown such regard for the formalities.[15]

If the opposition of the committees was almost nonexistent, that of the other members of the administration was as rare, and only two clear-cut cases were discovered. The committee of Cambrai released, among others, the municipal officers of Nouvion, as *laboureurs*. Lebon protested and said that the decree read *laboureurs-manouvriers*. When it was pointed out that there was a comma between the two words, he thundered out, "That comma is a crime of high treason; it is placed in such a way as to guillotine twenty committees."[16] The other incident, in a sense related to the first, was the suspension of the law by Duquesnoy and two ex-jurors of Lebon's tribunal, by a decree issued at Arras on 19 Thermidor. It also ordered the rearrest of the "large number of detained farmers" released by the committees of the district and canton capitals, notably Arras, Bapaume, Saint-Pol, Calais and Saint-Omer.[17]

Obstructionism of this kind was unusual, however. By the majority of committees the law was welcomed as an opportunity to repopulate the countryside, mitigate the labor shortage, and perhaps exorcise the specter of famine, never far away during the Terror. To only a very few was it an excuse to release persons who, they now realized, were unjustly held but whose liberty could be restored only by the representatives or the two Committees at Paris. For most of them the law was always present to check their impulses. Repeatedly they cited the statutory limitation of 1200 inhabitants in refusing petitions hopefully presented to them, even while declaring that the restriction was not a wise one. Just as often they refused the petitions of persons who had trumped up a case to prove

---

[15] Arch. Indre L 1552, 25, 29 Messidor.

[16] Paris, p. 587. The distinction is between persons who possibly could be simply landowners and actual farm-hands. Literally, *laboureur* means one who ploughs or tills — by extension, any farmer.

[17] Paris, p. 598 and note 3.

they were farmers — priests and landowners especially were refused. The committees were careful to inform themselves as to the exact status and offense of the suspect before acting, and as a result indiscriminate releases before 9 Thermidor were rare.

THERMIDOR

As the news of 9 Thermidor trickled into the cities and towns of the Republic, the committees conformed politely to this latest *coup d'état*, wrote congratulatory messages to the Convention, but changed little in their methods or their attitude toward the suspects they had imprisoned. The district of Narbonne on 27 Thermidor found it necessary to warn the committees of its jurisdiction against releasing some draft-evaders under the law of 21 Messidor, particularly since it was to be enforced only by the committees of the district capital, but no more violations of the law's intent were discovered.[18] The month of Thermidor, in short, saw no sudden conversion on the part of the committees. For them the fall of Robespierre meant no more than the fall of the Hebertists and of the Indulgents.

By the beginning of Fructidor, however, it was clear that times had changed and the committees with them — from conviction or expediency, it would be difficult to say. Aided by the law of 29 Thermidor, which removed the population restriction, they resumed their inquiries, and certain of them gave evidence of their change of heart.

A merchant was released at Péronne (Somme) because he worked with his hands (he was a *manouvrier*), an equivocal statement which not a few committees made use of (3 Fructidor). At Vienne (Isère), of forty-one released in four days, one was a priest and two were ex-nobles. On 18 Fructidor four ex-priests, removed from their positions in the local school for incivic teachings, were set at liberty by the same committee because they had no income and they must therefore work

[18] Arch. Aude L 2222, 27 Thermidor.

with their hands. Beaune on 7–8 Fructidor released some who worked with their hands and had only their business or profession to support them; they included a business man (*négociant*), two lawyers, and a former municipal officer. On the 9th, seven workers (*travailleurs*) released included three ex-Carmelites; on the 10th, five persons were freed, of whom one had an income of "only 700 *livres*," another had "a house with a garden in the *faubourg de l'Unité* and that where he resides . . . for which he still owes two-thirds of the purchase price"; still another had an income of 1600 *livres*. At Grasse, apothecaries and a perfumer were released under the law of 29 Thermidor.

The committee of the Section Maison Commune at Dijon released a musician on 13 Fructidor as an "artisan and artist" who had no other way of making a living. Limoges released the commandant of the military warehouse, dismissed for inefficiency. Since, however, he had been an artisan before his appointment, by his dismissal he became once more an artisan and was therefore subject to release. A noble was released at Orthez (Basses-Pyrénées) on 16 Vendémiaire III, the register revealing that "since the times have changed, the committee foresees no danger or inconvenience in granting him his liberty." On the following day, an apothecary sought his freedom by claiming to practice a "mechanical art," but the committee had the intelligence to motivate his release on the fact that he was cured of his counter-revolutionary opinions. And one last example: on 8 Frimaire III, the committee of Fontenay, basing its action on the law of 21 Messidor, released a woman with no other reason given save that she had a fever.[19]

Protest against these violations was rare. The national agents who during the Terror had been on the alert to call

[19] Ramon, p. 307; *Procès-verbaux du comité . . . de Vienne* (Grenoble, 1888), pp. 71–78, 83; Barbuat, *M. Soc. Beaune*, 1911, pp. 324–326; Combet, *Révol. Fr.*, LVII, 352; Arch. Côte d'Or L IV a 47/f, 13 Fructidor; Arch. Haute-Vienne L 844, 8 Vendémiaire III; "Registre des délibérations du comité de surveillance établi à Orthez," *B. Soc. Pau*, 2e série, XXX, 20, 22; Arch. Vendée L 1188, 8 Frimaire III.

the committees to account for such transgressions were now silent. Only Farez, the national agent of Cambrai, seemed to protest against this new indulgence. "You must know," he wrote to the district administration, "the extreme complaisance with which the revolutionary committee of Cambrai pronounces the release of those detained; you also know that instead of restricting itself within the limits of the laws of 21 Messidor and 29 Thermidor, the committee has released persons whom the law of 17 September seems to declare suspect and condemn to arrest." He had protested to the committee, but "either because it has been deceived, or because it thought that it was necessary to efface from memory its arbitrary arrests by acts of indulgence, it continues to release." [20] At Rouen the popular society in Fructidor made known its objections to the action of the committee in releasing such a large number of aristocrats. Otherwise, the committees were allowed to go their own way.[21]

These releases were not in any sense wholesale deliveries. They formed a small part of the number set free during Fructidor, for the majority restored to liberty were farmers or artisans, and released as such. Nevertheless, in comparison with the committees' scrupulousness during the Terror, the tendency is strongly toward moderation and reaction.

This rather long account of the law of 21 Messidor is intended to indicate the distance the committees and the administration had traveled since the turbulent winter of 1793. In those days, it was possible for a law not to be enforced at all, and if it was enforced, not infrequently it was altered to suit the ideas of the administration.

By the end of the Terror the orders of the Convention and the two great Committees were enforced swiftly and precisely in the majority of cases. There was no flouting of the laws, perhaps because the committees were themselves terrorized by

[20] Arch. Cambrai I, 9, 18 Fructidor.
[21] Clérembray, La Normandie, 1899.

the Terror, perhaps because they had been broken to administrative duties. The law of 14 Frimaire and the persistent effort of the Committee of Public Safety in enforcing its centralizing provisions had borne their fruit.

OPENING THE PRISONS

The releases ordered by the committees under the law of 29 Thermidor mark the beginning of the mass liberations which ended the Terror in the departments. Thermidor had seen little change in the attitude of most committees, and if there had been a transformation in their views it was not from action to reaction but rather to neutrality. The committee of Châlons-sur-Marne continued to arrest throughout Thermidor, and when on the 18th a member suggested a congratulatory address to the Convention, the committee declared without much enthusiasm that it had no objections. Pau's committee resisted the new indulgence as much as possible, refusing to coöperate with the more moderate municipality in releasing suspects. The members of the Uzès (Gard) committee went further and tried to convince the citizenry that 9 Thermidor meant nothing.[22]

The Convention, however, was more speedily convinced, and on 18 Thermidor it made the first assault on the system of surveillance. On the motion of Bourdon, amended by Bentabole, it ordered the committees to furnish all suspects with a copy of the charges which had led to their arrest. Now it was possible for the suspects to answer the accusations made against them, if they were definite enough; the mystery surrounding arrests was to disappear. Furthermore, it placed the committees on the defensive in some cases, for they had to produce charges for persons concerning whom they had no knowledge.

Critics of the committees have made great point of their

[22] Arch. Marne, Register of deliberations, 18 Thermidor; Rivarès, *B. Soc. Pau*, 2e série, IV, 512; M. Fabre, "La Réaction thermidorienne et la liquidation de la Terreur à Uzès," *M. Acad. Nimes*, 1922–23, pp. 71–72.

confessing ignorance of the charges against many suspects. In some cases this surprising situation resulted from the fact that the committee in office in Thermidor was not the same committee which had made the arrests. The law of 14 Frimaire altered some committees almost entirely, and there were in addition many "purges" which eliminated all twelve of the members. Furthermore, the registers of these suspended committees would be of unequal value in determining the reasons for arrests. Frequently there is only the brief mention, "On the report of a member . . ." or "On the motion of a member . . ." a certain citizen is declared suspect.[23]

In their quandary, the committees usually wrote some ambiguous statement after the suspect's name and considered their obligation discharged. At Quimper the committee, after receiving the petition of a suspect for the motives of his arrest, solemnly deliberated on the subject in the hope of discovering exactly why he had been arrested. This committee was, indeed, a bit backward about supplying the required copies, issuing them only on special petition. The Beaulieu (Corrèze) committee was even more reluctant. The women and servant-girls of the town had to stir up a small riot to force the committee to hold a meeting and issue the precious papers.[24] Usually, however, the committees made no official objections to their new duties and passed out to all suspects copies of the charges made against them, unsatisfactory as they may have been.

Armed with a semblance of an accusation, the suspects spent their idle moments drawing up petitions which commenced to pour in upon the committees in Fructidor. Almost without exception the committees followed the procedure of the Terror,

---

[23] It will also come as a surprise that the committees were not required by law to keep a register of their deliberations, according to a decision of the Committee of Legislation of 8 Messidor. Charles Porée, *Sources manuscrites de l'histoire de la Révolution dans L'Yonne, Archives nationales* (Auxerre, 1918), tome 1er, pp. 172–3. Registers for charges against those of the suspects not included in the law of 17 September, and for those to whom passports were issued by the law of 26–28 Germinal, were obligatory, however.

[24] Trévédy, *R. H. Ouest*, XII, 713–4; Cantouny, *B. Soc. Corrèze (Tulle)*, XLIV, 14–15.

noting their opinion on the petition and forwarding it to the representative. In certain districts, however, the deputies delegated to the committees themselves the power to release if it seemed desirable. Already Ingrand had granted to the committee of Fontenay the right to release those against whom there were no charges, an action undoubtedly inspired by the large number of mass arrests made in the troubled districts (Messidor). The same right was given to the district committee of Lyon, where a similar situation prevailed (Frimaire III). In the Var and the Bouches-du-Rhône, where an unusually large number of suspects were under detention, the representatives Auguis and Serres gave the new district committees the right to free "all those persons who, deceived and misled, committed errors which were not in their heart, and those who have retracted within a reasonable time" (4 Brumaire III).[25]

It was more usual, however, for the representatives to resort to a device they had used during the Terror, a commission to review arrests and petitions, sometimes including members of the committee, sometimes chosen outside its membership. In the Meurthe, Michaud established commissions which included the committee, members of the district administration, and twelve citizens from the popular society, the commission limiting itself to recommendations.[26] In the Seine-Inférieure, Sautereau ordered the committees to name three of their members to meet with delegates of the district administration in order to pass upon the petitions of the detained and make recommendations.[27] In none of these cases was the commission au-

[25] Arch. Vendée L 1186, 12 Messidor; Arch. Rhône, Register of deliberations of district committee, 18 Frimaire III; Arch. Bouches-du-Rhône L 1857, 11 Brumaire III; Patin, *B. Soc. Draguignan*, XVII, 111. Such sweet forgetfulness was exceeded only by an entry in the register of the Bayeux committee. A citizen had been arrested as implicated in "the pretended federalism which a thoroughgoing examination of the troubles which disturbed the departments has proven never existed." Arch. Calvados, Register of deliberations, 3 Nivôse III.

[26] Arch. Meurthe-et-Moselle L 3265, 17 Vendémiaire III; Denis, p. 122; Godchot, *Révol. Fr.*, LXXX, 295.

[27] Arch. Seine-Inf. L 5187, 5 Vendémiaire III; L 5391, 24 Vendémiaire III.

thorized to restore freedom to any of those detained. In conformity with the law of 14 Frimaire, they merely reported, favorably or unfavorably, to the deputy on mission in their department.

The opening of the prisons, the end of the Terror in the provinces, was, therefore, the work of the representatives. It could hardly have been otherwise. The committeemen had been terrorists of the terrorists in the sense that they were most compromised by the events of the preceding year. The law of suspects, frequently the levying of revolutionary taxes, the looting of churches, household inspections, snooping in private correspondence, the concern of the committees with the maximum and with deserters — their ubiquity, in short — roused the hatred of the citizens of their communes. The members had every reason to believe that they would be the first attacked. Some, like those of Cambrai, hoped by present clemency to obliterate memories of past severity. Others, and they were the majority in Thermidor, hoped, by stubborn refusal to compromise, to maintain the system intact even against the will of their fellow citizens.

CHAPTER XV

CONCLUSION

APOLOGISTS for the Terror from Robespierre to Mathiez have always pleaded extenuating circumstances, have demonstrated that the revolutionary government was the direct consequence of civil and foreign war, an expedient imposed upon France by the alarming plight in which she found herself. These writers have shown that the Revolutionary Tribunal, the Committees of Public Safety and of General Security, the committees of surveillance, the maximum, the law of suspects — in short, all the extra-constitutional devices which formed the Revolutionary government — sprang logically from the effort to defend the nation from enemies at home and abroad. For France to hold her own, a single will was necessary; to win this unity of purpose, there was no alternative save the Terror.

The revolutionary committees fit only imperfectly into this picture. The hatred of the foreigner and the conviction that he was largely responsible for the predicament in which France found herself resulted directly from the war, but it is our contention that the law which created the committees resulted equally from the abortive insurrection against the Gironde on 9–10 March, which had a purely political character. Furthermore, the particular character of the law, its indisputable weakness, can only be explained by the Gironde's distrust of the Paris sections and their committees of surveillance. The resulting impotence of the committees as institutions revealed itself in the departments during the spring and summer of 1793. Those committees whose functions were confined to the mere surveillance of foreigners enjoyed a placid, uneventful existence. Only the committees established by the representatives or the local authorities — either Mountain or Girondist —

engaged in the arrest of suspects, censored correspondence, and in general performed the functions usually associated with revolutionary committees.

When the law of 17 September assigned to them the duty of arresting suspects, the committees started upon an evolution in character which marked the majority of revolutionary institutions. It is a truism that in using institutions one transforms them, altering their nature by making new and different demands of them. These new functions denature the institution by shifting the emphasis in other directions, and there results a new organization, related historically, but not functionally, to the original conception. The Committee of Public Safety soon ceased being merely a body to coördinate the national defense and became a governing council, dictating the religious, political, social, and economic policy of the nation.

The powers of the committees of surveillance were similarly enlarged. After confining in houses of detention the suspects of the commune, the majority of them upper-class citizens and priests, the committees commenced to extend their prerogatives over a constantly widening field, partly by usurping powers, partly as a direct result of legislation. Their right of visaing certificates of civism, coupled with their power of arrest, enabled them to control the personnel of the administration and in many places the entire body of citizens as well. The right to examine the mail of suspects they often extended to any mail that looked suspicious. Their duty of visaing passports tightened the bonds in which they held the lives of the citizens of their communes.

The representatives on mission, called upon to reorganize these committees during the fall of 1793, set them new tasks, generally of a nature which can be described as Hebertist. The committees as a result took a hand in the dechristianization of the departments by inviting the abdication of priests and looting the churches; but more often they confined themselves to levying revolutionary taxes, forcing the wealthy to make "voluntary contributions" to the Republic and confiscating the gold and silver they had hidden away, all acts with a legal sanction but enforced with threats of coercive measures.

The uncontrolled violence of this movement in the departments threatened to transform the whole nation into a new Vendée. From Paris it was almost impossible to direct the acts of the representatives, for they were moving quickly from place to place, and satisfactory correspondence, even if that alone would have sufficed, was out of the question. The committees were responsible to no one, and the powers they enjoyed were the sole sanction for their acts.

The Convention, therefore, enacted the law of 14 Frimaire with the dual purpose of restraining the deputies and at the same time assuring the speedy enforcement of its orders to the committees by systematizing these hitherto improvised and haphazard organs of the revolutionary government.

The committees were henceforth forbidden to release those they had arrested — a precaution against indulgence and, at the same time, bribery. The national agents of the districts were designated as the center of the surveillance established over the entire administration, and by a system of reports by *décades* they were able to follow the course of the committees and restrain or direct their acts as the occasion required.

This law did not put an end to the irregular jurisdictions which had existed in the fall when committees had exercised their surveillance over entire districts and even departments. After the reorganization carried through in Nivôse, there still existed committees whose powers extended over entire districts or cantons. Because they realized the lack of capable men and distrusted the peasants who were dominated by the opinions of the large landowners, many representatives replaced the village committees with a single body in whose *sans-culottisme* they had faith.

Apart from this exception, the law of 14 Frimaire was observed in the departments, the committees refraining from releasing suspects, reporting regularly to the national agent, confining themselves to their jurisdiction, and excluding members of the administration from the membership. Indeed, they assumed an air of legality and quoted the law like judges.

As a result of this same law of 14 Frimaire, the committees were empowered, in collaboration with the municipalities, to administer all revolutionary laws. In certain communes, the committees were called upon to perform many routine duties usually carried out by the municipality. They assisted, not too eagerly, in enforcing the maximum, but to the problem of provisioning their communes during the food crisis of the Year II they brought more enthusiasm and ingenuity. To aid the overburdened military administration the committees undertook the duties of military police, rounded up deserters and draft evaders, and tried to regulate the movements of soldiers on leave. Some of them extended their supervision to the military depots and *étapes*, attempting to accelerate the movements of supplies and to eliminate what abuses they could. Their activity in this field of administration was extensive; they had, in short, escaped from the simple police function of repression and advanced to more constructive activities.

With the passing of the months, the committees became more and more reliable as administrative agents, enforcing the laws of Ventôse and those of 26–28 Germinal with a dispatch which, if not all that was desired by the committees of government, was decidedly better than could have been expected six months before. Three months later when they were called upon to enforce the law of 21 Messidor, the majority of the committees performed their task with more expedition and more scrupulousness than they had ever exhibited before. After the fall of Robespierre this same law served in some cases as an excuse to release favored suspects, but in general the majority of those detained were only released in Fructidor on the initiative of the representatives on mission.

This more condensed account of the committees gives a stronger impression of the diversity of their activities. Constantly the committees have been described merely as "arresting suspects" and visaing certificates of civism. If this study has done nothing else, it has at least restored to the committees a part of the credit — or blame — which is their due. In the lives of their fellow citizens they were omnipresent; with their decrees, requisitions, patrols, household searches, visaing documents of one kind or another, arresting, hearing petitions and so on and on, they intruded themselves upon the consciousness of the commune.

Ultimately, any moral judgment which one passes upon them must depend upon one's view of the Revolution. Any sententious remarks which might be made upon their crimes, any casuistical apology for their acts, would be fatuous. But consider them from a realist, positivist point of view and a certain appreciation for them must be confessed. They were called upon to remove from society certain members who, according to the opinions of the period, were dangerous. Quite simply they arrested these men and women, whose ability to harm was consequently reduced. Making use of the undoubted influence they exercised, they attacked another group of enemies — the wealthy, the indifferent — extorting money from them on one pretext or another. The rich they had mulcted were discreet enough not to protest until the committees were attacked by the Thermidorians in search of scapegoats; then only did the victims cry out, all the louder for having been pent up for so many months. Quite effectively the committees had shut the mouths of the enemies of the Revolution and imposed upon them a restraint in speech and act which the ordinary Frenchman must have found novel and uncomfortable. They had terrorized upon the assurances of Robespierre that terror was the only solution. Terror did not bring heaven to earth, and they and their *sans-culottes* friends were the dupes.

Our attempt to discover if there existed in the departments any overwhelming influence upon Paris comparable to that which Paris exercised over the departments has been only partly successful. We have seen that the passage of the law of 14 Frimaire was more than justified by the casual manner in which the local administration had played fast and loose with the decrees of the Convention during the first nine months of their existence. We have also seen that there existed in the departments a strong Hebertist movement which may in part explain the eagerness to subject the rest of France to the control of Paris. Otherwise, we must admit defeat, for of determining events of more than local significance, we found nothing not already known to the historians whom we so roundly denounced in our introduction.

Nevertheless, we have struck a few blows at the legend we criticized. We have shown that local influences were stronger than events in Paris in determining the intensity of the Terror in the departments, that the comings and goings of the deputies on mission were of more significance than the shoutings and rantings of the deputies in Paris. As a result, each region tends to have a "climate" of its own, periods of greater or less activity, especially during the early months of the Terror. To a large extent the cause can be found in the bewildering variation in the manner of enforcing — or not enforcing — the mass of laws poured out upon the heads of men quite unbroken to administrative duties. These irregularities have confirmed us in our conviction that the history of the committees, and, indeed, of any of the institutions of the Revolution, cannot be written from the laws as passed in Paris, and that any statement made simply on the basis of those laws will be at least misleading if not entirely incorrect.

We have also indicated that the fall of Robespierre did not convert the committees to indulgence overnight. Because they sought to protect themselves from the consequences of reaction, or because they still respected the system which was to bring them salvation, the majority did not take advantage of the law of 21 Messidor to release the suspects. Neither did the doors of the houses of detention burst open at the first trumpetings of the Thermidorians, who had at length discovered, to their evident amazement, that their victory was the triumph of mercy and justice. Not until Fructidor did the terrorists retreat, and from that time they were on the defensive, hooted in the streets by those who had once applauded them, chased from commune to commune, and then dragged back again to undergo the same punishment they themselves had meted out during the Terror. Only the guilty consciences of the Thermidorians who shared their crimes saved these men from the punishment so loudly demanded, and on 21 Vendémiaire IV the Convention voted an amnesty for all terrorists, and the play was played out.

APPENDICES

APPENDIX I

THE CHARACTER OF THE SOURCES

ANY statement made on the basis of the existing records must be taken *cum grano*. Barère, who kept the pay lists of the committees, says in his *Mémoires* (II, 324 note) that there were 21,500 committees in France. Today the documents of about 3,650 are extant, and this number includes hundreds of registers of village committees whose activities were negligible. Any comparative statements are consequently mere approximations.

Some of the documents were intentionally destroyed. At Lyon, though the catalogue of the collection shows a number of registers for the period of the Terror, the pages of many of them have been ripped in half. Generally the missing papers are, as in the case of Lyon, for the period of the Terror. Obviously the person responsible wished to remove compromising documents, and it was upon the official orders of the national agent that the records of the committees of the Haute-Loire were destroyed in Pluviôse IV. The subprefect of Autun on 15 Ventôse X mentioned in a report to his superior "documents or what answer for documents" of the committees and popular societies. "All searches," he admitted, "to legalize [these conclusions] in these registers would be fruitless. Could we have left in existence for such a long time the elements of hatred between citizens and the monuments of bitter memories?" [1]

Elsewhere, many of the documents followed the usual fate of old papers. Some of the archives of the Haute-Garonne were used by Wellington's soldiers to light their campfires. At another place they were sold to the junkman, in still others they crumbled into dust.

Nevertheless, for many committees in important centers the documents are still complete, including five or six registers of deliberations, the visaing of certificates of civism and passports, and of correspondence; files of letters, of petitions, of copies of law, and so on. In short, there is no embarrassment for material as such, and it is regrettable that the committee records are not used more frequently by local historians, for in them are related, as much as in the records of municipalities and other local authorities, the expressions of the life of the commune.

[1] Arch. Côte d'Or Q 904, 4.

APPENDIX II

THE LAW OF 21 MARCH 1793

Article 1 — A committee, composed of twelve citizens, shall be formed in each commune of the Republic and in each section of those communes divided into sections, at a time to be indicated in advance by the council-general of the commune.

Article 2 — The members of this committee, who shall not be chosen from either the clergy, or ex-nobles, or ex-lords of the locality, or their agents, shall be elected by ballot and by a relative majority of votes.

Article 3 — To be elected, the candidate must receive as many times one hundred votes as there are times a thousand inhabitants in the commune or section.

Article 4 — The committee of the commune, or each of the committees of the sections of a commune, will be charged with receiving, as regards its jurisdiction, the declarations of all foreigners at present resident in the commune, or who may later come there.

Article 5 — The declarations shall contain the name, age, profession, place of birth, and sources of income of the individual declaring.

Article 6 — They shall be made within the week following the publication of the present decree; a list of them shall be posted and printed.

Article 7 — Any foreigner who during the period prescribed above shall refuse, or neglect, to make his declaration before the committee of the commune or of the section in which he resides shall be required to leave the commune within twenty-four hours and the territory of the Republic within a week.

Article 8 — Any foreigner born in those countries with whose governments the French people are at war, who, in making his declaration, cannot present to the committee evidence of an establishment set up in France, or of a profession exercised here, or of real property purchased here, or of his civic opinions, by the testimony of six citizens domiciled for a year in the commune or the section, if the commune is divided into sections, shall also be required to leave the commune within twenty-four hours and from the territory of the Republic within a week. In the opposite case, he shall be granted a certificate authorizing his residence.

Article 9 — Foreigners who do not possess property in France, or who do not practice a useful profession, shall be required, under the penalties indicated above, to give, in addition to the certificate of six citizens, a bond to the amount of the half of their presumed fortune.

Article 10 — All those whom the provisions of the preceding articles

quired to indicate and prepare for this purpose, immediately after the receipt of this law.

Article 7 — The detained will be permitted to have transferred into those buildings the furniture which shall be absolutely necessary. They shall be kept there until peace is declared.

Article 8 — The salaries of the guard will be paid by the detained and will be shared among them equally. The guards shall, by preference, be men with families and parents of citizens who either are, or shall soon be, with the armies. The salary for each guard shall be fixed at the value of a day and half's labor.

Article 9 — The committees of surveillance shall send without delay to the Committee of General Security a list of persons whom they have arrested, with the reasons for their arrest and the papers taken from them.

Article 10 — The civil and criminal courts shall, if there is occasion, detain under arrest as suspicious persons and send to the houses of detention mentioned above, those whose cases have been dismissed or who have been acquitted of the charges brought against them.

APPENDIX IV

THE LAW OF 14 FRIMAIRE

SECTION II

THE EXECUTION OF LAWS

Article 8 — The application of revolutionary laws and of measures of general security and public safety is entrusted to the municipalities and to the committees of surveillance (or revolutionary committees) with the same duty of reporting every ten days in regard to the execution of these laws in the territory of their jurisdiction, since they are charged with their immediate surveillance.

Article 11 — It is expressly forbidden to any authority and to any public official to make proclamations, or to pass decrees, extending, limiting or contradicting the literal sense of the law, on the pretext of interpreting or supplementing them.

To the Convention alone belongs the right of interpreting decrees and it alone must be appealed to for this purpose.

Article 12 — The intermediary authorities, charged with supervising the execution and application of laws are also forbidden to pronounce any decision and order the release of citizens who have been arrested. This right belongs exclusively to the National Convention, to the Committees of Public Safety and General Security, to the representatives of the people on mission in the departments and with the armies, and to the courts by application of criminal laws and police regulations.

Article 17 — The national agents of the communes are required to make the same report (the report by *décades*) to the district of their locality and the presidents of the revolutionary committees of surveillance shall maintain the same correspondence with the Committee of General Security and the district charged with their surveillance.

SECTION III

THE COMPETENCE OF THE CONSTITUTIONAL AUTHORITIES

Article 7 — The president and the secretaries of the revolutionary committees of surveillance will also be replaced twice a month and can be reëlected only after an interval of a month.

Article 8 — No citizen already employed in the service of the Republic can exercise, or collaborate in the exercise of, powers of an authority entrusted with the surveillance, either direct or indirect, of his duties.

Article 9 — Those who exercise, or collaborate in the exercise of two functions in similar authorities, shall be required to choose between the two within twenty-four hours of the publication of this decree.

Article 15 — All constitutional authorities, all public officials, all agents employed in the service of the Republic are expressly forbidden to extend the exercise of their powers beyond the territory assigned to them, to perform acts which are not within their competence, to encroach upon other authorities and to go beyond the functions assigned to them, or to assume those which are not entrusted to them.

Article 16 — All constitutional authorities are forbidden to alter the character of their organization either by meeting with other authorities, or by delegates charged with forming central assemblies or by agents sent to other constitutional authorities. All relations between all public officials shall take place by correspondence.

Article 17 — Any congress or central meetings, established either by the representatives of the people, or by popular societies under whatever name they may assume, even of central committees of surveillance or of central revolutionary or military commissions are revoked and expressly forbidden by this decree, since they are subversive of the unity of action of the government and *tend to federalism*; and those in existence shall be dissolved within twenty-four hours following the publication of this present decree.

Article 20 — Armed forces, taxes, loans, forced or voluntary, can be levied only by virtue of a decree. The revolutionary taxes of the representatives of the people shall be executed only after having approved by the Convention, save in enemy or rebel territory.

APPENDIX V

DATES OF ENFORCEMENT OF THE LAW OF 21 MESSIDOR

THE law of 21 Messidor was put into execution on the following dates in the following communes of France:

23 Messidor
Montargis (Loiret)
Pithiviers (Loiret)
24 Messidor
Châlons-sur-Marne (Marne)
Douai (Nord)
25 Messidor
Baye (Marne)
Blamont (Meurthe-et-Moselle)
Caen (Calvados)
Cany (Seine-Inférieure)
Dieppe (Seine-Inférieure)
Lunéville (Meurthe-et-Moselle)
Nancy (Meurthe-et-Moselle)
Nîmes (Gard)
Vitry-le-François (Marne)
26 Messidor
Montivilliers (Seine-Inférieure)
Péronne (Somme)
27 Messidor
Beaune (Côte d'Or)
Darney (Vosges)
Orléans (Loiret)
Semur (Côte d'Or)
Vézelise (Meurthe-et-Moselle)
Vienne (Isère)
28 Messidor
Bayeux (Calvados)
Châteauroux (Indre)

Lisieux (Calvados)
Les Sables (Vendée)
29 Messidor
Arras (Pas-de-Calais)
Grenoble (Isère)
Hazebrouck (Nord)
Mirecourt (Vosges)
Romans (Drôme)
30 Messidor
Aix-les-Bains (Savoie)
Epernay (Marne)
1 Thermidor
Carcassonne (Aude)
3 Thermidor
La Châtaigneraye (Vendée)
Château-Salins (Meurthe-et-Moselle)
Dijon (Côte d'Or)
Draguignan (Var)
Fousseret (Haute-Garonne)
La Tour-du-Pin (Isère)
Uzès (Gard)
Villefranche (Rhône)
5 Thermidor
Fontenay-le-Comte (Vendée)
Mareuil (Vendée)
Saint-Marcellin (Isère)
7 Thermidor
Amplepuis (Rhône)

SOURCES AND BIBLIOGRAPHY

SOURCES AND BIBLIOGRAPHY

MANUSCRIPT SOURCES

Series L, the Revolutionary Period, in the following Archives:

Archives départementales de l'Aude
Archives départementales des Bouches-du-Rhône
Archives départementales du Calvados
Archives départementales de la Côte d'Or
Archives départementales de la Gironde
Archives départementales de la Haute-Vienne
Archives départementales de l'Indre
Archives départementales de l'Isère
Archives départementales du Loiret
Archives départementales de la Marne
Archives départementales de Meurthe-et-Moselle
Archives départementales du Nord
Archives départementales du Rhône
Archives départementales de la Seine-Inférieure
Archives départementales de la Vendée

PRINTED SOURCES

Archives parlementaires, Série I.

AULARD, F. A., *Recueil des actes du Comité de salut public, avec la correspondance officielle des représentants en mission et le registre du Conseil executif provisoire*, 26 vols. (Paris, 1889–1923).

—— *La Société des Jacobins. Recueil de documents pour l'histoire du club des Jacobins de Paris*, 6 vols. (Paris, 1889–1897).

CARON, P., *Paris pendant la Terreur*, 2 vols. (Paris, 1910–1914).

"Comptes décadaires du comité d'Angers," *Anjou historique*, VII (1906), 243–270.

"Correspondance du comité révolutionnaire d'Angers," *Anjou historique*, XXVI (1926), 37–47.

DESMOULINS, CAMILLE, *Le Vieux Cordelier* (reprinted, Paris, 1825).

DECHRISTÉ, L., *Douai pendant la Révolution, 1789–1802* (Paris, 1880).

DELMAS, J., *Registre du comité révolutionnaire du Cantal* (Aurillac, 1897).

GALMICHE, E., "Nouveaux documents sur le comité de surveillance de Saint-Brieuc," *Annales de Bretagne*, XXXVIII (1928–29), 398–424.

GALMICHE, E., "Quelques documents sur le comité de surveillance de Saint-Brieuc," *Annales de Bretagne*, XXVIII (1912–13), 585–596.

GUIGUE, G., *La Commission populaire républicaine et de salut public du Rhône-et-Loire, 30 juin–8 octobre 1793* (Trevoux, 1899). *Journal des débats*.

LOTTIN, D., *Recherches historiques sur la ville d'Orléans*, 6 vols. (Orléans, 1834).

Moniteur, réimpression.

PORÉE, C., *Sources manuscrites de l'histoire de la Révolution dans l'Yonne, Archives nationales* (Auxerre, 1918).

Procès-verbaux du comité de surveillance de Vienne-le-patriote, publiés par un vieux bibliophile dauphinois (Grenoble, 1888).

"Registre des délibérations du comité de surveillance établi à Orthez," *Bulletin de la société des sciences, lettres et arts de Pau*, 2e série, XXX, 1.

RIVARÈS, F., "Documents pour servir à l'histoire de la Révolution dans le Sud-ouest," *Bulletin de la société des sciences, lettres et arts de Pau*, 2e série, XI (1881–82), 1–39.

Papiers inédits trouvés chez Robespierre . . . supprimés ou omis par Courtois, 3 vols. (Paris, 1828).

VERMALE, F., et A. ROCHET, "Registre des délibérations du comité révolutionnaire d'Aix-les-Bains," *Mémoires et documents publiés par la Société savoisienne d'histoire et d'archéologie*, XLV (1907), 4e fascicule, XLVII (1909), 3–167.

SECONDARY AUTHORITIES

AFFRE, H., *Tableau sommaire de la Terreur dans l'Aveyron* (Rodez, 1886).

ARNAUD, G., *Histoire de la Révolution dans le département de l'Ariège* (1904).

BABEAU, A., *Histoire de Troyes pendant la Révolution*, 2 vols. (Paris, 1874).

BARBUAT, P. DE, "Le Comité de surveillance révolutionnaire de Beaune," *Société d'archéologie de Beaune, Mémoires*, 1911, pp. 155–366.

BAUMONT, H., "Le département de l'Oise pendant la Révolution," *Bulletin de la société d'études historiques et scientifiques de l'Oise*, V (1909), 1, 153, 289; VI (1910), 34, 155.

——— *Histoire de Lunéville* (Lunéville, 1904).

BELLONI, G., *Le Comité de Sûreté Générale de la Convention* (Paris, 1924).

BIERNAWSKI, L., *Un département sous la Révolution française — L'Allier de 1789 à III* (Moulins, 1909).

BLIARD, P., "Le Conventionnel Prieur (de la Marne) en mission," *Revue historique*, LXXXIII (1903), 38, 225.

BLOSSIER, H., "Le Comité de surveillance du département de Loir-et-Cher et la déchristianisation," *Bulletin historique et philologique du Comité des travaux historiques et scientifiques*, 1910, pp. 246–272.

BLUSSON, R., et A. MARCHANT, *La Société populaire du canton de Larche et de la Fraternité, 1793–95* (Tulle, 1905).

BOURCIER, E., "Essai sur la Terreur en Anjou," *Revue de l'Anjou*, VII (1872), 50.

BOUVIER, F., *Les Vosges pendant la Révolution* (Paris, 1885).

CALVET, H., "Les Rapports du comité de surveillance et des autorités constituées du département de Loir-et-Cher," *Annales historiques de la Révolution française*, V (1928), 430–441.

CAMPAGNAC, E., "Le Comité révolutionnaire de Bourges et l'affaire de la Guerche," *Révolution française*, LVII, 327–354.

—— "Le Comité de surveillance de Melun," *Annales révolutionnaires*, I (1908), 467; II (1909), 38, 541.

CANTOUNY, E., "Le Comité de surveillance de Beaulieu," *Bulletin de la société des lettres, sciences et arts de la Corrèze (Tulle)*, XLIII (1926), 203; XLIV (1927), 3.

CHAPUSIAT, E., "Une séance des comités révolutionnaires genevois en 1794," *Révolution française*, LVII (1907), 364.

CHASSIN, C. L., *La Vendée patriote*, 4 vols. (Paris, 1893–95).

CHAVIGNY, DESMÉ DE, "Histoire de Saumur pendant la Révolution," *Revue historique de l'Ouest*, VII–VIII.

CHEVALIER, U., *Le Comité de surveillance révolutionnaire et la société républico-populaire de Romans en 1793 et 1794* (Romans, 1890).

CLÉREMBRAY, F., "La Terreur à Rouen," *La Normandie*, 1897–1900.

COMBET, J., "Les Comités de surveillance du district de Grasse," *Révolution française*, LVII, 327–354.

"Le Comité de surveillance de La Cadière," *Bulletin de la société d'études scientifiques et archéologiques de Draguignan*, XXVIII (1910–11), liv–lvii.

"Le Comité révolutionnaire de Sancoins (Cher)," *Annales révolutionnaires*, V, 178, 492.

"Conflits entre le comité révolutionnaire d'Angers et la Commission militaire," *Anjou historique*, 1902–03, p. 646.

CONNAC, E., "La Révolution à Toulouse," *Revue des Pyrénées*, vols. XII–XIII.

CUZACQ, R., "Le Comité révolutionnaire de Bayonne," *Bulletin de la société des sciences, lettres et études regionales de Bayonne*, 1929, p. 5.

DARSY, F. J., *Amiens et le département de la Somme pendant la Révolution*, 2 vols. (Amiens, 1878–93).

DENIS, ALBERT, *Le Comité de surveillance révolutionnaire de Toul* (Toul, 1911).

PARIS, A. J., La Terreur dans le Pas-de-Calais et dans le Nord (Arras, 1864).

PASTOORS, A., Histoire de la ville de Cambrai pendant la Révolution, 2 vols. (Cambrai, 1908).

PATIN, M., "Le Comité de surveillance et la société populaire de Draguignan sous la période révolutionnaire," Bulletin de la société d'études scientifiques et archéologiques de la ville de Draguignan, XVII, 45.

PIONNIER, E., Essai sur la Révolution à Verdun (Nancy, 1905).

POMMERET, H., L'Esprit public dans le département des Côtes-du-Nord pendant la Révolution (Paris, 1921).

POUPÉ, E., "Le Comité de surveillance de la Roquebrussanne (Var)," Bulletin historique du Comité des travaux historiques et scientifiques, 1907, p. 289.

RAMON, G., La Révolution à Péronne (5e et 6e série) 1793–95 (Péronne, 1886).

RICHARD, A., "Le Comité de surveillance et les suspects de Dax," Annales historiques de la Révolution française, VII, 24.

—— Le Gouvernement révolutionnaire dans les Basses-Pyrénées (Paris, 1926).

RIFFATERRE, C., Le Mouvement anti-jacobin et anti-parisien à Lyon et dans le Rhône-et-Loire en 1793 (Lyon, 1912).

RIVARÈS, F., "Pau et les Basses-Pyrénées pendant la Révolution," Bulletin de la société de Pau, 2e série, IV, 405.

ROUVIÈRE, F., Histoire de la Révolution dans le Gard, 4 vols. (Nîmes, 1887–89).

SALLIARD, E., La Terreur à Poitiers (Paris, 1912).

SCHWAB, LEON, "Les Comités de surveillance dans les Vosges pendant la Révolution," La Révolution dans les Vosges, 22e–24e années.

SERRES, J. B., Histoire de la Révolution en Auvergne, 10 vols. (Mauriac, 1895–99).

TAINE, H., The French Revolution, 3 vols. (New York, 1885).

TRÉVÉDY, J., "Histoire du comité révolutionnaire de Quimper," Revue historique de l'Ouest, Notices, vols. XII–XIV.

UZUREAU, F., "L'Arrestation des fédéralistes angevins," Révolution française, LXVII, 230.

—— "Le Procès des terroristes angevins," Anjou historique, IV, 500.

—— "Les Victimes de la Terreur en Anjou," Anjou historique, IV, 278.

VELASQUE, A., "Carrier, le comité révolutionnaire et la société populaire Vincent-la-Montagne," Revue historique de la Révolution française, XV, 233.

—— "Du nombre des victimes de la Terreur à Nantes," Revue historique de la Révolution française, XIV, 161.

VIDAL, PIERRE, Histoire de la Révolution française dans le département des Pyrénées Orientales, 3 vols. (Perpignan, 1885–89).

VIÉ, L., "*La Société populaire et le comité de surveillance de Fousseret,*" *Revue de Comminges,* XXI, 129.

VIVIE, A., *Histoire de la Terreur à Bordeaux,* 2 vols. (Bordeaux, 1877).

WAITZEN-NECKER, E., "Le Comité royaliste de Palluau," *Revue du Bas-Poitou,* 1901, 1903–07, 1909–10, 1912–14.

WALLON, H., *Histoire du tribunal révolutionnaire,* 6 vols. (Paris, 1880–82).

—— *La Révolution du 31 mai et le fédéralisme,* 2 vols. (Paris, 1886).

INDEX

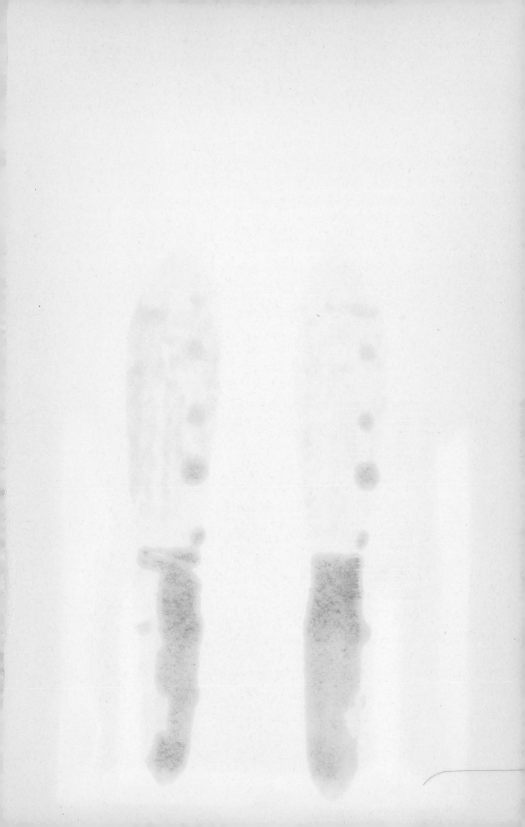

DATE DUE		
DEC 1 5 1999		
SEP 1 4 2009		